DORIE'S ANYTIME CAKES

DORIE GREENSPAN

Dorie's Anytime CAKES

HARVEST
An Imprint of WILLIAM MORROW

Illustrations by Nancy Pappas

HarperCollins books may be purchased for educational, business, or sales promotional use. For information, please email the Special Markets Department at SPsales@harpercollins.com.

FIRST EDITION

Designed by Melissa Lotfy
Illustrations © Nancy Pappas
Food styling by Mary Dodd

Library of Congress Cataloging-in-Publication Data has been applied for.

ISBN 978-0-06-334696-3

25 26 27 28 29 MAI 10 9 8 7 6 5 4 3 2 1

For Gemma and VV,
who are baked into my heart

Contents

Introduction

So much of this book was inspired by memories and so many of those spring from my mother's kitchen and the cakes that sat on the counter there. Not that my mother ever baked a cake—never ever—but there was always cake in the kitchen. When I was very young, it was something that my grandmother had baked. Often it would be a honey cake with almonds on top—my mother didn't like the cake, but she loved the almonds and picked them off before the cake was even out of its wrapper (I've got a honey cake reminiscent of my grandmother's on page 95); sometimes it would be my favorite apple cake, a recipe I've never been able to fully re-create, but one I haven't given up on yet (the cake on page 5 is different, but it brings back memories of the original). When Grandma no longer baked for us, there'd be a shop-bought cake in the kitchen—our counter was never bare.

I'd often come home from school to find my mom sitting in the kitchen with a friend, the aroma of coffee in the air and a bakery cake on the table. A marbled Bundt cake (see page 107 for my version). A lemon loaf that had cracked down the center in a way that I found beautiful even as a kid (try the one on page 61). A bready kugelhopf with raisins—my father would pull them out the way my mother snagged the honey cake's almonds. (It's funny, but the Olive Oil Dunking Bundt, page 103 so different from anything from my childhood, reminds me a bit of those kugelhopfs.) Crumb cakes, crumb cakes and more crumb cakes, some with fruit, some just covered with spice-scented nuggets. (I've never stopped loving crumbs and never stopped baking with them.) From time to time, there'd be a layer cake or a single round cake with frosting, and sprinkles if it was a special occasion. If there was a blackout cake from Ebinger's, the long-gone, legendary Brooklyn bakery, we kids would jockey to grab the biggest slice. (The Devil's Chocolate Cake, page 135, has a flavor that whispers Ebinger's.)

My mother loved cake, and she understood the power of cake, even the simplest ones—perhaps most especially the simplest ones—to welcome, warm and comfort the people she cared about.

Me, too. I believe in cakes' powers and charms.

I also believe in simplicity. My first and most enduring love is for simple cakes. I made a towering wedding cake with sleek frosted sides and cascading fresh flowers—once. I made a coal-black cake sculpted to look like Darth Vader—once. I made an oversized sheet cake with seventy-eight buttercream roses—once. But I've made hundreds and hundreds of simple cakes over the years. Loaf cakes and the kinds of cakes that you can serve right out of the pan, the ones that we now call snacking cakes. Brownies, for sure. Swirly Bundt cakes. Layer cakes and cakes that have only one layer. Little cakes—I made baby cakes for my granddaughter Gemma's first birthday (see page 215) and a mini-layer cake when her sister, VV, turned one (see page 219). Sometimes I frost the cakes and sometimes I fill them. Sometimes I top them with fruit. But most of the time I leave them plain, letting their color and shape, their bumps and dips, their baked-in personalities sparkle. These are the kinds of cakes you can cut into without fretting about precision—and go back to for another nibble. The kinds you can eat out of hand or put on a plate and break into morsels with your fingers. The kinds that go with coffee in the morning or tea in the afternoon. And even cakes to have with wine: salty, savory cakes; cheesy and herby cakes; mini muffins made with seaweed; and pull-apart scones with miso—each of them holds a little surprise and a full measure of deliciousness. (Please don't miss the Feta, Sumac and Za'atar Loaf on page 254.) They are truly "anytime cakes."

That these cakes are all simple to make is just another of their pleasures. For the recipes in this book, whenever I could, I found a way for you to make the cake by hand. While I'd never want to be without a mixer, there's something primally joyful about whisking eggs and sugar together, folding in flour and watching the ingredients come together into a batter. I've tried to make these cakes in pans you'll already have in your kitchen. And since I assume I'm not the only spur-of-the-moment baker among us—if I have a yen for a cake, I want to bake it immediately—my recipes rely on readily available ingredients. If you've got a baker's basics in your pantry (take a look at page xiv), most of these recipes can be whim-bakes for you, too.

Despite how long I've been baking simple cakes, I still find them alluring. Classic cakes still satisfy and comfort and, for me, an incorrigible tinkerer, still make a splendid springboard for playing around; for changing a little something here or there, a flavor, a shape, a filling, or a fruit; for adding a dash of the unexpected to a long-loved favorite; for making what will delight my family and friends most when they come into the kitchen for cake. And for telling the stories behind these cherished recipes.

This book brims with stories. Some come from discoveries—my first trip to Greece sparked ideas for cakes, as did a return visit to Italy; some come from the joy of finding fresh ideas closer to home—there are recipes from my life in Paris, of course, and from friends and places in America; and some come from sweet memories. There are stories about cakes that send me back to childhood, to old recipes that still delight (it made me so happy to surprise Michael with a cake that tasted just like the Charlotte Russe we both remembered from a small sidewalk stand in Brooklyn; see page 222) and to beloved recipes that I keep riffing on. I'm happy when I can take an old recipe and add something that makes it seem new again. (I think you'll love both the original Swedish Visiting Cake and my new rum-raisin version, page 53; and my two new takes on Bill's Big Carrot Cake, a recipe I've been making for more than forty years and have never stopped loving, page 185.) Because these recipes are special to me, and because I think you'll find the magic in them, too, they're marked "A Treasured Favorite" so that you won't miss them.

Over the years, making simple cakes, cakes I've come to think of as anytime cakes, has created lasting memories for me and the people I love. I so hope that it will be the same for you and everyone you bake for. When it comes to happiness, you can count on cake.

xoxo Dorie

BACKBONE BASICS

Good to Know Before You Start

There are a million reasons to love baking and one of them is that if you follow the rules, you're just about guaranteed to pull something good from the oven a little while later. Happily, the rules are simple. In fact, the rule of all rules is the simplest: Follow the directions—read the recipe through and then make it the way it's written. After that, if you want to play around, you'll have a good base.

When I give you a recipe, I've got only one wish: I want it to be a success for you. I want you to be proud of what you've made and proud of yourself for making it. I want you to have the same feeling about your cakes that I have about mine—I can barely wait for them to cool, because I can't wait to share them.

I've listed below what I think is important for you to know—think keys to success. Take a look at this section before you start. I've written detailed recipes in the hopes of covering all contingencies and leading you from start to deliciousness. If you choose basic ingredients that are the same as the ones I use in my kitchen, and if you measure them the way I do, you're bound to get cakes that are just like the ones I make. I can't emphasize enough how important measuring is in baking and how easy your baking life will be once you make a habit of using a scale. Extra-easy if you measure in metrics, which is just a matter of pressing a button on a digital scale—no math required.

Read, please. Bake, often. Share, always.

INGREDIENTS

The Fundamental Four

The four most important ingredients for a baker are flour, sugar, eggs and butter. If you have those, you can bake a cake. So that we start on the same page, though, here's a quick guide to the backbone ingredients in my kitchen. (There's more info in Pantry and Fridge Staples at the bottom of this page.)

FLOUR

My staple is unbleached all-purpose flour; my house brand is King Arthur. And, most important, for my recipes:

1 cup all-purpose flour = 136 grams

I know that you'll see other books with other measurements and that the weight of a cup of flour will vary from author to author and from brand of flour to brand of flour. Please, please, please, when you bake these recipes, use this conversion.

And if you are using a cup-for-cup gluten-free flour, please weigh the flour so that you know that it is truly cup-for-cup.

SUGAR

My standard sugar is granulated—if it's a different kind of sugar, I say so—and:

1 cup sugar = 200 grams

Many bakers like using superfine sugar. If that's what you stock, that's okay, but just make sure to use weight—not volume—measures.

I haven't distinguished between light and dark brown sugar here—they can be used interchangeably in these recipes. However, my preference is for light brown sugar:

1 cup brown sugar, light or dark = 200 grams

For crunch, a little sparkle and extra pleasure, I'll often sprinkle the tops of cakes with turbinado or raw sugar, demerara sugar or sanding sugar. These are sweet extras, not necessities.

EGGS

I test all of my recipes with large eggs. The color of the eggs doesn't matter, but the size does. It's just about impossible to get a precise weight for eggs, but this is close:

1 large egg (out of its shell) = approximately 50 grams
1 large yolk = approximately 20 grams
1 large white = approximately 30 grams

BUTTER

All of these recipes were tested with standard (not high-fat or cultured) American butter. Among the brands I used were Land O'Lakes; Cabot, a local brand for me in New England; Kirkland from Costco; and various supermarket-brand butters—all unsalted. It's good to know that:

1 tablespoon butter = 14 grams

If your favorite brand of butter is still packed in 8-tablespoon sticks, then:

1 stick butter = 113 grams

Pantry and Fridge Staples

These are the baker's everyday necessities. Stock them, and you'll always be able to bake on a whim.

CHOCOLATE

Dark chocolate is my first choice for everything from baking to eating, but I'm not a bittersweet tyrant: it's fine to use bittersweet and semisweet chocolate interchangeably in these recipes. If a recipe calls for milk or white chocolate, though, you should stick to the recipe. As for the brand of chocolate—your favorite should win every time. Keep chocolate tightly covered in a cool, dry place.

COCOA

I tested these recipes with Dutch-processed cocoa, using Valrhona, Guittard and Hershey's Special Dark. If you're using natural (non-Dutched) cocoa, you'll be fine—there's no need to change anything in the recipe. Cocoa has a tendency to clump, so it's wise to measure it out and then sift it. (I push it through a strainer.) But if you're only using a tablespoon or two, you'll probably be able to crack the clumps when you're whisking the cocoa into the other ingredients. Keep cocoa tightly covered in a cool, dry place—humidity is not cocoa powder's friend.

EXTRACTS

I always use pure extracts. Vanilla is often the flavoring that brings a recipe to life, the baseline flavor that helps everything else shine, and so it should be the best-quality vanilla you can find and afford. Vanilla's expensive, so when you get it, take good care of it—keep it tightly covered (like the perfume that it is) in a cool, dark place. Ditto almond extract. I also keep orange-blossom and rose water in my cupboard.

MILK AND BUDDIES

One of my hobbies is poking around the dairy fridge in markets to see if there's a fun ingredient to play with. My dairy regulars are milk, buttermilk—I love buttermilk—and yogurt, but I often use sour cream and sometimes ricotta or mascarpone. No matter what dairy I use, it's always whole, full-fat, rich and delicious. As for yogurt, it seems that these days, there are more brands of yogurt than ever and the majority of them are labeled "Greek." When I call for Greek yogurt, it's usually for really thick yogurt, the kind that looks as though you could cut it. (I often use Fage.) However, if you measure carefully, you'll have success with other yogurts here. Please don't avoid a recipe because you don't have the exact type of yogurt listed. Use what you've got!

SALT

I keep three kinds of salt within easy reach: fine sea salt, fleur de sel and flaky sea salt.

My daily baking salt is fine sea salt, specifically La Baleine. Oddly, some sea salts are saltier than others—taste whatever salt you're using and decide if you'd like more or less than I've suggested.

Fleur de sel is a sea salt. My favorite is fleur de sel from Guérande, France, but for years now fleur de sel has been produced by countries around the world, including America. What makes fleur de sel stand out is its mineral taste and its texture—the grains are firm and moist and you can feel each one when you rub a pinch between your fingers, and they hold a bit of their bite under heat. Fleur de sel is less salty than fine sea salt—when I use it, I measure out about twice as much as I would sea salt. This kind of salt is expensive and considered a finishing salt—don't use it for cooking pasta!

The best-known flaky sea salt is Maldon, which comes from England, but again, you can now find this type of salt from many places. If an ice crystal were salt, it would look like Maldon salt. Like fleur de sel, flaky salt is sprinkled, not spooned; it's often scattered sparingly on top of a sweet as an accent.

BEST PRACTICES

If you're new to baking, please take a minute to look through this section. It's a potpourri of small things to do to set yourself up for success, of important things to remember and of basic things, like pan sizes, oven quirks and instructions for measuring (as well as a plea for patience when baking). If you're an experienced baker, I hope you'll still give this a read. I always read this part of any cookbook first because I like to know if the author and I do things the same way, and when I'm making a recipe for the first time, I always follow the author's lead.

Temperature

Unless otherwise specified, all ingredients should be at room temperature.

Measurements and Measuring

If anyone were to ask me what one thing they could do to up their baking game, I'd say, "Buy a scale and use it to measure your ingredients . . . in metric." I'm not sure why so many people are so reluctant to use scales, but I know that everyone who does becomes a cheerleader for them. You've probably heard the arguments in favor of weighing—accuracy, ease, fewer bowls, faster process—so all I want to do is to beg you to take my advice and the advice of just about every other baker I know: Get a scale! Keep it within easy reach! And when you become a convert—as I know you will—preach the gospel of scales to everyone else.

Ovens, Ovens, Ovens, Temperature, Racks and Pesky Hot Spots

All of these recipes were tested in a conventional home (non-convection/non-fan) oven. Of course they can be made in a convection oven, but you'll need to lower the temperature. The question is always how much lower should you go, and I don't have a set answer. I've got two convection ovens—one a countertop and the other a small wall oven—and I lower the temperature for each of them by a different amount. If you've got one, follow the manufacturer's suggestions for how to convert temperatures from still to convection; if not, then you'll have to go for trial and error, the way I did. When you figure it out, remember to record the information and keep it someplace handy.

No matter what kind of oven you use, it's crucial that the temperature be right (I leave a thermometer in mine all the time) and that the oven be preheated to the correct temperature. Years ago, an oven repairman told me to wait for at least 15 minutes after the signal indicating that the oven's reached temp goes off. According to him, it hasn't or if it has, then only just. And since when you open the door to slide the pan in, the temperature will drop and it will take a while for it to come up and stay up, it's good to wait until the oven has had time to heat through thoroughly to start baking. The instant the urge to bake strikes, turn on the oven!

For cakes, I always bake in the middle of the oven—if

you've got a bunch of rack positions, find the middle one and stick to it.

Hot spots are annoying—they'll bake one side of a cake faster and darker than another—but there isn't much that you can do about them other than befriend them. Get to know them and plot a work-around—bake your cake in a different part of the oven or just turn your pan around midway through the bake. It's an "if you can't beat 'em, join 'em" kind of situation.

Baking Pans

My standard baking pans are metal. I avoid pans with dark interiors and I prefer nonstick pans, although I still prep them with baker's spray or butter and flour. If you've got glass or ceramic pans, of course you can use them, but your bake might be slightly different from mine.

What's most important is that your pan be the size called for in the recipe. It's a Goldilocks thing: too big, and the cake will bake too quickly and be low; too small, and the batter may overflow or not bake through properly. To check, measure round, square, rectangular, loaf and baking sheets at the top. It's best to measure Bundt pans by volume—fill the pan with water and see how many cups it holds.

No matter what kind of pan you're using, treat it nicely: Avoid cutting in it or, if you must (and there are those times), use a table knife and don't dig in. Wash the pan well after you use it and make sure that it's thoroughly dry before you put it away. (I'll often put a pan in the still-warm oven to dry.) And try not to ding or dent it—try really hard. If you're buying new pans, it's worth getting the best quality you can afford—if you buy good pans and take good care of them, you'll have them for years. And years.

THE BASIC PAN BATTERY

Loaf Pan: 8½ x 4½ x 2¾ inches
Loaf Pan: 9 x 5 x 2¾ inches
Mini-Loaf Pan: each well measures about 2¼ x 4 x 1¼ inches (I use a pan that has 8 wells)
Square Pan: 8 x 8 x 2¼ inches
Square Pan: 9 x 9 x 2¼ inches
Rectangular Pan: 9 x 13 x 2¼ inches
Baking Sheet: 12 x 17 x 1½ inches
Round Pan: 8 inches in diameter/2¼ inches high
Round Pan: 9 inches in diameter/2¼ inches high
Tart Pan: 9- to 9½-inch fluted with removable bottom
Skillet: 10- to 12-inch cast iron
Springform Pan: 8 inches in diameter/3 inches high
Springform Pan: 9 (to 9½) inches in diameter/3 inches high
Springform Pan: 10 inches in diameter/about 2½ inches high
Standard Muffin Tin: 12 wells, each 2 to 2½ inches in diameter
Mini Muffin Tin: 24 wells, each about 1¾ inches in diameter
Jumbo Muffin Tin: 6 wells, each about 3½ inches in diameter
Bundt Pans: 12 cups, 10 cups and 6 cups

SPRAYING OR BUTTERING PANS, AND LINING THEM, TOO

Getting ready to bake almost always requires getting your pans ready, often a two-step process: greasing the pan (or buttering it) and then lining it. There are some exceptions (and I know there are personal preferences), but generally you can either coat the inside of a pan with butter, dust it with flour and then tap out the excess, or use baker's spray, a mixture of oil and flour. One is faster than the other, but both are effective.

If you spray your pans: I take two quick extra steps when I use baker's spray. Since I never seem to be able to apply the spray evenly, I spray and then smooth the mixture over the inside of the pan with a silicone basting brush. And then I turn the pan over onto a paper towel until I'm ready to use it, so that if there's any excess spray, it doesn't pool in the bottom of the pan.

Lining pans: Covering the bottom and often two opposite sides of a prepped pan with parchment paper helps the cake bake evenly and makes unmolding easy—if you leave an overhang, you can use the paper as handles to lift the cake out of the pan. Also, there's something so satisfying about peeling parchment away from the bottom of a cake.

Test Early, Often and Properly

Whenever I can, I give you a range for baking times. Maybe your ingredients are a little cooler than mine were; maybe your pan is paler or darker, lighter or heavier; or maybe your oven cycles up and down in a rhythm that's not the same as mine—there are lots of variables that can affect baking time and it's impossible to take them all into account, so the final judgment has to be yours. Sometimes the best heads-up that a cake's done or approaching done is the fragrance wafting from the oven—if you can smell the cake, it's a sign that it's almost fully baked. Cakes turn golden brown (or many of them do) as they bake; they rise; they will feel springy when prodded; and they might pull away from the sides of the pan when tugged gently. These are all good doneness indicators to know about. Usually the definitive test is the toothpick plunge—poke a toothpick or thin bamboo skewer into the center of the cake, making sure you hit the midway point, then pull it out—unless I give you a different clue, if the pick is clean, the cake is done. I usually let the cake sit in the pan on a cooling rack for a few minutes before unmolding it—the recipe will tell you if you should actually unmold it immediately or how long you should wait.

Patience

Most cakes are best when they've cooled to room temperature. I won't be around to stop you if you grab for warm cake, but I think you'll find that the flavor is fuller and the texture more satisfying when the cake has had time to cool. Think of cooling as part of the baking process—it's the time when the cake relaxes, gathers itself and becomes what it's meant to be. The effects of a good rest are most pronounced with spice cakes—while they're often delicious the day they're baked, they can be magnitudes better a day later.

BEYOND BASIC TECHNIQUES

Over so many years of baking, I've discovered a few things that make baking easier, faster or more fun—sometimes all three come together. They're small things, but they make a sweet difference.

Melting Chocolate

Chocolate needs to be babied—you can melt it a couple of different ways, but no matter what method you choose, the heat has to be low. Also, it's best to start with small pieces of chocolate or chopped chocolate—the chocolate will melt faster and more evenly. To melt chocolate in a microwave, go slow—set the oven to half (or low) power and work in very short spurts, stirring after each spurt. Chocolate, particularly when you're melting it in a microwave, has a way of fooling you—it'll hold its shape, and you won't know it's melted until you prod it. To melt it in a double boiler—a method that gives you easy control—find a heatproof bowl that fits snugly over a saucepan of simmering water. Make sure that the water isn't touching the bottom of the bowl and that no water is bubbling up the sides and hitting the chocolate. Water is chocolate's nemesis: just a drop can irreparably seize your chocolate. The third method, direct heat, is easy and reliable only if you have a burner that goes low, low, low. No matter which method you use, you've got to be vigilant: stand by and watch. And if you're melting milk or white chocolate, you've got to watch more carefully—these chocolates can go from just melted to burned quickly, and once chocolate scorches, there's nothing you can do but mourn its loss.

Smush Trick

To get the very most flavor out of citrus zest, put the recipe's sugar in a bowl, grate the zest onto the sugar and then reach in and use your fingers to smush, mush, mash and press the zest into the sugar. Keep at it until you catch the aroma of the fruit. Depending on the amount of zest you've got, the sugar may become moist, and it might take on some color. I love this trick. I learned it from the remarkable French pastry chef Pierre Hermé about thirty years ago. As soon as I'd done it once, I knew I'd be doing it forever after—and I have.

Toasting Nuts

You can make any baking recipe that calls for nuts without toasting them, but you can make any recipe that calls for nuts better by a measure if you do toast them. Spread the nuts out in a single layer on a baking sheet and slide the sheet into a 350-degree-F oven for 10 to 15 minutes, stirring the nuts around after the first 5 minutes and checking in on them frequently after that. Sliced or slivered nuts will take less time to become golden brown than whole or chunky bits of nuts. Cool the nuts to room temperature before adding them to a recipe or processing them to make flour.

Making Nut Flour

Nut flours (sometimes called nut meals) add richness and deep flavor to recipes. While I use almond flour most often—I buy it ready-made—I like some other nut flours that are not easy to find on a whim. They are, however, easy to make. Measure out the nuts by weight, put them in a food processor with a little sugar (it can be additional sugar or some of the sugar called for in the recipe) and pulse away, stopping often to scrape down the bowl—make sure to slide your spatula around the "corners" of the bowl where the sides meet the base; the sugar helps keep the nuts from quickly going pasty. Pulse until you've got a fluffy flour—if you have a few mini nuggets of nuts here and there, that's fine and much better than turning the nuts into a paste. For added flavor, consider toasting the nuts before grinding them. (It's what makes the Toasted Almond Cake, page 14, a standout.)

Plumping Fruit

The thing about dried fruit is that if it starts out hard, it's going to finish hard: baking won't soften it. But hot liquids will. Dunk the dried fruit in very hot tap or boiling water for a minute or so, drain it and pat dry. If you'd like to add a little more flavor to the fruit, use tea as the soaker or make a mix of water and booze, put it in a small saucepan with the fruit and cook until the alcohol just about evaporates—this is the quick step that ups the flavor in the Rum-Raisin Visiting Cake (page 53).

Measuring Sticky Ingredients

As pleasurable as baking is, there are some things that can be truly annoying—I'm thinking about measuring sticky ingredients like honey. The easiest way to avoid battling with the stickies, and to get every last bit of them out of the measuring cup and into the batter, is to oil the measuring cup before you pour in the sticky stuff. You can grease the cup with neutral oil or give it a quick spritz of cooking or baker's spray. Or, if the recipe has oil in it, measure the oil into the cup and then pour it out and use the same cup to measure (and easily pour out) the honey or molasses or maple syrup.

Stirring/Folding

Sometimes I tell you to stir/fold ingredients into a batter. I don't know if there's a technical term for this motion, but it comes in handy when you've got a light batter and you've got to add more ingredients to it. Working with a flexible spatula, start to stir the ingredients in, and then, when they're almost incorporated, switch to folding, turning the batter a couple of times. There are no rules for this technique; it's just what I do when I want to be very gentle with a batter. Play around and see what's most comfortable and effective for you.

How to Make Jumbo Muffin-Tin Liners

I'm a fan of cupcake papers—use liners, and your cupcakes and muffins will bake more evenly. I'm also a fan of jumbo muffin tins, but it's hard to find liners for them (and they're often expensive). To make your own—a cute little arts-and-crafts project—find a glass or a can that fits into the muffin mold, then cut out as many 6-inch squares of parchment paper as you need. One way to shape the liners is to mold each piece of paper over the glass or can and then fit the paper into the tin. Another is to fold the square in half, so that it forms a triangle, press firmly against the folds and then fold the paper again, to form a smaller triangle, and press those folds. Fold again, if you'd like. Open up the triangle, put it in the muffin mold and press it into shape with the glass or can. It will pop up—it always does—but it will be fine once it's filled with batter. If you want to anchor it a little more securely, spray the pan before you fit the paper into it.

ROUND CAKES

BFF Brownie Cake

Makes 8 servings

16 tablespoons (8 ounces; 226 grams) unsalted butter, cut into chunks

8 ounces (226 grams) semisweet or bittersweet chocolate, coarsely chopped

4 large eggs, at room temperature

¾ cup (150 grams) sugar

½ teaspoon fleur de sel or ¼ teaspoon fine sea salt

½ cup (68 grams) all-purpose flour

Cocoa powder or confectioners' sugar for finishing (optional)

Something creamy for tagging along (optional)

Everyone needs a chocolate cake they can depend on. A dark, rich, creamy cake you can make easily and serve with delight. Preferably one that's as good eaten out of hand as it is dolled up with cream or glaze or fruit or something fussy. This one's mine. The cake's flavor is full-on chocolate, and its texture is lush—soft in the center and just a little firmer and cakier on the top and bottom. It has only six ingredients and comes together quickly. It can be served at room temperature or chilled. And, because it's so elemental, you can embellish it not just with toppings, but also with add-ins and flavorings. Make it once in all its glorious plainness, and then, if you want to fiddle, I've got some ideas to get you started; see Playing Around.

Center a rack in the oven and preheat it to 325 degrees F. Butter a 9-inch round cake pan (one with at least 2-inch-high sides) and dust the interior with cocoa, or coat with baker's spray and dust with cocoa; tap out the excess.

Gently heat the butter and chocolate together until melted and smooth. You can do this in a saucepan over super-low heat or in a heatproof bowl set over a pan of simmering water (the bottom of the bowl shouldn't touch the water), or in short spurts in a microwave set to low power. However you do this, keep an eye on it and be careful: you don't want to get the mixture so hot or cook it for so long that the butter and chocolate separate. When they're melted, remove from the heat.

Working in the bowl of a stand mixer fitted with the whisk attachment, or in a large bowl with a hand mixer, beat the eggs, sugar and salt together on medium-high speed until they triple in volume and are pale and creamy, about 5 minutes—when you lift the beater, the mixture should fall back onto the batter in a dissolving ribbon. With the mixer on low, pour the blended butter and chocolate into the bowl and continue to mix until you've got a lovely homogeneous batter. If you're using a stand mixer, remove the bowl from the stand. Spoon the flour over the batter and use a flexible spatula to fold it in gently but thoroughly. When you think the batter is finished, take a peek at the bottom of the bowl just to make sure there isn't any loose flour hiding down there. Scrape the batter into the pan and swivel the pan to level it.

Bake the cake for 20 to 22 minutes, or until the top is dry and feels set to the touch. A tester inserted into the center of the cake will come out with a smear of →

chocolate or a couple of moist crumbs—this is a case in which a little underbaked is fine. Transfer the pan to a rack and let rest for 15 minutes.

Put a piece of parchment on a cutting board or rack, turn the cake out onto the parchment and then invert the cake onto another rack. Allow the cake to cool until it's barely warm or has reached room temperature.

This cake cuts easily—most easily with a knife that's been run under hot water and wiped dry between cuts—and can be served plain. If you'd like, though, you can dust the top with cocoa or confectioners' sugar, and think about a dollop of cream as a go-along—whipped cream, crème fraîche, sour cream or ice cream are all good choices.

Storing: Wrapped, the cake holds for about 4 days at room temperature. If it's more convenient, you can keep it in the fridge—the texture will be firmer and fudgier, which is different from the original but nice. You can also wrap the cake airtight and freeze it for up to a month; thaw in the wrapper.

Playing Around

Flavor the sugar

To add another flavor, rub freshly grated orange zest into the sugar. Or rub in some tea leaves or even some very finely minced fresh herbs—thyme's a good choice.

Fold-in flavor

Chocolate loves spice. You can whisk ground spices into the measured-out flour—think cinnamon, ginger, allspice, cardamom or a small amount of star anise. Instant espresso or instant coffee are also good add-ins.

Top-off flavor

Double the pleasures of chocolate by scattering cocoa nibs over the top of the cake batter. Nibs are intensely chocolaty, and they also have crunch. For a softer addition, consider topping the batter with fresh raspberries, blackberries or even blueberries—they'll sink into the cake, or they may leave little divots on the surface, but you might find them as pretty as I do.

Sasha's Grated Apple Cake

This is one of the most unusual cakes I've ever made and one of the most nostalgic: it reminds me of my grandmother's soft apple cake, a cake I've come close to replicating but never fully achieved.

The recipe came to me from Darra Goldstein, a Russia scholar, who included it in her book *Beyond the North Wind*. Because I trust Darra, I trusted the recipe, but it felt like a leap of faith. For as many times as I've made it, I still don't understand how a recipe that follows almost none of the rules of cakedom can turn out such a splendid cake—it's a delightful conundrum. All of the liquid for the cake comes from grated apples and the bit of lemon juice you use to keep the apples from darkening. There are no eggs, no milk and no reason to think that by mixing together flour, farina, sugar, baking powder, salt and some spice, you'll end up with a cake. But you do! You sprinkle this dry mixture between layers of apples, dot the top with tiny pieces of cold butter and bake for an hour, then marvel at the transformative magic of heat. It feels like a culinary miracle, but it doesn't feel like a standard cake—there's no fluffy crumb, no layers. Still, what you get is a surprisingly moist, generously spiced cake with the seductive texture of pie.

Makes 6 to 8 servings

8 tablespoons (4 ounces; 113 grams) very cold unsalted butter

¾ cup (102 grams) all-purpose flour

½ cup (90 grams) fine farina or Cream of Wheat, *not* instant (see below)

½ cup (100 grams) sugar

1 teaspoon baking powder

½ teaspoon ground cardamom, cinnamon, ginger or the spice of your choice, or less to taste

¼ teaspoon fine sea salt

1½ pounds (680 grams) tart apples (3 to 5, depending on size), such as Granny Smith, halved and cored but not peeled

2 tablespoons freshly squeezed lemon juice

¾ cup (100 to 125 grams) moist, plump dried apple rings, finely chopped, dried cranberries or raisins

Confectioners' sugar for dusting (optional)

A word on farina: Farina is an old-fashioned breakfast porridge. The best-known brand is Cream of Wheat—it's what I use for the cake. That it's easy to find is a good thing, because there's no substitute for farina in this recipe.

Center a rack in the oven and preheat it to 400 degrees F. You need either an 8-inch springform pan or an 8-inch round cake pan with sides that are at least 2 inches high. (Please don't try to make the cake in a 9-inch pan—it will be too thin.) If you're using a springform, butter the pan and place it on a baking sheet lined with parchment paper to catch any drips (springforms are not always leakproof). If you're using a cake pan, butter the pan, line the bottom with a circle of parchment and butter the parchment. Alternatively, you can use baker's spray, but butter's the first choice here.

Cut 7 tablespoons of the butter into tiny pieces and keep them in the refrigerator while you start to put the cake together. Keep the remaining tablespoon at the ready in the fridge. It's hard to know whether or not you'll need a bit more butter as the cake bakes, so it's best to be prepared. →

In a medium bowl, whisk together the flour, farina, sugar, baking powder, cardamom or other spice and salt.

The apples need to be coarsely grated, a job you can do using the large holes of a box grater or in a food processor with the grating blade. If you're grating by hand, grate the apples into a large bowl; if you use a processor, scrape the grated apples and whatever liquid has accumulated into a large bowl. Stir in the lemon juice and mix well, then stir in the dried apples (or whatever dried fruit you're using).

Now comes the odd part: Sprinkle one-third of the flour mixture evenly over the bottom of the pan. Top with half of the apples, then cover with half of the remaining flour mixture. Spoon on the remaining apples. If you've got a little liquid from the apples in the bowl, add it—if you've got a lot (unlikely, but . . .), just add a spoonful or two. Cover the apples with the last of the flour mixture. Scatter the bits of butter evenly over the top, taking care to cover the entire surface.

Slide the cake into the oven *and immediately lower the temperature to 350 degrees F.* Bake for 30 minutes, then take a peek at the cake. If you notice some dry spots, cut the reserved tablespoon of butter into bits and pop them onto the dry patches. Continue to bake the cake for 30 minutes longer, or until golden. The cake doesn't get very dark and it's really too soft to be tested reliably with a toothpick or skewer, so you must go with time and appearance. Transfer the pan to a rack and let the cake cool for about 20 minutes.

If you made the cake in a springform, run a table knife between the sides of the pan and the cake, then remove the ring of the pan. If you've made the cake in a regular cake pan, place a piece of parchment on a cooling rack or cutting board and have a serving plate or another rack or board covered with paper at hand. Run a table knife between the pan and the cake, unmold the cake onto the covered rack or board, peel away the round of parchment and then gently invert the cake onto your plate or the other parchment-covered rack or board. If you used a springform and want to remove the base (it's a doable but delicate procedure), follow the instructions for turning the cake over onto a parchment-lined surface.

The cake is ready to serve when it is slightly warm or has reached room temperature. Dust the top with confectioners' sugar, if you'd like.

Storing: The cake is best the day it is made, but if you have any left over, cover and refrigerate it—it's very good cold the next day. (I'm a fan of the next-day cake.) This cake isn't a good candidate for freezing.

Olive Oil and Orange Grab-and-Go Cake

Makes 10 to 12 servings

1¾ cups (238 grams) all-purpose flour

1 teaspoon baking powder

1 teaspoon fine sea salt

½ teaspoon baking soda

1¼ cups (250 grams) sugar

1 large orange

4 large eggs, at room temperature

½ cup (about 115 grams) plain whole-milk Greek yogurt, preferably at room temperature

2 tablespoons Campari or Aperol (or 2 tablespoons more orange juice)

¾ cup (180 ml) olive oil, mild or full-flavored

This cake is ample and tall; it's got the give and spring that are part of what endears oil cakes to us; and it's got an edge that comes from the orange and a small shot of bitter Campari or Aperol. There's just a splash of booze, but it changes the cake enough to make you stop for an instant and wonder what you're tasting.

If I didn't know myself better, I'd be tempted to declare this just-a-little-rough, just-a-little-rustic olive oil cake the final entry in my personal olive-oil–cake canon, but I know I'm an incurable fiddler and that there's bound to be another one. Or two. In part, it's my curiosity, but mostly it's the nature of olive oil that keeps me playing with it. The oil changes a cake's texture, adds flavor either subtle or strong and can be used to make something refined and delicate, like Pierre Hermé's Lemon Cake (page 50), or as casual as this hefty round.

I imagine this as a picnic cake. Or a breakfast cake—Michael likes it toasted and covered with salted butter. Or a dessert cake—serve it with a few spoonfuls of orange salad (see Playing Around) and maybe even with a spritz alongside.

Center a rack in the oven and preheat it to 350 degrees F. Coat the interior of a 9-inch springform pan with baker's spray or butter it, dust with flour and tap out the excess, and line the bottom with a circle of parchment paper.

Whisk the flour, baking powder, salt and baking soda together.

Put the sugar in a large bowl and grate the orange zest over it, then reach into the bowl and use your fingers to mash and press the zest into the sugar. Halve the orange and squeeze 2 tablespoons of juice into a separate bowl.

Add the eggs to the bowl of orange sugar and whisk vigorously to incorporate them. One by one, whisk in the yogurt, juice, Campari or Aperol and olive oil, whisking until each ingredient is blended in before adding the next. Spoon half the dry ingredients into the bowl and whisk gently—if you'd like, you can use a flexible spatula here—until the flour mixture just disappears into the batter. Add the →

remaining dry ingredients and mix to incorporate. You'll have a thick, shiny, pale apricot-colored batter that ribbons on itself when stirred and lifted. Scrape the batter into the pan and swivel the pan to even it.

Bake for 43 to 46 minutes, or until the top of the cake is honey-nut brown and it can be pulled away from the sides of the pan when gently tugged. The top will have crowned, and a tester inserted into the center of the cake should come out clean. Transfer the pan to a rack and wait for 10 minutes, then run a table knife around the edges of the cake, open the springform ring and remove it. Turn the cake over onto the rack and peel away the paper, then turn the cake right side up onto another rack; allow to cool. You can cut the cake when it's warm or wait for it to come to room temperature.

Storing: Wrapped, the cake can be kept at room temperature for at least 5 days. If you want to keep it longer, wrap and freeze it for up to 1 month; thaw in the wrapper.

Playing Around

Orange Salad

Count on 1 large orange for every 2 or 3 people. Cut a slice off the top and bottom of each orange, then stand one orange on a cutting board. Slice away the peel and cottony white pith by cutting from top to bottom all around the orange, following the contours of the fruit—you want to cut deep enough to expose the fruit. Now, cupping the orange in one hand and working over a bowl, cut between each segment and the membranes to release the fruit, letting it drop into the bowl. When all the segments are in the bowl, squeeze the membranes to get the last little bit of juice out of them, and repeat with the remaining oranges. For the salad, toss the oranges with a little sugar, maybe give them a squirt of lemon juice and sprinkle over a little Campari or Aperol. Add a little minced fresh rosemary, crushed thyme leaves or chopped fresh mint, if you'd like.

Olive Oil and Orange Party Cake

The cake is delicious with Yogurt Topping (page 269) or a generous covering of Cream Cheese Frosting (page 264). It's even nicer when the yogurt is flavored with orange-blossom water. If you'd like to really fancy up this simple cake, split it in half, spread orange marmalade over the bottom layer, cover with the top layer and finish with the frosting or yogurt topping and maybe some orange segments, too.

Paradise Cake

I came back from a week in Italy ready to make pasta and pizza, but it turned out that what I was really ready to make, maybe even meant to make, was this cake. It's a glorious member of the sponge cake family and known among Italian bakers as Paradise Cake—a tough name to live up to, but it's been holding its own for a very long time. I'd never heard of it when I set off to Italy and never even tasted it while I was there. Paradise might have eluded me—or maybe I might have eluded Paradise—had I not grabbed a brochure promoting flour and been stopped by a picture of the cake. I loved that it was taller than most single-layer cakes, that its crumb looked tender in the close-up and that it contained potato starch, an ingredient that my Russian grandmother always had in her cupboard, and one I'd rarely used. The original recipe called for Type 00 flour, a finely milled flour most famously used for pizza and often for pasta. That I choose to use cake flour might land me in bakers' jail in Italy, but it makes a fine cake in America.

This is one of those cakes that's so much better than you'd expect, since most of the ingredients are basic and the only add-in, citrus zest, is optional. Its texture, classically dry in the European tradition, is as light and lovely as a birthday cake, its crumb fine and golden because of the soft flour and potato starch, the combination of energetic and gentle mixing and all those eggs. Its flavor is hard to describe—you might think it's plain, but you'll find yourself taking bite after bite to make certain.

The cake bakes up close to a full 2 inches high and looks striking covered with a cloak of powdered sugar—it looks even more striking set on a cake stand. It can also be cut into layers and filled with cream or made into a spectacular shortcake (see Playing Around).

Makes about 10 servings

FOR THE CAKE

1 cup (125 grams) cake flour

⅔ cup (125 grams) potato starch

2 teaspoons baking powder

¼ teaspoon fine sea salt

Finely grated zest of 1 lemon or 1 orange (optional)

1¼ cups (250 grams) sugar

18 tablespoons (9 ounces; 254 grams) unsalted butter, cut into chunks, at room temperature

5 large eggs, at room temperature, lightly beaten

FOR THE SWEETENED CREAM FILLING OR GO-ALONG (optional)

1¼ cups (300 ml) heavy cream

½ cup (120 ml) sweetened condensed milk

1¾ teaspoons pure vanilla extract

Confectioners' sugar for topping

A word on temperature and on getting the best of both worlds: The cake's texture is truly paradisical at room temperature. If you fill it, the cake will need to be refrigerated, which will tighten the crumb a bit—happily, though, the cake will still be a heavenly treat. To get the best of both worlds, serve the cake at room temperature with the (optional) cold sweetened cream on the side.

To make the cake: Center a rack in the oven and preheat it to 350 degrees F. You need a 9-inch round cake pan with at least 2-inch-high sides or a 9-inch springform for this cake. Butter and flour the pan and tap out the excess flour, or lightly coat it with baker's spray; line the bottom with a circle of parchment paper. →

Whisk the cake flour, potato starch, baking powder and salt together. If the ingredients look even the teensiest bit lumpy, pass them through a sieve.

To add the lemon or orange zest, work in the bowl of a stand mixer, or in a large bowl if you're using a hand mixer, and rub the sugar and zest together with your fingers until the sugar is fragrant; if you're skipping the zest, put the sugar in the bowl. Drop in the butter. If you're using a stand mixer, fit it with the paddle attachment. Beat the sugar and butter at medium speed, scraping the bowl and beater(s) occasionally, for about 3 minutes—the mixture will be light and fluffy. With the mixer still on medium, slowly pour in the eggs and beat for about 4 minutes. At this point the batter will look as though it's deciding whether or not to curdle—ignore it. Scrape the bowl, add half the dry ingredients and mix on low until they just start to blend in. Add the remainder of the dry ingredients and beat on low until they disappear. Give the bowl and beaters a last scrape and stir the batter a couple of times with a flexible spatula just to make sure it's thoroughly mixed. Scrape the batter into the pan and smooth the top.

Bake for 38 to 42 minutes, or until a tester inserted into the center of the cake comes out clean, the sides pull away from the pan when gently prodded and the cake springs back just a bit when gingerly poked in the middle. Transfer the pan to a rack and wait for 5 minutes, then run a table knife around the edges of the cake (if you've used a springform, remove the ring) and turn it over onto the rack. Peel away the paper and invert the cake onto another rack. Allow the cake to cool to room temperature before topping or filling.

To make the (optional) filling or topping: Working in the bowl of a stand mixer fitted with the whisk attachment, or in a large bowl with a hand mixer, beat the cream, condensed milk and vanilla together until you've got firm peaks. You can make the cream a few hours ahead of time and keep it covered in the refrigerator—just give it a few brisk beats with a whisk to pull it back into shape before using.

To fill the cake or to use the filling as a go-along: If you want to fill the cake, use a long serrated knife to slice the cake in half at its midpoint. Spoon and smooth the filling over the bottom layer and cap with the top layer. You can serve the cake now or pop it into the fridge for a few hours until you're ready for it. Just before serving, shower the top of the cake with confectioners' sugar.

Or, if you want to use the filling as a go-along, top the cake with confectioners' sugar and serve it at room temperature with a hearty spoonful of the filling alongside or in a bowl that you can pass at the table.

Storing: Wrapped, the unfilled cake will keep at room temperature for about 3 days; if you've filled the cake, it will still keep for about 3 days, but it needs to be refrigerated. In either case, you'll probably want to dust the top of the cake with confectioners' sugar again before serving. You can wrap the unfilled cake airtight and freeze it for a month; thaw in the wrapper.

Playing Around

Paradise Shortcake

Cutting the cake into layers and filling them with whipped cream and berries will give you both a stunning dessert and a delectable oxymoron: a very tall shortcake. Do this, and you might want to brush each layer with Simple Syrup (page 282). If you make the shortcake with berries, try a Kirsch syrup; make it with peaches, and a brandy syrup is nice.

Toasted Almond Cake

Makes 8 servings

FOR THE CAKE

2 cups (200 grams) whole, slivered or sliced almonds or almond flour (see below)

14 tablespoons (7 ounces; 200 grams) unsalted butter, at room temperature

1 cup (200 grams) sugar

1 teaspoon fleur de sel or ½ teaspoon fine sea salt (if you love salt, use 1¼ teaspoons fleur de sel or ¾ teaspoon sea salt)

4 large eggs, at room temperature

1 to 2 tablespoons rum or 2 teaspoons pure vanilla extract

⅓ cup (45 grams) all-purpose flour

FOR THE GLAZE (optional)

¾ cup (90 grams) confectioners' sugar, sifted if lumpy

About 3 tablespoons water, rum or milk

Blanched almonds, whole or halved, for decoration (optional)

I first tasted this cake at the Salon de l'Agriculture in Paris, a huge annual fair that showcases animals big and small, farm tools and tractors and so much good food from every region of France. There are oysters from Brittany, cheeses from Normandy and dried sausages from everywhere, and one year there was this cake from Pithiviers, in the center of France. It was, as so many French cakes are, slender and plain, so plain that I almost passed it by. Had I missed this simple, elegant cake, I would have missed the pleasure of its soft, slightly chewy texture and its full almond flavor. I also would have missed getting the recipe—it was tucked into the cake's wrapper.

The original recipe called for store-bought almond flour, and that's what I used for years. Then recently, low on almond flour, I decided I'd just grind my own, measuring out the weight in whole almonds and whirring the nuts in a food processor with just a bit of the recipe's sugar. It was only later that I realized I'd ground roasted salted almonds—actually, what I'd ground were wildly expensive Marcona almonds from Spain. Not surprisingly, they made a great cake—such a great cake that I rejiggered the recipe to be able to always get that exceptional flavor even when starting with almonds from the grocery store. The shortcut to greatness is toasting the almonds, not grinding them uniformly—the cake is best when you've got some tiny pieces of nuts—and then adding more salt (preferably fleur de sel) to the batter.

Since I discovered the cake, I've seen different versions of it with different glazes. Truly the cake needs no embellishments, but it deserves to be fussed over, so I usually glaze it and often crown it with a ring of blanched almonds.

A word on the almonds: You can make this cake with 2 cups (200 grams) almond flour and it will be a good cake, but if you start with whole, slivered or sliced almonds (blanched or not), toast them and then whir them in a food processor, the cake will be better. A lot better.

A word on the temperature: To get the best texture, make sure that all of your ingredients are at room temperature.

A word on the glaze: You can play around with the amount of liquid you use to make the glaze. Start with just enough to make the mixture spreadable and then add more water, rum, or milk to get the consistency you want. And the opacity. A glaze like this is a little-more-a-little-less kind of thing.

Center a rack in the oven and preheat it to 350 degrees F.

If making your own almond flour, spread the nuts out on a baking sheet (I usually line the pan, but it's not necessary) and bake them for 10 to 15 minutes—less if you're using slivered or sliced almonds. You want them to be golden brown; keep checking on them and stir them around at least once. Let them cool, then toss them into a food processor with a spoonful of sugar (you can use some of the sugar you've measured out for the cake) and pulse, scraping the bottom of the bowl often, until the nuts are finely ground. You'll have a few discernible pieces here and there, and that's fine—nice, actually.

To make the cake: Butter a 9-inch round cake pan or coat it with baker's spray; line the bottom of the pan with a circle of parchment paper.

Working in the bowl of a stand mixer fitted with the paddle attachment, or in a large bowl with a hand mixer, beat the butter, sugar and salt together on medium speed until smooth and creamy, about 4 minutes; give the bowl and beater(s) a scrape now and then as you blend the ingredients. Add the almond flour (homemade or store-bought) and beat for another minute or so. One by one, add the eggs—drop them in and beat for a good minute after each addition to incorporate them. Beat in the rum or extract; you'll have a billowy batter. Then, either continuing with the mixer on low speed or switching to a flexible spatula, blend in the flour. Scrape the batter into the pan and shimmy it to smooth the top.

Bake for 35 to 38 minutes, or until the cake is deeply golden brown and starting to come away from the sides of the pan; a tester inserted into the center will come out clean. Set the pan on a rack and wait for 5 minutes, then gently run a table knife between the edges of the cake and the pan. Turn the cake over onto the rack and peel away the paper. If you're going to glaze the cake, leave it upside down on the rack until it cools to room temperature; if you're going to serve it plain, turn it right side up.

To make the (optional) glaze: Put the confectioners' sugar in a bowl, sprinkle over most of the 3 tablespoons of liquid and stir with a flexible spatula (see page 14). You want a glaze that will flow easily off the tip of the spatula or a spoon, so add more liquid little by little, if necessary. When you've got the consistency you like, pour it over the cake. You can let the glaze run down the sides of the cake in here-and-there drips or you can smooth the glaze on the sides with an icing spatula. If you'd like, circle the edges of the cake with a ring of almonds. Allow the glaze to set before serving.

Storing: Covered, the cake will keep at room temperature for about 5 days. I like it more the day after it's been baked than freshly baked. If you haven't glazed the cake, you can wrap it well and freeze it for up to 1 month; thaw in the wrapper.

Beach-Vibe Tropical Cheesecake

I grew up in New York City, the home of cheesecakes that are famous across the country, if not the world—mention Junior's or Lindy's, and old-time Gothamites still sigh. We're talking big cheesecakes—I don't think I ever saw one of them cut into slices that were less than gargantuan. I have a childhood memory of standing on a chair to get to the top of the cheesecake for a forkful. It was an adventure! And because cheesecake isn't an everyday dessert, it should always be an adventure—like this cake, which carries you away from city life. While it's got the best qualities of a New York cheesecake—it's ultracreamy, smooth, decisively rich and, yes, big—its flavors are tropical. Summery. Beachy. And bright—even the traditional graham-cracker crust has perky ginger in it. You can serve this plain, like a classic cheesecake from the Big Apple. But I hope you'll go the extra step and finish the cake with a layer of citrus curd and maybe even some summer berries. They're the perfect top-off—not just beautiful, but delicious.

A word on the cream cheese: I've made this cake with several different kinds of cream cheese, including store brands, and I've found that Kraft Philadelphia Cream Cheese makes the best cake.

A word on the zest: I like to use a lot of zest and I like a mix of lemon, lime and clementine, but if you've only got one kind of citrus or a different kind of orange, don't let that stand in your way. Whatever citrus you've got, you want a rounded tablespoon or so of zest (and 2 tablespoons juice).

A word on working ahead: It takes almost no time to make a cheesecake but a lot of time until it's ready to eat. The cake bakes for 90 minutes and then rests in the oven for an hour, after which it has to cool to room temperature, and then, finally, it's chilled for about 5 hours. Keep this in mind when you decide to put this on your menu.

Makes 16 servings

FOR THE CRUST

About 2⅔ cups (10 ounces; 280 grams) graham cracker crumbs OR 2 sleeves/18 full-size graham crackers, crushed or processed to fine crumbs

2 tablespoons sugar

¾ teaspoon ground cinnamon

½ teaspoon ground ginger

½ teaspoon fine sea salt

8 tablespoons (4 ounces; 113 grams) unsalted butter, melted (it's fine if it's still warm)

FOR THE CHEESECAKE

1 cup (200 grams) sugar

2½ teaspoons ground ginger

½ teaspoon ground cinnamon

½ teaspoon fine sea salt

Grated zest of 1 lemon, 1 lime and 1 clementine (see left; hold on to the fruit for the juice)

1½ pounds (680 grams) cream cheese, at room temperature

2 tablespoons citrus juice (squeezed from the zested fruit)

2½ teaspoons pure vanilla extract

3 large eggs, at room temperature

1 cup (240 grams) full-fat sour cream, at room temperature

Mixed Citrus Curd (page 275) for topping (optional)

Berries for finishing (optional)

To make the crust: Butter a 9-inch springform pan and wrap the pan in a double layer of foil. Cut two long pieces of aluminum foil and lay one on top of the other to form a cross, put the pan in the center and pull the foil up around the sides of the pan, crimping the foil as needed. Get the foil as high up and as tight against the sides as you can.

Mix the crumbs, sugar, spices and salt together in a large bowl, then pour in the butter. You need to mix everything together until the crumbs are moist and hold together when squeezed, a job best done with fingers. Turn the mixture out into the springform pan and press the crumbs over the bottom and about halfway up the sides of the pan—I like to get a layer of crumbs on the sides before I press the rest into the bottom, but it'll work any way you do it. The sides probably won't be even, and they may be above or below the midway point—that's not a problem, and I think the cake is actually prettier when the crust zigs and zags. Put the pan in the freezer while you preheat the oven.

Center a rack in the oven and preheat it to 350 degrees F. Find a roasting pan that has sides that are almost or just as high as the springform and that can hold the pan comfortably. Put the springform in the pan.

Bake the crust for 10 minutes. Carefully lift the springform out of the roaster onto a rack and let the crust cool while you make the batter. Keep the roaster at hand.

Reduce the oven temperature to 325 degrees F.

To make the cheesecake: Put a pot of water on to boil—you need a fair amount of water because you're going to fill the roaster about halfway.

Put the sugar in the bowl of a stand mixer or in a large bowl that you can use with a hand mixer and stir in the ginger, cinnamon and salt. Add the citrus zest to the sugar. Set aside.

Reach into the bowl and smush and mush everything together with your fingers until the sugar is moist and fragrant. Cut the cream cheese into chunks and add it to the bowl. If you're using a stand mixer, fit it with the paddle attachment. Beat the sugar and cream cheese together on low speed to blend, about 2 minutes, scraping the bowl and beater(s) as needed—making a cheesecake filling like this is as much about scraping as it is about blending, so scrape early and often. Still on low, beat in the 2 tablespoons juice and the vanilla. Add the eggs one by one, beating for about 30 seconds or so after each one to incorporate it. Don't forget to scrape! The mixture should be beautifully smooth and velvety; if it's not, scrape again, then raise the speed to medium for just a nanosecond—you don't want to beat air into the batter. Add the sour cream and mix on the lowest speed for 1 minute to finish the batter. Scrape the bowl well, particularly the bottom, then pour the batter into the crust and swivel the pan to level it (or give it a few sweeps with a spatula).

Make sure that you lowered the oven temperature and that it's at 325 degrees F.

Put the pan in the center of the roaster and pour enough hot water into the roaster, taking care not to spatter the top of the cake, to come halfway up the sides of the springform. Carefully slide the setup into the oven. (Some people find it easier to pull out the oven rack, put the roaster and springform on the rack and fill the pan with water, then slide the rack back into the oven. Do whatever you've got the strength and nerves to handle.)

Bake the cake for 90 minutes, testing your ability to keep the oven door closed the whole time—don't peek! The cake will rise a little, it will brown a little and it may even crack here and there. If it cracks, I hope you adopt my attitude on this matter: I don't care! I think a crack is like a fingerprint—it says the cake was made with your hands.

Turn off the oven and slip in a wooden spoon that will keep the oven door open just a bit. Leave the cake in its water bath in the turned-off oven for 1 hour. →

After an hour, carefully remove the roaster from the oven and even more carefully lift the springform out of the water bath. No matter how diligently you wrapped the pan, some hot water is bound to have seeped between the layers of foil, so pay attention. Discard the foil, then transfer the springform to a rack and allow the cheesecake to cool to room temperature.

Lightly cover the cooled cake and refrigerate it for at least 4 hours—longer is better.

I think the best way to remove the sides of the springform is to warm them with a hair dryer set to hot and then release the ring. You can also wrap the sides of the pan with kitchen towels dampened with hot water. When the sides are off, you've got a choice—serve the cake on the pan's base or lift it off the base and onto a platter. The cake looks better without the base but getting it off can be tricky—I rely on a large cake lifter, a spatula and prayer. See what works for you.

If you are going to top the cake, give the citrus curd a good stir to loosen it, then spoon and spread it over the top of the cake. It's a loose curd and some of it may slither its way down the sides of the cake—celebrate its random beauty. Finish with berries, if you'd like.

Storing: Wrapped well and kept away from foods with strong odors, the cake will hold in the fridge for at least 4 days. If you haven't topped the cake, you can freeze it. I like to put it in the freezer to get it firm before wrapping it airtight. It will keep for up to 1 month; thaw in the wrapper in the refrigerator.

Pudding Puff Cake

Think of this as a great big, shareable éclair. And really, that's what it is. The layers are made with the same dough used to make éclairs, cream puffs and profiteroles, but here it's spooned into two cake pans and swirled around so that it bakes into two supersized puffs with extravagant hills and valleys, peaks and dips. When the layers are cool, they are turned out of their pans and sandwiched—a job that's a giggle: the layers are so delightfully wonky that figuring out how to balance them feels like a trick.

Like éclairs or cream puffs, the cake can be filled with whatever makes your heart sing. Since I'm married to Michael, who would trade any dessert for a serving of chocolate pudding—and since I'm also crazy about pudding (and about Michael, too)—I'm likely to choose chocolate more often than not. But the filling can be whipped cream—I like a combination of whipped cream and mascarpone for this, or pastry cream, or you can channel profiteroles and sandwich the layers with ice cream. If you do, I think the rule book says that you've got to pour hot chocolate sauce (page 276) over each generous portion.

If chocolate is all that you dream about, you could make chocolate layers (see Playing Around). For a little fun, you could use just one layer and top it with chocolate pudding, then top the pudding with whipped cream and cover the whipped cream with chocolate shavings. Do that, and you can tuck the second cake layer into the freezer, where it can wait for the next proverbial rainy day.

Makes 6 to 8 servings

FOR THE LAYERS

⅓ cup (80 ml) water

⅓ cup (80 ml) whole milk

6 tablespoons (3 ounces; 85 grams) unsalted butter, cut into 6 pieces

1 tablespoon sugar

½ teaspoon fine sea salt

¾ cup (102 grams) all-purpose flour

3 large eggs

1 large egg white

FOR THE FILLING

Dark Chocolate Pudding Filling (page 274), Mascarpone Whipped Cream (page 285), Vanilla or Chocolate Pastry Cream (page 272 or 273), Whipped Cream (page 284) or another filling

Confectioners' sugar for dusting

Whipped cream for serving (optional, or maybe not really)

A word on serving: If you fill the cake with chocolate pudding, whipped cream or pastry cream, you can serve it right away, but I think it's nicer if you give it at least an hour in the fridge. (The pudding- and pastry-cream-filled cakes can chill for up to a day.) If ice cream is your choice, you'll need to soften it so that you can scoop and spread it, and then you might need to pop the whole cake into the freezer to reset it. The layers are surprisingly good frozen and then left at room temperature for about 10 minutes before serving.

To make the layers: Center a rack in the oven and preheat it to 400 degrees F. Line two 8-inch cake pans (the sides should be at least 2 inches high) with parchment paper. There's no need to grease the pans.

Put the water, milk, butter, sugar and salt in a medium saucepan and set it over medium heat. Cook until the butter melts and the liquid comes to a boil, then add the flour all at once, grab a sturdy spatula or wooden spoon and start stirring the ingredients, which will form a ball. You want to stir diligently and nonstop for about 2 minutes to essentially dry and cook the mixture; unless you're using a nonstick pan, a white film will form on the bottom of the pan. Scrape the mixture into the bowl of a stand mixer fitted with the paddle attachment or into a large bowl that you can use with a hand mixer. (You can certainly make this by hand, continuing with the spatula or spoon, but it's easier to get a smooth dough with a mixer.)

Let the dough cool for 5 minutes or so. While it's cooling, stir the eggs and white together to break them up.

With the mixer on medium, beat the eggs in a little at a time. Scrape the bowl and beater(s) often, and when you do, you might take a minute to enjoy how the batter goes from pasty to smooth, shiny and flowing. Divide the batter evenly between the two pans. Using an offset spatula or the back of a spoon, push the batter around so that it covers the bottom of the pans and then circle around it as though you were swirling frosting on a cake.

Bake for 35 minutes—without opening the oven door! Look at the cakes—they should be golden brown and firm to the touch. If you think they need a couple more minutes, bake them a bit longer. Transfer the pans to a rack and let the cakes cool to room temperature. They'll deflate a bit—it's inevitable.

To fill the cakes: If you're using chocolate pudding or pastry cream, give it a few beats with a flexible spatula to soften it; if you're using whipped cream, check to see if it needs a little whisking to firm it. When the cakes are absolutely cool, run a table knife between the cakes and the sides of the pans, making sure you get down to the bottoms. Turn the cakes over, remove the parchment and return them right side up to the rack. The bottoms of the cakes won't be flat—they'll be hilly and craggy and look like the custardy inside of a cream puff, which is what they are. Decide which layer you like best and set it aside, then put the other layer, wavier side up, on a serving platter. Turn the filling out onto the layer and spread it as best as you can across the top. Obviously, you'll end up with more filling in the valleys and less on the mountains—it's one of the delights of this quirky cake. Top the filling with the second layer, wavier side up, gently pressing it into place.

If you've got time, chill the cake for at least an hour—more, if you'd like. Playing against type, I like this cake served cold. (If you've filled the cake with ice cream, you'll have to freeze it and then leave it at room temperature for just a little bit to soften the ice cream.) When you're ready to serve, dust the top generously with confectioners' sugar—it highlights the up-and-down texture—and, if you'd like, have a bowl of whipped cream ready to pass around the table.

Storing: You can make the layers up to 1 day ahead—leave them in the pans and lightly cover them. Alternatively, you can freeze the layers for up to 1 month—wrap them once they're frozen and then thaw them in their wrappers. If they seem wilted, give them a quick reheat in a hot oven, cool and then fill. The assembled cake can be kept covered in the refrigerator for up to 2 days.

Playing Around

Chocolate Puff Cake

Sift or strain the flour for the puff layer together with 1¾ tablespoons cocoa powder.

Black Forest Puff Cake

Make chocolate layers (as for the Chocolate Puff Cake, above), and when they're cool, fill with sweetened whipped cream (Mascarpone Whipped Cream, page 285, is lovely here)—if you'd like, you can flavor it gently with a teaspoon of rose water. Dot the cream with pitted and halved fresh dark cherries, or use jarred cherries (drained and patted dry), and cover them with a little more cream. Finish the cake with whipped cream and chocolate curls.

Makes 8 to 10 servings

FOR THE CAKE

3 tablespoons instant espresso powder

1 tablespoon very hot water

1¼ cups (170 grams) all-purpose flour

½ cup (68 grams) whole wheat flour

2 teaspoons ground cinnamon (or 1 teaspoon cinnamon and ½ teaspoon ground cardamom)

½ teaspoon baking soda

½ teaspoon fine sea salt

¼ teaspoon freshly grated nutmeg

2 to 3 very ripe medium bananas, peeled

⅓ cup (79 grams) coconut oil, melted and at room temperature

¾ cup (150 grams) sugar

1 large egg, at room temperature, lightly beaten

1½ teaspoons pure vanilla extract

¾ cup (90 grams) toasted shredded coconut, sweetened or unsweetened

FOR THE FROSTING (optional)

4 ounces (113 grams) cream cheese, at room temperature

8 tablespoons (4 ounces; 113 grams) unsalted butter, at room temperature

1½ teaspoons pure vanilla extract

1 teaspoon instant espresso powder

¼ teaspoon ground cinnamon

¼ teaspoon fine sea salt

2 cups (240 grams) confectioners' sugar, sifted if very lumpy

Toasted shredded coconut for topping (optional)

Banana Cappuccino Cake

When the cooking website *Simply Recipes* was getting ready to celebrate its twentieth anniversary, its founder, Elise Bauer, asked a few bakers to riff on the site's all-time most popular recipe, her Banana Bread. Because we were celebrating a milestone, I wanted to make something a little more festive than a bread, but I didn't want to stray too far from the classic. I changed the shape from loaf to layer; fiddled with the texture, so that it was definitely a cake, not a bread; and played with the flavors. Thinking about the adage "What grows together goes together," I found tropical mates for the banana, among them coconut, coffee, cinnamon and vanilla: think banana cappuccino. And I made sure there was frosting. Espresso-cinnamon frosting. Lots of it. Keeping the spirit of the cake but going rogue around the edges got me a cake with big flavor and great texture. Also, one that looks good with candles.

To make the cake: Center a rack in the oven and preheat it to 350 degrees F. Coat a 9-inch round cake pan with baker's spray. Or, if you prefer, butter and flour the pan (tap out the excess flour), or use coconut oil to grease it, but heads up—the oil can leave spots of residue on the cake.

Put the espresso powder in a small bowl, pour over the hot water and stir until the powder dissolves; set aside.

Whisk the all-purpose and whole wheat flours, the cinnamon (and cardamom, if you're using it), baking soda, salt and nutmeg together.

Working in a large bowl, mash the bananas with a fork until they're smooth; you'll have 1¼ to 1½ cups. Pour in the melted coconut oil and, using a mixing spoon or a flexible spatula, stir to blend. One by one, stir in the sugar, beaten egg, espresso mixture and vanilla. Stir with intention, so that everything is fully incorporated. Spoon half the dry ingredients over the batter and, using a motion that's somewhere between stirring and folding, gently blend it in. Do the same with the remaining flour mixture. Finish by stirring in the toasted coconut. The batter will be lumpy, bumpy and very fragrant. Pour it into the pan and use the spatula to smooth the top.

Bake for 23 to 25 minutes, or until the cake has risen and turned a gorgeous shade of deep brown—it should feel springy to the touch and pull away from the sides of the pan when you tug it lightly; a tester inserted into the center of the cake should come out clean. Transfer the pan to a rack and let rest for 5 minutes, then run a table knife around the edges of the cake and unmold it onto the rack. Turn the cake over onto another rack and let it cool completely before serving or frosting.

To make the (optional) frosting: Working in the bowl of a stand mixer fitted with the paddle attachment, or in a large bowl with a hand mixer, beat all of the ingredients *except* the confectioners' sugar together on medium speed. Add the sugar and pulse the mixer on and off to start incorporating it—you might want to drape the bowl with a kitchen towel to keep the sugar from flying about. When the risk of a sugar shower has passed, beat the frosting on medium until it's smooth and velvety.

To frost the cake: You've got plenty of frosting, so swoop away. My preference is to frost the top and leave the sides bare, but the cake's yours to play with, of course. If you want to dust the top with toasted coconut, do it now while the frosting is fresh and the shreds will stick.

The cake is ready to be served as soon as it's frosted, but it can wait.

Storing: Covered, the cake will keep at room temperature for about 3 days. If you've frosted it, it's best to keep it in the fridge. If it's been in the fridge, it's good to let it come to close to room temperature before serving. Not that it's not good chilled—it's really fine. Wrapped airtight, the cake—frosted or plain—can be frozen for up to a month. Thaw, still wrapped, in the refrigerator overnight (ideal) or on the counter.

Choose-a-Fruit Cake: The Blueberry Edition

Every once in a while, I work on a recipe and end up with something that can become almost anything: a recipe, like my Classic French Yogurt Cake (page 94), with enough wiggle room to accept a bounty of whims. I knew this was a wiggle cake after I'd made it with apricots in Paris and blueberries in Connecticut, with apples and pears in winter and cherries in summer. The cake itself is plain, unspiced, flavored with only vanilla and almond extract. But it can take a little spice, if you'd like; poppy seeds, if they're in your freezer; or some streusel on top, if you're in a crumbcake mood. It will always be the kind of cake that you'll bring on a picnic, take to a friend's house, put out for dessert or nibble through the day. Here's the berry version, but play, play, play!

Makes 6 servings

- ⅔ cup (91 grams) all-purpose flour
- 1 teaspoon baking powder
- ¼ teaspoon fine sea salt
- ¾ cup (75 grams) almond flour
- 2 large eggs, at room temperature
- ½ cup (100 grams) sugar
- ½ teaspoon pure vanilla extract
- ¼ teaspoon pure almond extract
- 7 tablespoons (3½ ounces; 100 grams) unsalted butter, melted and cooled
- 1½ cups (about 225 grams) blueberries (or other fruit; see headnote)
- Sliced almonds for sprinkling (optional)
- Turbinado sugar for sprinkling (optional)

Center a rack in the oven and preheat it to 350 degrees F. Butter an 8-inch round cake pan with at least 2-inch-high sides or coat it with baker's spray. To make it easier to remove the cake from the pan, cut two wide strips of parchment, each about 12 inches long, and crisscross them in the bottom of the pan, so that the overhang forms handles, or line the pan with a sheet of parchment, pressing it against the bottom of the pan and allowing it to extend above the pan's rim—the parchment will pleat, and that's fine.

Whisk the all-purpose flour, baking powder and salt together, then whisk in the almond flour.

Working in a large bowl with a whisk, beat the eggs and sugar together for 2 minutes. Whisk in the vanilla and almond extracts. Switch to a flexible spatula and stir in half of the dry ingredients. The mixture will be thick, so it will take a few turns—be gentle. When the ingredients are almost completely incorporated, stir in the rest of the dry mixture. Pour the melted butter over the dry ingredients and thoroughly blend it in. Take a peek at the bottom of the bowl to be sure that no butter has slithered its way down and pooled there.

Scrape the batter into the pan and smooth the top. Scatter over the berries and, if you'd like, top them sparingly with almonds and a dusting of turbinado sugar. →

Bake for 35 to 38 minutes, or until the cake is golden brown, pulls away from the sides of the pan when gently prodded and, most important, leaves no crumbs on a tester inserted into the center. (If you're using wetter fruits, the cake may take a bit more time—trust the tests.) Transfer the cake to a rack and let it rest for 5 minutes, then run a table knife around the edges of the cake and use the parchment overhang to lift it out of the pan and onto a rack to cool. Serve the cake when it is only just warm or at room temperature.

Storing: Wrapped, the cake will keep at room temperature for a day. You can refrigerate the cake for about 2 days—try to let it warm up a bit before eating—or freeze it for up to 1 month; thaw in the wrapper.

Breton Buckwheat Butter Cake

When it comes to baking in France, it's easy to know when something is from Brittany—the saltiness is the tell. The Bretons use salted butter in and on everything and they use it generously. I think it's one of the reasons I fell in love with their shortbreads at first bite. For years, I made my version of their famous cookies—they were buttery, lightly crunchy and salty. I made the cookies thin and thick; I made them plain; and I made them with jam in the centers. Then I baked them in a large pan, the size and the longer baking time softening the crunch only a tad. I fiddled and fussed and never made a version I didn't love, but there was never one that I loved as much as I like this newer recipe, built on the shortbread blueprint, nudged into cakedom and, in the process, made even more Breton by showcasing the region's hometown favorite flour: buckwheat.

Buckwheat flour tastes nutty and, when mixed with all-purpose flour, as it is here, produces an appealingly tweedy-looking crumb. I've flavored the cake with freshly grated nutmeg, a strong spice, but one that blends beautifully with buckwheat, and fleur de sel, the pride of Brittany. Together, they tilt the cake's axis—it's still sweet, but you catch a savory hint now and then.

The batter for the cake—a soft, sticky affair—is pressed into a tart pan, so that it bakes into a thin layer with pretty rickrack edges. Before it goes into the oven, you can sprinkle the top with kasha (roasted buckwheat), more sea salt and some turbinado sugar, if you'd like. When it's cool, you can slick it with chocolate ganache, drizzle it with hot fudge, speckle it with crushed berries, dollop it with jam or eat it the way I like it best—neat! And out of hand.

Makes 8 servings

FOR THE CAKE

- ¾ cup (102 grams) all-purpose flour
- ¼ cup (30 grams) buckwheat flour
- 1¼ teaspoons baking powder
- ¼ teaspoon freshly grated nutmeg
- 1 large egg, at room temperature
- 2 large egg yolks, at room temperature
- 10 tablespoons (5 ounces; 140 grams) unsalted butter, at room temperature (see below)
- ⅓ cup (67 grams) sugar
- ⅓ cup (67 grams) brown sugar
- ½ teaspoon fleur de sel or ¼ teaspoon fine sea salt, or more to taste

FOR THE GLAZE AND TOPPING (optional)

- 1 large egg yolk
- Kasha (optional)
- Fleur de sel
- Turbinado sugar

A word on the butter: Since every brand of salted butter seems to have a different level of saltiness, I use unsalted butter and then add fleur de sel to the batter. If you want to play around, try making the cake with European salted butter, which is usually noticeably saltier than American butter, and adjust the amount of fleur de sel to get what you like.

To make the cake: Center a rack in the oven and preheat it to 350 degrees F. Butter a 9- to 9½-inch fluted tart pan with a removable bottom. (Butter is preferable to baker's spray here.) Or, if you don't have a tart pan, use a springform or a regular round cake pan and line the bottom of the buttered pan with a circle of parchment paper. Line a baking sheet with parchment. →

Whisk together the all-purpose and buckwheat flours, baking powder and nutmeg. Put the egg and yolks in a small bowl and beat them lightly with a fork so that they're pourable.

Working in the bowl of a stand mixer fitted with the paddle attachment, or in a large bowl with a hand mixer, beat the butter, both sugars and the salt together at medium speed for about 3 minutes, scraping the bowl as needed. With the mixer on medium, gradually pour in the beaten eggs (pour them down the side of the bowl to keep spatters at bay) and then beat until fully incorporated; don't fret if the mixture looks as if it's on the verge of curdling. Stop the mixer, add the dry ingredients and pulse the mixer a few times to get things started. Working on low speed, beat until the flour almost disappears into the batter, then grab a flexible spatula and finish the mixing by hand. Scrape the sticky batter into the pan and use a spatula (an offset is good here) to get it into all the pan's crannies and to smooth the top.

To glaze and top the cake (optional): Using a fork, break up the yolk, add a splash of cold water and mix until blended. Brush the glaze over the top of the cake, taking care to keep the glaze from dribbling down the sides and gluing it to the pan. Sprinkle the top sparingly with kasha, if you're using it, fleur de sel and turbinado sugar.

Put the pan on the lined baking sheet, slip it into the oven and bake for 30 to 35 minutes, or until the cake is uniformly puffed (it will sink as it cools, but the puff is a good hint of doneness at this point) and gives a bit when you poke it in the center. A tester inserted in the middle of the cake will come out clean. If in doubt, go for underbaked rather than overbaked. Transfer the pan to a rack and let rest for 5 minutes before unmolding. After you've removed the sides of the tart pan, removing the cake from the base can take a little cajoling: gently work the bottom of another tart pan, a cake lifter or a long wide metal spatula between the cake and the base, going around the edges and then slowly moving it to the center to make certain the entire bottom is free. Lift the cake onto the rack and let cool until it is only just warm or has reached room temperature.

Storing: Wrapped well, the cake will keep for up to 3 days at room temperature. It can be frozen for up to 1 month; thaw in the wrapper.

Grammy's Easy Cake

It was my friend Berna Feuerstein who gave me this recipe and it was her mother, "Grammy" Shirley Spector, who gave it to her. I wish I knew where the recipe originally came from or when Grammy got it (Berna does, too). Nothing about the way you make this eggless cake plays by the rules as we know them—it's a wild way to end up with a great cake. But if you follow these directions, minimal as they are, you'll have a golden-crusted moist, buttery cake that hugs whatever fruit you've topped it with it—even if on the first try, like me, you're sure it's not going to work. At the end of the recipe that Berna sent me, she wrote, "VOILA!" She might just as rightly have said, "TA-DA!" Or "HA!" The cake is such a surprise.

Makes 6 to 8 servings

12 tablespoons (6 ounces; 170 grams) unsalted butter, cut into chunks

1 cup (136 grams) all-purpose flour

1 teaspoon baking powder

½ teaspoon fine sea salt

¼ teaspoon baking soda

¾ cup (150 grams) sugar

¾ cup (180 ml) whole milk

About 1½ cups (225 grams) blueberries or other fruit (see below)

Lightly whipped cream or ice cream for serving (optional)

Center a rack in the oven and preheat it to 350 degrees F. Have a 9-inch deep-dish glass, ceramic or pottery pie pan at hand. You're going to serve the cake from the pan, so if you've got a pretty one, use it.

Toss the butter into the pie pan, slide the pan into the hot oven and heat until the butter is melted—about 5 minutes.

Meanwhile, whisk the flour, baking powder, salt, baking soda and sugar together in a large bowl. Add half of the milk and whisk to moisten the dry ingredients—the mixture will be thick. Pour in the remainder of the milk and whisk until smooth.

Pour the batter into the pan over the butter—do not mix. Or, as Berna wrote, "DO NOT MIX!" And don't be concerned when the butter slides up and around the batter. Scatter the berries over the top and, again, "DO NOT MIX!"

Bake the cake for 44 to 48 minutes, or until the butter has been absorbed, the cake is beautifully golden and, most important, a tester inserted into the center of the cake comes out clean. The edges of the cake, which will pull away from the pan if tugged gingerly, will be firmer and darker than the center—good reason for you to check the middle of the cake carefully. Transfer the cake to a rack and let it cool until it's only just warm or has reached room temperature. The cake is too soft and fruit-filled to unmold, so serve it from the pan.

If you decide to serve the cake with lightly whipped cream or ice cream, I think Grammy would approve.

A word on the berries: Berna said that her mother's "go-to" were blueberries. When I asked if Mom ever used frozen, she answered emphatically, "Never!" But Berna did concede that other berries are acceptable. Also, soft fruits, such as plums, apricots or peeled peaches, work as long as you cut them into bite-size pieces.

Storing: Try to serve the cake the day you make it—that's really when it's best. If you've got leftovers, cover the pan tightly and keep the cake at room temperature; it may be a bit heavier when you serve it, but it will still be tasty.

Makes 10 to 12 servings

1 cup (136 grams) all-purpose flour

¼ cup (34 grams) whole wheat flour

1 teaspoon baking powder

½ teaspoon ground cinnamon

¼ teaspoon baking soda

8 tablespoons (4 ounces; 113 grams) very soft unsalted butter

¾ cup (150 grams) turbinado or demerara sugar

¾ teaspoon fleur de sel or ½ teaspoon fine sea salt

3 tablespoons natural almond or peanut butter (or other nut butter; see below), well stirred

1 large egg, at room temperature, lightly beaten

4 ounces (113 grams) semisweet or bittersweet chocolate, coarsely chopped

⅓ cup (about 50 grams) almonds (or other nuts; see below), coarsely chopped

About 3 tablespoons salted caramel topping (store-bought is perfect here) for finishing

Fleur de sel or flaky salt for finishing

A word on the nut butter and nut topping: François uses hazelnut butter and chopped hazelnuts from Piedmont for the cake, but he said that it's fine to use peanut butter. It's my go-to, but I love the cake with almond butter and think cashew butter would work as well. I like to match the nut to the nut butter, but you can mix and match.

A Ritzy Cookie Cake

Say "cookie" in France (or even *en français*—it's the same word in both languages), and the first thing that pops into any French person's mind is "chocolate chip cookie"—one is shorthand for the other there. And, indeed, this could be called a chocolate chip cookie, but since it was created by François Perret, the pastry chef at the famous Ritz hotel in Paris, it's a more sophisticated and much more surprising cookie than you'd expect. It's chockablock with good things and big enough for the whole family to share. In fact, before the cookie became a sensation at the Ritz, Perret made it only at home for his kids. Adorably, he told me he decided on one big cookie so that his children wouldn't fight over whose cookie might be microscopically bigger than the other's.

Baked in a tart pan or the ring of a springform pan, the recipe transforms the cookie we think we know into a chewy cake, with everything we love in that classic cookie and more. Because Perret uses turbinado sugar in the dough, each bite has a bit of crunch. And in very Parisian fashion, the chef flips the American favorite upside down—instead of mixing the chocolate chips and nuts into the dough, he bakes them on top of the cake and then, when it cools, he drizzles, spatters or dots the top with caramel and a light shower of sea salt. It's extravagant. It's playful. And it's fun for a party or for the whole family—which is just what Perret intended.

This recipe is pretty much the same as the one François Perret gave me—*merci*, Chef—with the exception of the whole wheat flour, which I added to play up the chewiness that I love in the cake. Everything else is his, including the advice to use very soft butter—it's important for the cake's lovely texture.

Center a rack in the oven and preheat it to 350 degrees F. Line a baking sheet with parchment paper. Then line a 9- to 9½-inch tart pan with a removable bottom with a circle of parchment. Alternatively, you can use the ring from a 9-inch springform pan—turn the ring upside down so that the ridge is at the top. Whichever pan you're using, put it on the baking sheet. →

Whisk the all-purpose and whole wheat flours, baking powder, cinnamon and baking soda together.

Working in the bowl of a stand mixer fitted with the paddle attachment, or in a large bowl with a hand mixer, beat the butter, sugar and salt together on medium speed for about 2 minutes, until smooth. Add the nut butter and beat for 2 minutes more, scraping the bowl as needed. Add about one-third of the dry ingredients and mix on low until blended, then pour in the beaten egg and mix to incorporate. Add the remainder of the dry ingredients and mix only until they're no longer visible. Give the dough a couple of good stirs with a flexible spatula and then scrape it into the pan or into the springform ring. Use your fingers (my first choice) or the spatula to spread the dough as evenly as you can. It's sticky, so it's not easy to work with, but try to get it smooth without pressing on it too much or too heavily. Scatter over the chocolate and then top with the nuts.

Bake for 22 to 24 minutes, or until a tester inserted in the center of the cake comes out clean. If you used a tart pan, slide it onto a rack and let rest for 5 minutes, then remove the sides of the pan (you can leave the cake on the pan bottom and remove it when you're ready to serve). Or, if you used a springform ring, carefully remove it, leaving the cake on the baking sheet. Let the cake cool to room temperature.

When you're ready to serve, top the cookie cake with dabs of caramel—a few or a lot, it's up to you. If the caramel's too thick to drop easily from a spoon, give it a 10-second burst or two in a microwave or heat it gently on the stovetop. Finish with a light sprinkle of fleur de sel or flaky salt.

If you know you won't be polishing off the cake all at once, the best move is to cut it as you go.

Storing: Wrapped well, the cake will keep at room temperature for at least 4 days.

Pears, Nuts and Rye, Oh My

Makes 8 servings

- 2 medium pears
- Freshly squeezed lemon juice
- ¾ cup (100 grams) spelt flour (or all-purpose)
- ¾ cup (90 grams) rye flour
- 1½ teaspoons baking powder
- ½ teaspoon fine sea salt
- ½ cup (56 grams) hazelnut flour
- 4 large eggs, at room temperature
- 1¼ cups (250 grams) brown sugar
- 8 tablespoons (4 ounces; 113 grams) unsalted butter, melted
- 2 tablespoons dark rum, brandy, Calvados, Armagnac or other aromatic liquor (or 1 more teaspoon pure vanilla extract)
- 1 teaspoon pure vanilla extract
- ¼ teaspoon pure almond extract
- ½ cup (120 ml) whole milk, at room temperature
- ¼ cup (30 grams) chopped hazelnuts
- Honey for drizzling, plus more (optional) for serving
- Confectioners' sugar for dusting (optional)
- Yogurt Topping (page 269) for serving (optional)

The first time I made this pear coffee cake–ish cake was in Paris, and I was so in love with it that I'd make another cake as soon as the one on the counter was on the verge of disappearing. I served it after light dinners, took it to friends, nibbled on it as I worked and looked forward to it in the afternoon the way a kid scrambles for an after-school snack. There's something about the cake that's inviting to the extreme. In part it's because both the fruit and the cake that cradles it have distinct but delightfully compatible personalities. And both are confident. The fruit, which can so often be merely decorative, bakes to a warmth and juiciness that permeates the cake. Also, there's a scattering of nuts and a drizzle of honey, adding flavor, texture, shine and presence. And the cake itself is a little wonder. It's earthy—the (switch-up-able) combo of spelt, rye, and nut flour grounds the cake and even gives it a touch of sweetness. And it's packed with the kinds of flavors that slow things down and make life feel comfier: brown sugar, vanilla and a couple of spoonfuls of a really aromatic liquor, like Armagnac.

While you could play with the fruit and flavors and devise a cake for the heat of summer, I never do—for me, this is the chill-in-the-air cake. If I had a fireplace, I'd sit in front of it, a slice of cake in hand. But if you want a summer cake with similar charms, try the Choose-a-Fruit Cake, page 27.

Center a rack in the oven and preheat it to 350 degrees F. Coat the interior of a 9-inch springform pan with baker's spray. Alternatively, butter the pan, dust the interior with flour and tap out the excess. No matter how you prep the pan, put it on a parchment-lined baking sheet—a precaution against drips and leaks.

Peel, halve and core the pears. Cut each one lengthwise into 6 to 8 slices and sprinkle them lightly with lemon juice to help keep them from darkening; set aside.

Whisk the spelt and rye flours, baking powder and salt together, then whisk in the hazelnut flour.

Working in a large bowl, whisk the eggs and sugar together for about 2 minutes, until the sugar dissolves. Switch to a flexible spatula and stir in half of the dry ingredients, then incorporate the remaining dry ingredients. Stir in the melted butter in two additions, being gentle but thorough. Stir the liquor (if using), vanilla and almond extracts into the milk, then add the milk to the batter in three additions—a light touch is good here.

Stir everything one last time to be certain that there's no liquid hiding at the bottom of the bowl, then scrape the batter into the pan, swiveling the pan to even and smooth it. Arrange the pear slices over the batter: I usually make a circle around the edges of the pan and leave the center bare, but there isn't a rule for this. (Also, there's every chance that the batter will bake up, around and maybe over your prettily arranged pears—so fuss, but not too much.) Sprinkle the chopped nuts over the pears and batter and top with honey—drizzle, don't drench.

Slide the cake into the oven and bake for 30 minutes. (You'll be lowering the oven temperature after the cake bakes for a while, so don't leave town.) Turn the oven temperature down to 300 degrees F and bake for another 25 to 30 minutes, or until the cake is deeply and beautifully golden and risen. It will spring back when lightly prodded and pull away from the sides of the pan when gently tugged; a tester inserted into the center of the cake will come out clean.

Transfer the pan to a rack and let it sit for 5 minutes, then run a table knife around the edges of the cake and remove the sides of the pan. Turn the cake over onto another rack, remove the bottom of the pan and flip the cake right side up onto a rack to cool to room temperature. Dust with confectioners' sugar before serving, if you'd like.

The cake is good plain or you can doll it up. Whole or cut into slices, the cake is extra delicious with spoonfuls of yogurt topping (for this cake, I leave the sugar out of the topping) and honey.

Storing: Wrapped, the cake will keep for a max of 2 days at room temperature (the pears cut the keeping time short) or for up to a month in the freezer; thaw in its wrapper.

Playing Around

While I urge you to keep the rye in the mix, you can substitute all-purpose flour for the spelt and almond or pistachio for the hazelnut flour, although I think hazelnuts are particularly nice with pears. Then again, you can play with the fruit, too—apples are an easy swap. Finally, play around with the alcohol that you add—go for a favorite or for what you've got on hand, but choose one that's got a beautiful nose. (Should you decide to nix the booze, add another teaspoon of vanilla to the batter.) If you change one ingredient, think about changing others to go with it.

Baked-in-a-Skillet Gingerbread

Makes about 12 servings

2 cups plus 2 tablespoons (288 grams) all-purpose flour

½ cup (68 grams) whole wheat flour

2 teaspoons ground ginger

1 teaspoon ground cinnamon

½ teaspoon baking soda

½ teaspoon fine sea salt

¼ teaspoon ground cloves (or freshly grated nutmeg)

⅔ cup (133 grams) sugar

⅓ cup (67 grams) brown sugar

5 tablespoons (2½ ounces; 70 grams) unsalted butter, at room temperature

⅓ cup (80 ml) neutral oil

1 large egg, at room temperature

⅓ cup (80 ml) unsulfured molasses

¾ cup (200 grams) apple butter, plain or spiced

¼ cup (60 ml) full-fat buttermilk (well shaken before measuring), at room temperature

⅓ cup (45 grams) finely chopped crystallized ginger (see left)

About 2 tablespoons sanding or turbinado sugar for topping (optional)

About 3 tablespoons Swedish pearl sugar for topping (optional)

For me, this cake might just as well be an official proclamation announcing the start of the holiday season. It's the ginger and molasses—the classic flavors of gingerbread—of course, but it's more. It's the look—a skillet cake is immediately inviting. It's the fragrance—intoxicating just out of the oven and no less haunting after even a couple of days on the counter. And the flavor. I've mixed things up, so that the cake is unmistakably a gingerbread in good standing, but more complex than most. There are the traditional spices as well as buttermilk (I love its sharpness here) and earthy whole wheat flour. For extra heat, there's crystallized ginger. And there's apple butter—the secret ingredient that brings moisture, keepability and a different kind of sweetness.

With all this, the only thing the cake needs is a crowd happy to nibble away at it over a weekend. But if you want a go-along, consider whipped ricotta (try mixing it with some apple butter) or thick yogurt, a dab of cream cheese or a slice of Cheddar. Or, if you're bringing it out for dessert, serve it with whipped cream, ice cream or hot fudge.

A word on the pan: While I love how this cake looks made in a cast-iron skillet, it will bake nicely in a 9-inch springform pan. Watch the baking time; it will need between 40 and 45 minutes in the oven—start testing at the 40-minute mark.

A word on the crystallized ginger: Like all dried fruit, crystallized ginger can harden, and hard fruit is unpleasant. To soften the ginger if it's tough, soak it in very hot water for a minute, then drain and pat dry.

A word on the topping: I'm crazy about the crunch you get when you double up the sugar with a layer of turbinado sugar under Swedish (or pearl) sugar. It's a wonderful touch, but an extra one—the cake is fine left plain or dusted with confectioners' sugar just before serving.

Center a rack in the oven and preheat it to 350 degrees F. Coat a 10-inch cast-iron skillet with baker's or cooking spray. If you don't have a skillet, use a 9-inch springform pan (see page 41).

Whisk the all-purpose flour, whole wheat flour, ginger, cinnamon, baking soda, salt and cloves together.

Working in the bowl of a stand mixer fitted with the paddle attachment, or in a large bowl with a hand mixer, beat the granulated and brown sugars together with the butter at medium speed for about 3 minutes—you'll have a pasty mixture. Pour in the oil and beat for another 2 minutes—the batter will thin out and become creamy. (Don't wash the measuring cup—use it for the molasses. The oily slick that's left in the cup will help the molasses slide out easily.) Scrape the bowl and beater(s) now and again—this is sticky business. Add the egg and beat for a minute. With the mixer on low, beat in the molasses, followed by the apple butter and another scraping. Add half the flour mixture and mix until it just disappears into the batter. Blend in the buttermilk, followed by the remainder of the dry ingredients. When they're almost incorporated, mix in the ginger. You'll have a thick, fragrant batter—take a beat to enjoy the aroma. Scrape it into the pan, nudging it into the corners and smoothing the top. Sprinkle over the sanding or turbinado sugar and then top with the pearl sugar, if you're using these (and I hope you do).

Bake for 43 to 48 minutes (if you've used a springform, start checking after 40 minutes), or until the top of the gingerbread is uniformly puffed all the way to the middle, the cake pulls away from the sides of the pan with a gentle tug and, most important, a tester inserted into the center of the cake comes out clean. Transfer the skillet to a rack and let the cake cool until it's just warm or has reached room temperature before cutting.

Storing: Left in the skillet (or springform) and well covered, the cake will keep at room temperature for about 5 days. The apple butter, molasses and oil will help to keep it moist and delicious for a long time. You can also wrap the cake well and freeze it for up to 1 month, but if you've topped the gingerbread with sugar, the sugar might melt (not tragic, just a little less pretty). Thaw the cake in the wrapper.

Pont-Aven Pistachio Cake

One summer day, Michael and I were having coffee at a guesthouse in the Breton village of Pont-Aven. We'd come for the museum that tells the story of Paul Gauguin's years there. For the town's proximity to Belon and its famous oysters. And to visit nearby friends. But I'd go back for this cake, which the proprietor brought out from the kitchen while it was still warm, tempting us with its plain good looks and nutty aroma and then telling us that we couldn't have a taste until it cooled. Like disappointed but obedient children, we went off exploring and returned to have the cake with tea.

Madame's cake got its primary flavor from ground pistachios and some pistachio cream. Its crumb owed its little bounce to unwhipped egg whites, and its richness came from melted butter. And there were bright, fresh raspberries in the cake—a nod to summer, not a year-round addition. That afternoon, Madame dusted the top of the cake with powdered sugar and gave each of us a generous slice. She also gave me the recipe.

In Brittany, the cake would be made with salted butter, but since it's saltier than most American butters, I use unsalted butter and add salt to the batter—either fleur de sel from Brittany or a smaller measure of fine sea salt. The cake is elegant served on its own, but it's perfect for a bit of celebratory embellishment: a cushion of raspberry jam in the middle and a slick of white chocolate on top. More fresh berries, too. This is a recipe that takes to change-ups; see Playing Around (page 46) for some ideas.

A word on the pistachio flour: You'll need ⅔ cup (about 3¼ ounces/90 grams) pistachio flour. You can either buy pistachio flour (sometimes labeled pistachio meal) or whir 3¼ ounces (90 grams) of shelled pistachios with a bit of sugar in a food processor to make your own. Pulse, scrape and be careful not to overdo it—a few nubbins of nuts are better than a paste.

A word on the pistachio cream: Using either pistachio cream or pistachio butter will deepen the cake's flavor and boost its color a bit. Both are available in some supermarkets, Italian specialty stores and online. For the most flavor, choose the cream with the highest percentage of pistachios. (You might want to keep the Crumble-Topped Pistachio Cake, page 86, in mind—it uses pistachio cream, too.)

Makes 6 to 8 servings

FOR THE CAKE

8 tablespoons (4 ounces; 113 grams) unsalted butter, cut into chunks

⅔ cup (90 grams) all-purpose flour

1 teaspoon culinary-grade matcha (optional, but good for enhancing the cake's color)

¾ teaspoon baking powder

¾ teaspoon fleur de sel or ½ teaspoon fine sea salt

¼ teaspoon baking soda

¾ cup (150 grams) sugar

⅔ cup (about 90 grams) pistachio flour (see left)

6 large egg whites, at room temperature, stirred to break them up

1 teaspoon pure vanilla extract

2 tablespoons pistachio cream (see left)

About ¾ cup (100 grams) fresh raspberries

FOR THE FILLING (optional)

About ½ cup (160 grams) raspberry jam

FOR THE GLAZE AND TOPPING (optional)

5 ounces (142 grams) high-quality white chocolate, chopped

1 teaspoon neutral oil

A handful of fresh raspberries

Confectioners' sugar

To make the cake: Center a rack in the oven and preheat it to 350 degrees F. Coat an 8-inch round cake pan, preferably one with at least 2-inch-high sides, with butter, dust the interior with flour and tap out the excess. Or, if you prefer, coat the pan with baker's spray. No matter which you choose, fit a circle of parchment paper into the bottom of the pan.

Put the butter in a small saucepan and bring it just to a boil over medium heat, then set the pan aside in a warm place. (Or leave it on the turned-off burner, as I usually do.) Alternatively, you can melt the butter in a microwave.

Working in a large bowl, whisk the flour, matcha, if you're using it, baking powder, salt and baking soda together. Whisk in the sugar and then the pistachio flour. (If the pistachio flour is lumpy, rub it to break up the clumps.) Switch to a flexible spatula and stir in one-third of the egg whites, followed by the vanilla. Stir in half of the remaining whites, add the pistachio cream and stir that in. Stir in the last of the whites—you might have to use a tad more energy than you're accustomed to in order to work in the whites at this point, so don't be afraid to give it a little muscle. You'll have a batter that flows off the spatula. Fold in the butter a little at a time—I do this in three additions. Once you get it incorporated—it seems like a lot of butter, but it'll all go in—you'll have a smooth batter with a satiny sheen. Gently fold in the raspberries, scrape the batter into the pan and smooth the top.

Bake the cake for 40 to 45 minutes, or until it is nut-brown and pulls away from the sides of the pan when gently tugged. A tester inserted into the center of the cake will come out clean. Transfer the pan to a rack and let it sit for 5 minutes, then run a table knife between the sides of the pan and the cake and unmold it. Carefully peel away the paper and leave the cake on the rack (right side up or bottom side up, either is fine) to cool.

Serve the cake plain, glaze it or cut it, fill it and glaze it or not—it's good no matter what you do.

To fill the cake (optional): Using a serrated knife and a gentle sawing motion, cut the cake in half through its belly. Stir the jam to loosen it, then spoon it onto the center of the bottom layer and spread it evenly to the edges with a small offset spatula or a table knife. Top with the upper half.

To glaze the cake (optional): Place the cake on a rack (slip a sheet of parchment under the rack to catch chocolate drips) or a serving plate and have an offset spatula or table knife at hand. Stir the chopped chocolate and oil together in a heatproof bowl. Place it over a pan of gently simmering water—the water shouldn't touch the bottom of the bowl—and heat, stirring often, until the chocolate is melted and smooth. Be careful—white chocolate is finicky and burns quickly, so stay close and pull the bowl from the heat as soon as you've got a velvety glaze. (You can do this in a microwave, but you've got to work on low power in short spurts and you've got to watch it with a hawk's eye.) When the glaze is ready, pour it onto the center of the cake and nudge it to the sides with the spatula (or knife). Run the spatula over the top or don't—the cake looks pretty either pristine or not-so-neat. Scatter (or carefully arrange) the fresh raspberries over the top. The glaze will get firmer—it will never dry completely—if you leave the cake at room temperature for about an hour. If you'd like to speed up the process, slip the cake into the fridge for about 30 minutes. While it's gilding an already gilded cake, you can dust the berries with confectioners' sugar before serving.

Storing: Unglazed, the cake will keep at room temperature for about 4 days—wrap it well. With the glaze, it'll be good for about 2 days—it's the berries that go quickly. The plain cake can be wrapped airtight and frozen for 1 month; thaw it in the wrapper.

Playing Around

Cherry or Apricot or No-Fruit Pont-Aven Cake

When raspberries aren't at hand, make the cake without them, or go for another fruit—halved cherries or cubed apricots are lovely with pistachio. You can use dried fruit in the batter—just make sure it's moist and plump and cut into small pieces (you'll need about ½ cup). If you change the fruit, change the jam filling, too. If you've chosen fresh fruit, you can use it as a topping. Think about melting a little jam with a splash of water and using it to glaze the fruit on top.

Hazelnut or Almond Pont-Aven Cake

You can swap the pistachio flour for hazelnut or almond. Do that, and you'll want to omit the matcha and use hazelnut or almond butter instead of the pistachio. For fun, make the cake with hazelnut flour and fill it with Nutella. I think a milk chocolate instead of a white chocolate glaze would be nice with either of these variations.

Chocolate and Almond Tabby-Not-Tiger Cake

I'm finally setting the record straight on this cake: it is NOT a tiger cake. Never mind that it's what I called it from the day I first tasted a version of it in Paris more than twenty years ago. The cake is based on the financier, the famous mini-cake, which was created in Paris in the nineteenth century by a pâtissier whose shop was near the stock exchange. Every afternoon, the financiers—the stockbrokers—would come in for a snack, and every afternoon they'd eat quickly and take special care not to get crumbs on their cravates. In an act that combined generosity with brilliance and great business sense, Lasne, the pastry chef, created a small cake that could be eaten out of hand in a few bites, neatly and without the risk of telltale crumbs. He made the cakes as rich as his clients and baked them in small molds that resembled gold ingots. While their origin story may have faded, affection for the cakes has endured—you can find them, or a riff on them, all over France. (The Pont-Aven Pistachio Cake, page 43, is essentially a big financier.)

But it was the riff that folds chocolate through the cake batter that tripped me up. It's called *tigré* and I instantly read—and translated—the word as *tiger*. Never mind that I couldn't find the stripes in the cake; once I got "tiger" in my head, it stuck . . . until I was so puzzled that I looked the word up. Oof! I wasn't so far off—it was just a matter of size. A tigré is a small tabby cat.

The thing I didn't get wrong was the cake's deliciousness—this is really one of my favorite cakes. Of course, adding chocolate to make the stripes—or, in this case, the spots—and finishing the cake with chocolate ganache, as I usually do, means that smudges and smears are almost inevitable. Cover those cravates!

Or, if you're looking for something plainer, simply omit the glaze, and you've got a perfect snacking cake.

Makes 8 servings

FOR THE CAKE

5 tablespoons (2½ ounces; 70 grams) unsalted butter, cut into chunks

¾ cup (150 grams) sugar

½ cup (68 grams) all-purpose flour

½ teaspoon baking powder

¼ teaspoon baking soda

¼ teaspoon fine sea salt

⅔ cup (70 grams) almond flour

6 large egg whites, at room temperature, lightly whisked to break them up

1 teaspoon pure vanilla extract

5 ounces (142 grams) semisweet or bittersweet chocolate, finely chopped

FOR THE GANACHE (optional)

⅓ cup (80 ml) heavy cream

1½ teaspoons light corn syrup

3 ounces (85 grams) semisweet or bittersweet chocolate, finely chopped

½ cup (48 grams) sliced almonds, toasted

To make the cake: Center a rack in the oven and preheat it to 350 degrees F. Butter a 9-inch round cake pan and dust the interior with flour, or coat the pan with baker's spray. Line the bottom with a circle of parchment paper.

The butter needs to be melted and then added to the batter while it's still warm, so bring it just to a boil in a small saucepan, or do this in the microwave. You can cook the butter a little longer, until it turns golden brown, if you'd like—browned butter's flavor is a little toastier and nuttier. Remove from the heat and keep the butter warm while you make the cake batter. (Because I do this on the stovetop, I usually leave the pan on the turned-off burner.)

Working in a large bowl, whisk the sugar, flour, baking powder, baking soda and salt together until thoroughly blended. Add the almond flour and whisk—if the almond flour is lumpy, use your fingers to break up the clumps. Switch to a flexible spatula and add the whites in three or four additions, stirring until the batter is smooth and flows off the spatula. Stir in the vanilla. Add the butter in three additions, folding and stirring until it is completely incorporated and you've got a smooth batter with a light sheen. Finally, stir in the chopped chocolate, blending well. Scrape the batter into the pan and use the spatula to smooth the top.

Bake for 37 to 40 minutes, or until the cake is golden brown, is evenly risen and pulls away from the sides of the pan when gently prodded. A tester inserted into the center of the cake will come out clean. Transfer the pan to a rack and leave for 5 minutes, then run a table knife between the cake and the sides of the pan. Flip the cake over onto the rack, peel away the parchment and invert the cake onto another rack. Let the cake cool to room temperature.

To make the (optional) ganache: Put the cream and corn syrup in a small saucepan and bring just to a boil (or do this in the microwave). Turn off the heat, add the chocolate and stir the mixture gently until blended, thick and shiny.

Pour the ganache over the cake and use an offset spatula or table knife to spread it across the top. I like to cover the top with the ganache and then, if some slides over the edges of the cake, I consider it a win. Scatter over the toasted almonds or arrange them in whatever fanciful pattern pleases you. You can leave the cake on the counter to let the ganache set a bit (it will never be really firm) or refrigerate it for about 15 minutes to set it.

Storing: You can keep the ganache-topped cake, loosely covered, on the counter for up to 2 days (the unglazed cake will keep for about 4 days) or refrigerate it for 3 or 4 days. If you've chilled the cake, I think you'll enjoy it more if you let it warm up a bit before serving. You can also freeze the cake, plain or glazed. If it's glazed, freeze it unwrapped until firm and then wrap it well. The cake will keep in the freezer for up to 1 month; thaw in the wrapper and, if you'd like, puff a little heat from a hair dryer over the glaze to restore its shine.

Makes 10 to 12 servings

FOR THE CAKE

1¾ cups (238 grams) all-purpose flour

1½ teaspoons baking powder

1 cup (200 grams) sugar

2 lemons

4 large eggs, at room temperature

3 tablespoons whole milk, at room temperature

7 tablespoons (3½ ounces; 99 grams) unsalted butter, melted and still warm

⅔ cup (160 ml) mild extra-virgin olive oil

1 pint (about 250 grams) fresh raspberries

Confectioners' sugar for dusting (if you don't use the meringue)

FOR THE MERINGUE (optional)

1 large egg white, at room temperature

¼ cup (50 grams) sugar

Confectioners' sugar

Fresh raspberries or a mix of berries for serving (optional)

♥ A TREASURED FAVORITE

Pierre Hermé's Lemon Cake, The One with Olive Oil

This is a cake that I first made with the French pastry chef Pierre Hermé in the mid-1990s, when we were working on our book *Desserts by Pierre Hermé*. I remember being surprised all those years ago that in addition to melted butter, the cake had a generous amount of mild olive oil. Pierre told me that the oil was there for flavor, of course, but also to make the crumb supple. The cake, like so many of Pierre's creations, is quietly brilliant. Without the meringue, it looks humble, like something you'd grab for an afternoon snack and eat out of hand, a desk treat to break up a workday. It doesn't call attention to itself, but one bite in, and you can't ignore it. The golden color is reminiscent of yellow cake, and that supple texture is tender and gentle and alluring. But then, just when you think you've got a sweet little comfort cake, along comes a jolt of lemon and the sharp edge of raspberries. Nothing about this cake is what you expect.

You've got choices here. You can serve the cake simply with a dusting of confectioners' sugar. Do this, and you might want to flip the cake over before dusting it—the cake domes, so the bottom gives you an even surface for sugaring. Or you can serve it a bit less simply by covering the top with a quickly made meringue. Either way, spooning some fresh berries over or around the cake before serving it is a nice touch.

To make the cake: Center a rack in the oven and preheat it to 350 degrees F. Coat the interior of a 10-inch round cake pan or springform pan with baker's spray, or butter it, dust the interior with flour and tap out the excess.

Whisk the flour and baking powder together.

Place the sugar in the bowl of a stand mixer or in a large bowl that you can use with a hand mixer and grate the zest of both lemons over it. Halve one lemon and squeeze to get 1 tablespoon juice (use the second lemon, if necessary); set the juice aside in a separate bowl. →

Reach into the bowl of sugar and use your fingers to mash and press the ingredients together until the sugar is moist, grainy and very aromatic. If you're using a stand mixer, fit the bowl onto the stand and put the whisk attachment in place. Add the eggs and beat on medium-high speed for about 3 minutes, until the mixture is pale and thick. Scrape the bowl and beater(s). Working on low speed, blend in the milk. Stop the mixer, add half of the dry ingredients and beat on low just until they're almost incorporated. Stop the mixer and repeat with the remaining dry ingredients. Continuing on low speed, add 1 tablespoon of the reserved lemon juice, followed by the warm melted butter and, finally, the olive oil, beating only until blended, and scraping the bowl and beater(s) as you work.

Pour about one-third of the batter into the pan—you want just enough to form a thin, even layer. Top with the berries, then pour on the rest of the batter, using a flexible spatula to gently spread the batter so that it runs between the berries and just covers them. You'll have a very thin top layer, and that's the way it's supposed to be.

Bake for 30 to 33 minutes, or until the cake is pale golden—it doesn't really brown much—has domed a bit and pulls away from the sides of the pan; a tester inserted into the center of the cake should come out clean. Remove the pan from the oven and immediately run a table knife around the edges of the cake, then unmold it onto a rack; turn it over onto another rack so that it's right side up and allow it to cool to room temperature.

Once it has cooled, the cake is ready to dust with confectioners' sugar or decorate with the meringue. (If you're going to skip the meringue, consider flipping the cake over and sugaring the flat side.)

To decorate the cake with the (optional) meringue: Center a rack in the oven and preheat it to 475 degrees F. Place the cake on a parchment-lined baking sheet.

Working with a mixer, beat the egg white until it holds soft peaks. Add the granulated sugar in a slow, steady stream and continue to beat until the meringue forms firm, glossy peaks. Immediately spread the meringue over the top of the cake.

Dust the meringue with confectioners' sugar and bake for 3 to 6 minutes, or until it's lightly browned. Don't go anywhere—meringue goes from pale to overbaked in a flash! Alternatively, you can brown the meringue using a kitchen torch. Before serving, top or surround the cake with berries, whole or sliced, if you're using them.

Storing: Without the meringue, the cake can be wrapped and kept at room temperature for about 4 days or frozen for up to 1 month; thaw in the wrapper. Once the cake is meringued, and especially if it's got strawberries, it won't keep well.

♥ A TREASURED FAVORITE

Rum-Raisin Visiting Cake

The minute my friend Ingela Helgesson walked into my kitchen with this cake, I knew it was going to be one I'd be making for a long time to come: it's now twenty-five years and counting. It's still a great cake and it came with a great story. Ingela, who grew up in Sweden, told me that her mother would bake the cake often because it was so good and because it could be made so quickly. Her mom claimed that you could start making the cake when you saw guests coming up the road and that it would be ready by the time they settled down for coffee.

For many years, hewing to the adage, "If it ain't broke, don't fix it," I followed Ingela's recipe to the letter (I include instructions for that on the next page so that you can, too). And then, for reasons lost to time, I gave the recipe a plump-up. I started by increasing the volume of the cake. The cake's texture always had a bit of chew—it was a lovely characteristic of the original—and now, because there's more cake, there's more chew and it's even more lovely. Then I added fruit—specifically, rum-soaked raisins. Heating the raisins in water and rum transforms them from commonplace to voluptuous, and they take on the lingering flavor of the tropical rum. But with more volume and the addition of dried fruit, the flavoring needed a rebalance, too. The new cake hits decidedly more almond, and that's just right—the flavor is strong, but not pushy; it picks up the sprinkle of almonds on top of the cake; and it's good with the vanilla and rum. Finally, I scattered cubes of apple across the top of the cake before baking—it was a spur-of-the-moment addition, inspired by propinquity: the apple was at hand. I thought I'd then make the apple optional forever after, but it's too good not to always include it. It adds a little more texture, a little more sweetness and another layer of flavor; subtle but, in the end, essential. Well, essential, but not immutable—because you've got raisins, which are sun-dried grapes, in the cake, you might consider fresh grapes on top; see Playing Around for more ideas for fiddling.

Makes 8 servings

FOR THE RAISINS

1 cup (about 160 grams) raisins

⅓ cup (80 ml) water

2 tablespoons dark rum

FOR THE CAKE

12 tablespoons (6 ounces; 170 grams) unsalted butter

1 smallish apple (about 160 grams), such as Fuji, Gala or Golden Delicious

1⅓ cups (266 grams) sugar

3 large eggs, at room temperature

½ teaspoon fine sea salt

¾ teaspoon pure almond extract

½ teaspoon pure vanilla extract

1½ cups (204 grams) all-purpose flour

About 3 tablespoons sliced almonds for the top

2 to 3 tablespoons raw, turbinado or sanding sugar for the top

Center a rack in the oven and preheat it to 350 degrees F. Coat the interior of a 9-inch round cake pan with baker's spray or butter it, dust with flour and tap out the excess flour; line the bottom with a circle of parchment paper.

To make the raisins: Put the raisins and water in a small saucepan, bring the water to a simmer over medium-high heat and cook, stirring, until it just about evaporates, about 6 minutes. Still over steady heat, add the rum and cook, stirring, until it boils away. Scrape the raisins onto a plate or into a bowl and set aside to cool while you work on the cake.

To make the cake: Melt the butter in a microwave or on the stovetop over very low heat; set aside to cool.

Peel the apple, cut it into quarters, remove the core and cut the fruit into small chunks—I like them to be approximately ½ inch on a side. You'll have about 1 cup of chunks; set aside.

Put the sugar in a large bowl and add the eggs one at a time, whisking vigorously after each egg goes in. Give the mix a few extra beats after the last egg is incorporated and then whisk in the salt and both extracts. Switch to a flexible spatula and gently stir in the flour in three additions, mixing until it disappears into the batter—the batter will be thick. Now work in the melted butter: I usually do this in four additions, using a motion that's somewhere between folding and stirring. It's a lot of butter for a relatively small amount of batter and you might have doubts about being able to get it all in, but stir on—the butter will blend in and you'll have a thick, satiny, very pretty batter. Stir the raisins and any liquid that has accumulated into the batter.

Scrape the batter into the pan and smooth the top. Scatter the apple chunks evenly over the top of the batter, then strew the almonds over the apples. Finally, give the top a dusting of raw (or turbinado or sanding) sugar.

Bake for 45 to 50 minutes, or until the cake has risen all the way to the center, the top is deeply and beautifully browned and, most important, a tester inserted into the center of the cake comes out clean. Transfer the pan to a rack and let the cake rest for 5 minutes, then run a table knife between the sides of the pan and the cake. Turn the cake out onto the rack, peel away the paper and flip the cake onto another rack; let it cool to room temperature.

Storing: Wrapped, the cake will keep for about 2 days at room temperature. It will hold for a little longer, but because of the apples, it will soften a bit (which I don't mind). You can wrap it well and freeze it for up to 1 month; thaw in the wrapper.

Playing Around

The Original Swedish Visiting Cake

The ingredients for Ingela's recipe are: 8 tablespoons (4 ounces; 113 grams) unsalted butter, 1 cup (200 grams) sugar, the grated zest of 1 lemon, 2 large eggs, ¼ teaspoon salt, 1 teaspoon vanilla extract, ½ teaspoon almond extract and 1 cup (136 grams) all-purpose flour. You'll need 3 tablespoons sliced almonds and 2 to 3 tablespoons raw, turbinado or sanding sugar for the topping. Follow the directions for mixing the batter above and bake the cake for 25 to 30 minutes.

Fruit Match-Ups

You can play around with the fruit inside and on top of the cake. Keep the rum raisins, but top the cake with sliced seedless grapes. Or swap the raisins for dried cherries and flavor them with Kirsch instead of rum; pit fresh sweet or tart cherries and put them on top, whole or cut. Or try cooking dried apricots in amaretto and using cubes of fresh apricots on top. Or cook dried pears with brandy and put sliced fresh pears on top of the cake.

LOAF CAKES

Double-Down Chocolate Loaf

Makes 8 to 10 servings

4 tablespoons (2 ounces; 56 grams) unsalted butter, cut into 4 pieces

4 ounces (113 grams) bittersweet chocolate, coarsely chopped

1¼ cups (170 grams) all-purpose flour

⅓ cup (28 grams) unsweetened cocoa powder, sifted if lumpy

2¼ teaspoons baking powder

¾ teaspoon fine sea salt

1 cup (200 grams) sugar

⅓ cup (67 grams) brown sugar

½ cup (120 grams) full-fat sour cream

3 large eggs, at room temperature

⅓ cup (80 ml) neutral oil

½ cup (120 ml) boiling water

I think the title says everything you really need to know about this cake: it's for chocolate lovers. The foundation of the cake is basic, but its heart is dark, make-no-mistake-about-it chocolate, a double dose of it: there's cocoa powder for depth and bittersweet chocolate for edge. The cake needs nothing more than it's got, but it's not insistently independent—it welcomes glaze and is happy to sport a layer or two of frosting: try splitting the cake in half, filling the middle and lavishly swirling the top. Cream Cheese Frosting (page 264) is perfect for this.

Center a rack in the oven and preheat it to 350 degrees F. Butter a 9-inch loaf pan, dust the interior with flour and tap out the excess, or coat the pan with baker's spray.

Put the butter in a heatproof bowl set over a pan of gently simmering water (make sure the water isn't touching the bottom of the bowl) and scatter the chopped chocolate over it. Cook over low heat, stirring now and then, until the butter and chocolate have melted and the mixture is smooth and glossy. Alternatively, you can do this in a microwave or on the stovetop if you've got a super-low setting. Set aside for the moment.

Whisk together the flour, cocoa, baking powder and salt.

Working in a large bowl, whisk both sugars and the sour cream together until smooth. Scrape the melted chocolate into the sugar mixture and whisk until it's thoroughly incorporated. One by one, add the eggs, whisking well after each one goes in. By the time the third egg is incorporated, the batter will look like unset chocolate pudding—which is fine.

Switch to a flexible spatula, add half of the dry ingredients and stir to blend. Add the remaining dry ingredients and stir until everything—including any ingredients that may be lurking at the bottom of the bowl—is fully blended. The batter will be thick, so you might have to work a little to blend in the last of the flour mixture. Just keep going, and don't be concerned if, when you're finished, you see some tiny bumps and lumps—the boiling water will be the end of them. →

Pour in the oil and, starting at the center of the bowl and working in increasingly wider circles, stir until the batter is homogeneous. As before, you might need to stir a bit longer and with a bit more intention than you normally do with a cake. Pour the boiling water over the batter and, using the same circular whirlpool motion that you used to incorporate the oil, stir until the water is blended in. The reward for this work will be a lovely, thinnish batter with a satiny sheen. Pour it into the pan and shimmy the pan to even the batter.

Bake for 53 to 57 minutes, or until a tester inserted deep into the center of the cake comes out clean or with just a few crumbs. Transfer the pan to a rack and let it sit for 15 minutes. Run a table knife between the cake and the sides of the pan to loosen the cake, invert it onto the rack, then turn right side up. Let the cake cool to room temperature.

Storing: Wrapped well, the cake will keep for about 3 days at room temperature or for up to 1 month in the freezer; thaw in the wrapper.

Mix-It-Up Citrus Loaf Cake

Makes 8 to 10 servings

- 1¾ cups (238 grams) all-purpose flour
- 2 teaspoons baking powder
- ½ teaspoon fine sea salt
- ¼ teaspoon baking soda
- ⅓ cup (67 grams) sugar
- About 3 citrus fruits (see headnote)
- 3 large eggs, at room temperature
- ½ cup (120 ml) honey
- ½ cup plus 2 tablespoons (150 ml) olive oil OR ½ cup (120 ml) olive oil plus 3 tablespoons (1½ ounces; 42 grams) unsalted butter, melted
- Citrus marmalade for glazing (optional)

This delight of a cake came from a treasure of a Paris boutique, L'Agrumiste, a shop built on one man's passion for *agrumes*, or citrus. The sunny shop, which looks like a gallery, has pyramids of yuzu, oranges of all sorts, lemons of many kinds, tiny caviar limes and citrons as large as softballs, as well as jams, teas, elixirs, syrups and pastries to nibble while you chat with the vendors, marvel at the fruits and dream up ideas for how to enjoy them. To get you started, L'Agrumiste had a beautifully designed little pamphlet that includes a recipe for an orange loaf cake. Of course I made the cake as soon as I got back home to my kitchen. But inspired by seeing so many joyously colored fruits, I couldn't resist tinkering with the recipe a bit. I used lemon—orange's peppier sister—and the smush trick: I smushed the citrus zest into the sugar to get even more flavor from it.

And then I made the cake again and again—sometimes with lime, once with grapefruit, often with clementines and most often with a mix of citrus fruits. It has always been lovely.

The cake, which can be made with olive oil or a combination of oil and melted butter, bakes to a deeply golden brown. It's sturdy, bright and just this side of sweet. Because I love the shine and the easy polish it gives this simple cake, I routinely glaze the top with melted marmalade (I like Korean honey-citron marmalade for this), and I often serve it with curd (page 275) or sometimes with both ice cream *and* curd. As with so many cakes of this kind, its flavor is improved with an overnight rest.

Center a rack in the oven and preheat it to 350 degrees F. Butter an 8½-inch loaf pan or coat the interior with baker's spray and place it on a baking sheet.

Put the flour, baking powder, salt and baking soda in a large bowl and whisk to blend.

Put the sugar in another bowl. Finely grate the zest from the citrus over the sugar—you want about 3 tablespoons of zest—and then reach in and use your fingers to smush and press the ingredients together until the sugar is moist and fragrant. →

Halve the fruits and squeeze to get ⅓ cup (80 ml) juice.

Add the eggs and honey to the sugar and whisk until smooth, then blend in the juice. Add the egg-sugar mixture to the dry ingredients in three additions, using a flexible spatula to gently mix the batter. Then slowly incorporate the olive oil (or the blend of oil and melted butter). You'll have a thick, smooth batter with a light sheen. Pour it into the pan and gently jiggle the pan to even the batter.

Bake for about 50 minutes, or until the cake is tall, dark and handsome and a tester inserted deep into the center comes out clean; check the cake after 30 minutes, and if it's getting too dark too quickly, tent it lightly with foil or parchment. Transfer the cake to a rack and let sit for 5 minutes, then unmold it and turn it right side up onto the rack. If you want to glaze the cake, do it now; otherwise, just allow the cake to cool to room temperature.

To make the (optional) glaze: Bring a few spoonfuls of marmalade with a splash of water just to a boil in a saucepan, stirring to melt the jam, or do this in a microwave. Brush the glaze over the warm cake.

Storing: Wrapped well, the cake will keep for about 3 days at room temperature. If you have the patience, wrap it and wait a day before slicing and serving. You can freeze it for up to 1 month, but if it's been glazed, the jam might get a bit watery—not fatal. Thaw the cake in the wrapper.

Playing Around

The most play-aroundable ingredient in this recipe is the citrus, of course. See what you like most—maybe it'll be the sharpness of lemons and limes or the sweetness of oranges, or a mix of both. I like a mild olive oil in this cake, but you might want to play up the olive flavor by using a stronger oil. And you might want to add a little vanilla or maybe a shot of dark rum or an aromatic orange liqueur.

Morning, Noon and Night Thanksgiving Cake

Makes 8 to 10 servings

FOR THE CAKE

- 1½ cups (204 grams) all-purpose flour
- ⅓ cup (45 grams) whole wheat or spelt flour (or additional all-purpose flour; see below)
- 1¾ teaspoons baking powder
- ½ teaspoon baking soda
- ½ teaspoon fine sea salt
- 1 teaspoon ground cinnamon
- ¼ teaspoon ground cloves or freshly grated nutmeg
- ⅔ cup (133 grams) brown sugar
- ¼ cup (50 grams) sugar
- 1 clementine or orange
- ½ cup (120 ml) neutral oil
- ¼ cup (60 ml) pure maple syrup
- 3 large eggs, at room temperature
- 2 cups (270 grams) lightly packed grated peeled sweet potatoes or yams (see below)
- ½ cup (about 60 grams) pecans or walnuts, preferably lightly toasted, chopped fairly fine
- ½ cup (60 grams) moist, plump dried cranberries (optional)

(ingredients continue)

This is like the little cake that grew and grew. It started as a spice loaf that got its moist texture from grated sweet potatoes. Then the sweet potatoes made me think about Thanksgiving, easy jump, and the much-loved side dish of mashed sweets topped with marshmallows. And whoosh—just like that I had a cake that embraced the spirit, flavors and even the marshmallows of Thanksgiving.

It also invited choice. The basic cake, made with the sweet potatoes, maple syrup, citrus zest, spices and nuts—dried cranberries, too, if that's your fancy—turns out a nibble loaf, a cake that can be eaten for breakfast (try slices toasted, buttered and drizzled with maple syrup), packed into lunch boxes or munched on the go.

Because the cake has so much flavor but not all that much sweetness, it welcomes sweet toppings. Add the orange-juice glaze, and you've got an afternoon cake that's good with coffee, tea or mulled cider. Top the glaze with marshmallow frosting and put the cake on a pretty platter, and it's ready to be set out for dessert—it's nice to have a "non-pie" on the holiday table. Any way you make it and anytime you serve it, it'll be right. Even if it's not Thanksgiving.

A word on the sweet potatoes: Of course you can use a food processor to coarsely grate them, but I prefer to use the large holes of an old-school box grater, mostly because the cleanup is easier.

A word on the flour: I like mixing a small amount of whole wheat or spelt flour in with the all-purpose—it adds a touch of heartiness to the cake. However, if you don't have either of these flours, don't run out to buy them: the cake is great made with only all-purpose.

Center a rack in the oven and preheat it to 350 degrees F. Coat a 9-inch loaf pan with baker's spray or butter, then press a piece of parchment paper over the bottom of the pan and up the two long sides, leaving enough of an overhang to use as lifters when the cake is baked.

Whisk together both flours, the baking powder, baking soda, salt, cinnamon and cloves or nutmeg.

Put both sugars in a large bowl and grate the zest of the clementine or orange over them. (If you're going to make the glaze, halve the fruit and squeeze the juice; cover and refrigerate until needed.) Reach into the bowl and squish the zest and sugar together until the mixture is moist and fragrant. Whisk in the oil—give this a bit of energy to incorporate it smoothly—and then do the same with the maple syrup. You'll have a thick blend. One by one, whisk in the eggs—the mixture will get thinner as each egg goes in. Gently whisk in about one-third of the dry ingredients. When they're blended in, whisk in half of the remaining dry ingredients. Switch to a flexible spatula and stir in the rest of the flour mixture. When it's almost incorporated, add the grated potatoes or yams, chopped nuts and cranberries, if you're using them, and stir everything together to blend evenly. Scrape the batter into the pan and smooth the top.

Bake for 53 to 58 minutes, or until the top is honey brown (it will crack), the cake pulls away just a bit from the sides of the pan and, most important, a tester plunged into the center of the cake comes out clean. Transfer the pan to a rack and let sit for 10 minutes, then gently lift the cake out of the pan, peel away the parchment and set the cake right side up on the rack.

If you're going to glaze the cake, you can do it now, while the cake is hot, or wait until it cools. If your plan is to serve the cake just as it is, wait until it cools completely before cutting. In fact, if you can wait a day, that would be even better—wrap the plain cake, tuck it away for a day and you'll have a more flavorful cake—spiced cakes like to have time to come into their own.

To make the (optional) glaze: Put all the ingredients in a small saucepan set over medium heat, stir, bring the mixture to a boil and let bubble away for 2 minutes, keeping watch and stirring occasionally to dissolve the sugar. The bubbles will get bigger and the glaze will thicken. Remove from the heat. (If you prefer, you can make the glaze in a microwave. It will take about 2½ minutes and you'll need to stop and stir it every 30 seconds.) →

FOR THE GLAZE (optional)

½ cup (100 grams) sugar

¼ cup (60 ml) clementine or orange juice (reserved from the fruit for the cake)

3 tablespoons water

1 tablespoon maple syrup

FOR THE MARSHMALLOW FROSTING (optional)

2 tablespoons (1 ounce; 28 grams) very soft unsalted butter

¼ cup (30 grams) confectioners' sugar (plus maybe a bit more)

½ cup (50 grams) marshmallow crème

¼ teaspoon orange-blossom water (optional)

½ teaspoon pure vanilla extract

A word on the frosting: Like the glaze, the frosting is optional, although I highly recommend that you make both. The recipe for the frosting makes just enough to cover the top of the cake with a thin layer. If you want more frosting, double the recipe.

Brush the top of the cake generously with glaze. You'll have more glaze than you need, but it's hard to make a smaller amount. Hold on to the leftover glaze—it's great mixed with butter and spread on slices of cake, especially if you toast them.

To make the (optional) marshmallow frosting (see page 65 for a word on quantity): Put the butter and sugar in a small bowl and, using an electric mixer, a whisk or a flexible spatula, beat until you've got a smooth and creamy mixture. Getting a good blend will look unpromising at the start, but keep at it. Using a spatula, stir in the marshmallow crème, orange-blossom water, if you're using it, and vanilla. The frosting should be creamy, have a beautiful sheen and beckon swoops. If it's too thin—humidity can affect the consistency—beat in a little more sugar. Cover the top of the cake with as little or as much of the frosting as you'd like—if you've made a double recipe, the layer will be generous.

Storing: Wrapped well, the plain or glazed cake will keep for at least 4 days at room temperature. You can also wrap it airtight and freeze it for up to 1 month; thaw in the wrapper. If it's been frosted, it's a bit harder to keep. If you don't mind smushed frosting, you can wrap the cake and hold on to it at room temperature for about 3 days. And since the frosting will keep, covered, in the fridge for a couple of days, you can set a little aside and touch up the cake if the original frosting's gotten too messy for you.

Bourbon Brown-Butter Cake

Some recipes entice us long before we get to taste them. With this cake, the enchantment begins as soon as you brown the butter, toast the pecans and add a little bourbon to the bowl—such heady aromas. Then there's the look of the batter—lustrous. And the way the cake bakes—high, cracked along the center and burnished around the edges. Finally, there's the quiet flavor of the bourbon-tinged caramel; think butterscotch. It's a cake that can bring warmth to a chilly evening. The romantic me imagines having it fireside with a snifter of bourbon and a good book to read, while the real me is happy to have it with coffee or tea in the afternoon and with ice cream at night. For a knockout dessert, toast slices of the cake, top with coffee or butter pecan ice cream and pour over some chocolate or caramel sauce.

Makes 10 servings

- 11 tablespoons (5½ ounces; 155 grams) unsalted butter, cut into chunks
- 1 cup (120 grams) pecans, very coarsely chopped
- ½ teaspoon fine sea salt, plus a pinch
- ½ teaspoon ground cinnamon, plus a pinch
- 1¾ cups (238 grams) all-purpose flour
- 1½ teaspoons baking powder
- 4 large eggs, at room temperature
- 1 cup (200 grams) sugar
- ¼ cup (50 grams) brown sugar
- ½ cup (120 ml) heavy cream, at room temperature
- 1 tablespoon pure vanilla extract
- 2 tablespoons bourbon (see below)

A word on the bourbon: No sooner did I think of brown butter and toasted pecans than I thought of bourbon, but you might think of dark rum or whiskey—they'd be good, too. If you'd rather skip the liquor, do—you needn't change anything in the recipe, although you might want to add ¼ teaspoon pure almond extract to the batter.

Center a rack in the oven and preheat it to 325 degrees F. Line a baking sheet with parchment paper. Coat a 9-inch loaf pan with baker's spray. Run a piece of parchment paper over the bottom of the pan and up the two long sides, leaving some extra to use when it's time to lift the cake out of the pan. Alternatively, you can butter the pan, dust the interior with flour, tap out the excess and line it with paper.

Put the chunks of butter in a small saucepan and set the pan over medium heat. Once the butter melts, allow it to keep bubbling away until it turns a deep golden brown. At this point, you might have a few dark butter dots at the bottom of the pan, and for sure you'll catch a whiff of nuts—both are lovely characteristics of brown butter. Remove the pan from the heat.

Mound the pecans on the lined baking sheet and drizzle 1 tablespoon of the brown butter over them. Toss to coat the nuts, then sprinkle over the pinch of salt and pinch of cinnamon and toss again. Spread the nuts out. Bake for 8 to 10 minutes—keep an eye on the nuts and shake or stir them around after 5 minutes—or until they are just toasted. Remove from the oven and set aside to cool.

Increase the oven temperature to 350 degrees F.

Whisk the flour, baking powder and the remaining ½ teaspoon each salt and cinnamon together. →

Working in a large bowl, whisk the eggs and both sugars together for 2 to 3 minutes, or until thoroughly blended. Pour the cream into the bowl in a steady stream, whisking as you go, and when it's in and the batter is smooth, whisk in the vanilla and bourbon. Add half of the dry ingredients to the bowl, switch to a flexible spatula and gently stir until they have almost disappeared into the batter. Add the remainder of the dry ingredients and stir until they're just about incorporated. Gradually pour in the browned butter, stirring and making sure to get to the bottom of the bowl with every few strokes—butter has a way of hiding out there. I like a motion that's halfway between stirring and folding when I'm working to get this much butter into a mixture. When all the butter is incorporated and you've got a smooth, satiny batter, stir in the toasted pecans. Scrape the batter into the pan and level it.

Bake the cake for 58 to 63 minutes, but take a look at it around the 40-minute mark—if it looks as though it's getting too dark too fast (this cake bakes dark), tent it loosely with parchment or foil. The cake is done when it's risen and the top is cracked (it can crack quite dramatically, and that's nice), it's firm to the touch and you can tug it gently from the sides of the pan. Most important, a tester inserted into the center of the cake will come out clean. Transfer the pan to a rack and wait for 5 minutes, then use the parchment handles to help you lift the cake out of the pan onto the rack. Peel away the paper and turn the cake right side up on the rack to cool to room temperature.

Storing: Wrapped, the cake will keep at room temperature for at least 3 days, and it can be frozen for up to 1 month; thaw in the wrapper. If the cake seems a little dry, toast slices, butter them and smile.

Apple Custard Cake

Makes 8 servings

- 4 to 6 apples (about 1¾ pounds; 800 grams; see below), peeled
- ¾ cup (102 grams) all-purpose flour
- 1¼ teaspoons baking powder
- ¾ teaspoon ground cinnamon
- ¼ teaspoon fine sea salt
- ½ cup (100 grams) sugar
- 1 small orange or 1 clementine or tangerine (or a lemon, if you prefer)
- 3 large eggs, at room temperature
- ½ cup (120 ml) whole milk, at room temperature
- ½ teaspoon pure vanilla extract
- 2 tablespoons (1 ounce; 28 grams) unsalted butter, melted and cooled
- Demerara or turbinado sugar for sprinkling (optional)

After tasting this cake, my Parisian friend Hélène said, "You better warn bakers that this isn't a cake-cake—it's really more like a pudding or a custard." She's right about this loaf, so consider yourself warned. Although "warning" sounds ominous, when everything about this cake is come-hithery. It's a recipe with a lot more apples than batter and, if you choose soft, low-crunch apples, they'll almost disappear into the cake, making a dessert that's true to its French name, Gâteau Invisible. It's a kind of magical cake—you make a custardy batter, slice a bunch of apples into it and mix, mix, mix, then pack everything into the pan. The sorcery happens in the oven: the apples, which somehow emerge aligned no matter how higgledy-piggledy they were at the start, drink up most of the batter and what's left of it bakes to a soft . . . a soft what? Cake? Custard? Does it matter? And if you serve it plain or with dollops of whipped cream or scoops of ice cream? Does it matter? Nope—it's always a delight. For a savory version of this kind of cake, take a look at the Zucchini and Chèvre Invisible Cake (page 246).

A word on the apples: If you choose soft, juicy apples, like Gala or Golden Delicious, the darling of French bakers, the apples and the cake will be almost indistinguishable from one another. Choose a firmer apple, say a Honeycrisp or Pink Lady, and the slices will retain some of their firmness. The choice is yours.

And a word on slicing the apples: Slicing the apples for this cake is a great job for a mandoline or a Benriner-type slicer. (A food processor fitted with a slicing disk works, too—cut the apples in half and core them before slicing.) If you cut the apples by hand, aim for thin slices—thin enough to bend but not break. Don't worry about precision—it's the thinness that counts here. If you're using a knife, it's best to cut the apples before you mix the batter; if you're using a tool to slice them, you can place it over the bowl of batter and slice the apples directly into the bowl—so convenient.

Center a rack in the oven and preheat it to 400 degrees F. Coat an 8½-inch loaf pan with baker's spray or butter and flour the pan (tap out the excess flour), then run a piece of parchment over the bottom and up the two long sides of the pan, leaving enough of an overhang to use as lifters when the cake is baked.

If you're using a knife for the apples, peel, core and slice them now (see page 71).

Working in a large bowl—eventually it will have to hold all the apples, too—whisk the flour, baking powder, cinnamon and salt together.

Put the sugar in a medium bowl and grate the orange (or lemon) zest over it. Smush the sugar and zest together with your fingers until you catch the scent of citrus. Drop the eggs into the bowl and whisk for 2 to 3 minutes, until pale and slightly thickened. (You can use an electric mixer for this job, if you'd like.) Whisk in the milk and vanilla, followed by the melted butter.

Pour the wet ingredients into the bowl with the flour and stir with a flexible spatula to blend. Place the mandoline or other slicer across the top of the bowl and slice the apples into the batter. (Leave the apples whole to slice them. When you get to the core on the first side—you don't want core or pits in the mix—turn the apple and continue slicing; turn the apple each time you come to the core and then discard the little rectangle of apple and core that remains.) Stop after every 2 apples to stir the mixture—stirring the apples in will give you space for more fruit. Continue until all of the apples are in and then, using the spatula, stir to coat the apples with batter. This will take a couple of minutes, and you're not going to catch every slice—there are more apples than batter—but make your best effort.

Using a large kitchen spoon, transfer the apples to the pan: spoon up some fruit, let the batter drain back into the bowl (don't be too meticulous here), drop the slices into the pan and use the spoon to even out the layer. Continue until all of the apples are in, then wiggle them with the spoon to fill the corners and even the top. Pour in the remaining batter, jiggle the apples again and give the pan a few good raps against the counter to coax the batter into all the crevices. Sprinkle the top with demerara or turbinado sugar, if you'd like.

Bake the cake for 30 minutes and then take a peek at it—if you think it's getting too brown too quickly, tent it loosely with parchment or foil. The cake needs to bake for a total of 50 to 60 minutes—you'll know it's done when it's set, is deeply golden brown and pulls away from the sides of the pan when you tug it ultragently. Transfer the pan to a rack and let the cake cool for at least 1 hour before unmolding.

When you're ready to lift the cake out of the pan, carefully run a table knife around the edges, then use the parchment to pull the cake out of the pan and onto a cutting board; peel away the paper from the sides of the cake and leave the bottom paper in place until you're ready to serve.

The cake can be served when it's still slightly warm, at room temperature or chilled—each temperature has its charm. Serve plain, like a snack cake, or top each slice with ice cream or whipped cream. If you're a cake-for-breakfast type, you might want to griddle a thick slice in butter.

Storing: Wrapped in plastic, the cake will keep for a day or two at room temperature or for about 4 days in the refrigerator—it's not a good candidate for freezing.

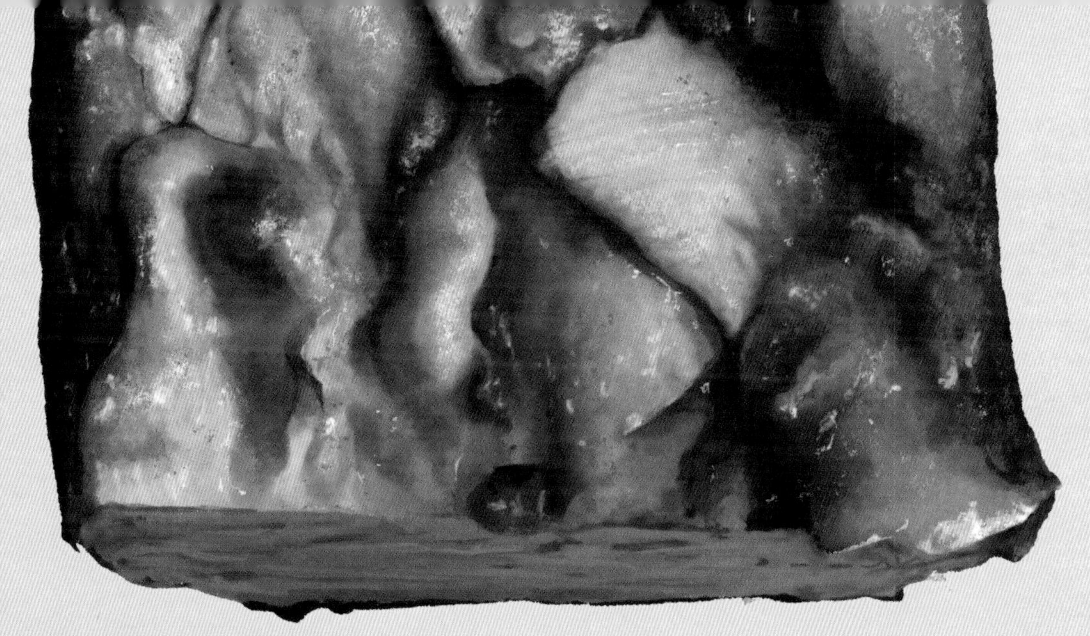

Cocoa-Cherry Thyme Cake

Cocoa, cherry and thyme. I love this combination. But this cake could be cocoa-raspberry. Or blueberry. Or mixed berry. Or even mango. Or peach. Or almost any other fruit you can find in the supermarket freezer. I committed to cherry for the basic cake because I was afraid that if I kept imagining the possible combinations, I'd end up cakeless. Some recipes are like that—they make you dream about mixes and matches, and if the recipe is solid, those ideas can become real. This is a solid recipe for a cocoa loaf cake that you can keep coming back to and keep tinkering with.

I like chopped fresh thyme in the cake—I like the herb with the cocoa, and I like that it's good with most soft fruits, red or yellow. But it's changeable—think about basil or minced rosemary—or skippable, if a touch of herbs in a sweet cake is not what you love. In fact, if deciding which fruit to use makes your head spin, you can even skip that and make a plain chocolate cake for an everyday snack. No matter how you play this cake, serving it with ice cream or crème fraîche is an easy and always welcome idea. And if you go with the cherry version and finish each slice with whipped cream, you can think of it as the easiest Black Forest cake ever.

Makes 8 to 10 servings

- 1½ cups (204 grams) all-purpose flour
- ⅓ cup (28 grams) unsweetened cocoa powder, sifted if lumpy
- 2 teaspoons baking powder
- ½ teaspoon fine sea salt
- ¼ teaspoon baking soda
- 1 cup (200 grams) sugar
- 1 to 2 tablespoons finely chopped fresh thyme (or another herb; see headnote)
- ½ cup (120 ml) neutral oil
- 3 large eggs, at room temperature
- ½ cup (120 ml) buttermilk (well shaken before measuring), at room temperature
- One 12-ounce (340 gram) bag frozen pitted whole cherries, sweet or tart, not thawed (see below)
- Whipped cream, ice cream or crème fraîche for serving (optional)

A word on the fruit: The recipe uses a 12-ounce pouch of frozen berries or fruit, and the fruit should go into the batter frozen—it will bake better that way. If for any reason the fruit has defrosted, turn it into a strainer set over a bowl to drain, then discard the juice and pat the fruit as dry as you can.

Center a rack in the oven and preheat it to 350 degrees F. Coat a 9-inch loaf pan with baker's spray or butter, flour it and tap out the excess flour, then run a piece of parchment paper over the bottom and up the sides of the pan, leaving enough excess to serve as lifters when the cake is baked.

Whisk the flour, cocoa, baking powder, salt and baking soda together.

Put the sugar in a large bowl and sprinkle over the thyme, then reach in and use your fingers to mash, press and smush the herb into the sugar. Pour in the oil and whisk energetically to blend—the mixture will look slushy. One by one, whisk in the eggs, beating well to make sure each egg is incorporated before you add another; the batter will be smooth and shiny. Still using the whisk, or switching to a flexible spatula, add the cocoa mixture in three additions and the buttermilk in two, beginning and ending with the dry ingredients and stirring only until each addition just disappears into the batter. Give the batter about a dozen brisk beats to →

bring it all together and then stir in the frozen fruit with a spatula, making sure that the fruit is evenly coated with batter. Immediately turn the batter into the pan and swivel it a bit to even the top.

Bake for 63 to 68 minutes, or until a cake tester inserted deep into the center of the cake comes out clean. Transfer the pan to a rack and let it rest for 5 minutes. Then, if necessary, run a table knife between the cake and the sides of the pan to loosen the cake, lift it out of the pan and onto the rack and pull away the paper. Cool to room temperature.

Slice and serve with whipped cream, ice cream or crème fraîche, if you'd like.

Storing: Wrapped, the cake will keep for up to 4 days at room temperature or for up to 1 month in the freezer; thaw in the wrapper.

Moko Cake-O

This is my cakeified version of a cookie I love from a place I love: the rye and poppy seed cookie Moko Hirayama makes at her Paris restaurant, Mokonuts. Mine's a loaf that, like Moko's cookies, is big on flavor and surprises. The top of the loaf is craggy and sparkly—the last-minute prebake sprinkle of demerara sugar and flaky salt picks out the crackles and makes them shine. Inside, it's a party of poppy seed speckles, marbly chocolate swirls and dried cranberries for taste, chew and the occasional pop of color. The rye's there to ground everything. Like Moko's cookies, the loaf is simple and looks homey and, like her cookies, it throws a couple of curveballs and packs a bundle of delights.

A word on the poppy seeds: You need a lot of them, so buy a bagful (or a large container), not a little jar from the supermarket's spice section, and after you've used them, wrap the bag well and store it in the freezer (or refrigerator). Cold storage keeps poppy seeds at their best for a long time; even so, because they're naturally oily and can go rancid, you should smell and taste them before adding them to a recipe. If you've bought a sack and are wondering how you'll ever use them, take a look at the adorable Poppy Seed Baby Bundts (page 121).

Makes about 10 servings

- 6 tablespoons (3 ounces; 85 grams) unsalted butter
- 2 tablespoons neutral oil
- 1¼ cups (170 grams) all-purpose flour
- ½ cup (60 grams) rye flour
- 1½ teaspoons baking powder
- ¾ teaspoon fine sea salt
- ½ teaspoon baking soda
- 2 large eggs, at room temperature
- ½ cup (100 grams) sugar
- ½ cup (100 grams) brown sugar
- 1 cup (230 grams) plain whole-milk Greek yogurt or 1 cup (240 grams) full-fat sour cream, drained of excess liquid, at room temperature
- 1½ teaspoons pure vanilla extract
- 4 ounces (113 grams) semisweet or bittersweet chocolate, chopped into chip-size morsels
- ½ cup (60 grams) moist, plump dried cranberries
- ⅓ cup (50 grams) poppy seeds (see left)
- Demerara, turbinado or sanding sugar for sprinkling
- About 1 teaspoon flaky sea salt, such as Maldon, for sprinkling

Center a rack in the oven and preheat it to 350 degrees F. Coat a 9-inch loaf pan with baker's spray or butter, then run a piece of parchment paper over the bottom of the pan and up the long sides, leaving enough extra paper to use as lifters when the cake is baked.

Melt the butter in a small saucepan (or in a bowl in the microwave), stir in the oil and set aside to cool a bit.

Whisk the all-purpose and rye flours, baking powder, salt and baking soda together.

Working in the bowl of a stand mixer fitted with the paddle attachment, or in a large bowl with a hand mixer, beat the eggs and both sugars together on low speed for about 2 minutes, scraping the bowl and beater(s) as needed. Add the yogurt or sour cream and blend it in. Keeping the mixer on low, blend in the cooled butter-oil mixture, along with the vanilla. Spoon in the dry ingredients in two or three additions, mixing just until the ingredients disappear into the batter.

Continuing to work with the mixer or switching to a flexible spatula, mix in the chocolate, cranberries and poppy seeds.

Scrape the bumpy batter into the pan, then plunge your spatula in and out of it in a few places to settle it into the corners. Smooth the top as best as you can and sprinkle with the demerara (or turbinado or sanding) sugar and flaky salt.

Bake for 53 to 58 minutes, or until the top is golden and crackly and a tester inserted into the center of the cake comes out clean. (The sides may or may not pull away from the pan, so trust the color and tester on this one.) Transfer the pan to a rack and let the cake rest for 10 minutes, then carefully run a table knife around the edges of the cake. Using the parchment handles, lift the cake out of the pan and onto the rack. Peel away the parchment and let the cake cool to room temperature on the rack.

Storing: Wrapped well, the cake will keep at room temperature for about 4 days. It can be wrapped airtight and frozen for up to 1 month; thaw in the wrapper.

Franco-American Banana Bread

Makes 8 servings

- 1⅓ cups (177 grams) all-purpose flour
- ¾ teaspoon baking powder
- ½ teaspoon fine sea salt
- ¼ teaspoon baking soda
- 1 teaspoon ground cinnamon
- ½ teaspoon coarsely ground black pepper
- ¼ teaspoon freshly grated nutmeg
- ⅛ teaspoon ground cloves
- 4 large eggs, at room temperature
- 1 cup (200 grams) brown sugar
- 3 very ripe medium bananas, peeled, plus (optional) 1 ripe banana, peeled, for decoration
- 14 tablespoons (7 ounces; 200 grams) unsalted butter, melted
- Turbinado or sanding sugar for sprinkling (optional)

This banana bread is my rendition of the French author and food critic François-Régis Gaudry's rendition of one made at the Loyal Café-Cantine in Paris. Having never tasted the first- or second-generation cakes, I can only vouch for this American-born grandbaby: it's so very good. And so different from most of the banana breads I've ever had or made. It's fine-grained and springy—more like a sponge cake than an open-crumb quickbread. It's richer than the normal banana bread—it's got four eggs and a hefty measure of melted butter. Its spice is recognizably French. And I don't think I'm imagining it, but it seems to have a bigger banana flavor, maybe because the bananas are crushed with the loopy end of the whisk, so that little bits of banana are scattered throughout the bread; come upon a morsel, and you get banana's fullest flavor and perfume.

Making French recipes work in American kitchens is tricky business—different flour, leavening, pan sizes and ovens, and in this recipe, spice. Gaudry uses pain d'épices, a spice blend that is easy to pick up at the grocery, if your grocery is in France; harder to find in America. It can be frustrating to pin down the spices that go into the blend because there are no set rules. Gaudry says his mix includes cinnamon, black pepper, nutmeg and cloves, but there are some that include ginger and anise, too. Make this for the first time and see if you'd like to add or subtract anything. Make a change, and you can call it your house blend.

It almost goes without saying that the reason so many cafés serve banana bread is because it's such a good match with coffee. Good, strong coffee.

Center a rack in the oven and preheat it to 350 degrees F. Coat a 9-inch loaf pan with baker's spray, or butter it, dust the interior with flour and tap out the excess, then run a piece of parchment paper over the bottom and up the two long sides, leaving enough extra paper to use as lifters when the cake is baked.

Whisk together the flour, baking powder, salt, baking soda and the four spices.

Pull out a sturdy whisk and a large bowl and roll up your sleeves. Drop the eggs into the bowl and beat for a minute to blend. Add the sugar and beat for a couple of minutes to dissolve it and to get a homogeneous mix. Add the flour mixture about one-third at a time, whisking only until each addition is just incorporated before adding more. Now here's the fun part: using your hands—or, more neatly, a knife—one by one, squish or cut the bananas into chunks, add the chunks to the bowl and use the whisk the way you would a pestle to pound the fruit and then stir the morsels into the batter. You don't want to be too thorough—one of the nicest things about this cake is the way the banana chunklets dot each slice. Continue until all the banana is in and then pour in the melted butter, stirring with the whisk to blend. Give the batter a last couple of beats and then pour it into the pan, plunging the whisk into the batter here and there to even it.

If you'd like to decorate the top of the cake with the banana, cut the banana in half the long way and place the halves cut side up on top of the batter. Generously sprinkle the top with turbinado (or sanding) sugar, if that's your druthers.

Bake for 55 to 60 minutes, or until the cake is golden—the top might crack prettily—and just comes away from the sides of the pan when gently tugged; a tester inserted into the center of the cake will come out clean. It will also come out looking a little oily—it's fine. Transfer the pan to a rack and wait for 10 minutes, then run a table knife around the edges of the cake. Using the parchment overhang, lift the cake out of the pan and onto the rack; gently peel away the paper.

Let the cake cool to room temperature before you slice it. In fact, if you've got the time, wrap the cooled cake in plastic and let it sit on the counter for a day—both the taste and texture improve with a day's rest.

Storing: Wrapped, the cake will keep for about 4 days at room temperature or for up to 1 month in the freezer; thaw in the wrapper.

Matcha Latte Loaf

Makes 8 servings

- 1¾ cups (238 grams) all-purpose flour
- 1¼ teaspoons baking powder
- ½ teaspoon fine sea salt
- 7 tablespoons (3½ ounces; 99 grams) unsalted butter, at room temperature
- 1 cup (200 grams) sugar
- 3 large eggs, at room temperature
- 3 tablespoons neutral oil
- 2 teaspoons pure vanilla extract
- ½ cup (120 ml) full-fat coconut milk (see left; shaken and mixed well before measuring)
- 4 teaspoons matcha green tea powder (see left), whisked if lumpy

Marble cakes are like snowflakes—all recognizable as members of a family, but each one different. You could try to get the same pattern every time, but the odds are against you, and besides, unpredictability is a marble cake's constant and one of its primary delights. Here the delights are multiplied by the tender crumb—the cake has a pound cake's spring and a cupcake's delicacy; by the beautiful colors—pale green and white; and by the flavors, which teeter between subtle and strong. It's matcha, green tea powder, that gives the green swirls their color and flavor, and coconut milk that gives the whole cake its sophistication, taming some of matcha's power and adding its own slightly sweet, almost fruity flavor.

While marble cakes are often made with the lion's share of the batter given to the quieter flavor (see Old-Fashioned Marble Cake, page 107, for a delicious example), I knew I could trust the coconut milk to bring everything into balance, so I went half-and-half. Making the flavors equal partners made the cake more beautiful, more surprising and more delectable.

A word on matcha: Please, please, please use culinary-grade matcha powder for this cake. First-quality matcha (often labeled "ceremonial") is very expensive and meant to be savored on its own in a tea. Its most prized characteristics would be lost in this cake.

A word on coconut milk: Look for full-fat coconut milk—its flavor is deep and its texture is satiny.

Center a rack in the oven and preheat it to 325 degrees F. Coat the interior of an 8½-inch loaf pan with baker's spray or butter it, dust it with flour and tap out the excess.

Whisk the flour, baking powder and salt together in a medium bowl.

Working in the bowl of a stand mixer fitted with the paddle attachment, or in a large bowl with a hand mixer, beat the butter and sugar together on medium-high speed for 3 minutes, or until creamy, scraping the bowl and beater(s) frequently—this is a batter that needs diligent scraping. Drop the speed down to medium and add the eggs one by one, beating for a minute or so after each goes in. With the mixer running, pour in the oil, followed by the vanilla, and mix until blended—the batter will be thin and satiny and have a pretty sheen. Add one-third of the dry ingredients and mix on low speed until they are almost incorporated, then mix in half of the coconut milk. Stop the mixer, scrape, add half of the remaining flour mixture and beat until it's almost blended in. With the mixer still on low, pour in the rest of the coconut milk and, when it's almost incorporated, add the last of the dry ingredients. Give the batter a few turns with a flexible spatula and then scrape half of the batter into a bowl.

Sprinkle the matcha powder over one of the portions of batter and stir it in with the spatula, mixing until the batter is uniformly green and you're no longer mesmerized by the beautiful swirling patterns you're making.

You're going to dollop the two batters into the pan and you can do this with a large spoon or a cookie scoop (my favorite tool) or two pastry bags (no need to insert any tips). I like to drop some white scoops into the pan, fill the in-between spaces with green batter and then continue filling the pan by topping the white scoops with green and the green with white. But that's just my game—you can make up your own. When all the batter is in, run a table knife, a bamboo skewer or a long toothpick through the batter to marble it. Make just one or two passes—more than that, and you won't have distinct marbling.

Bake for about 60 minutes (check the cake at 55 minutes, but it will probably need more time), or until it's risen and can be gently nudged from the sides of the pan; a tester poked into the center of the loaf will come out clean. And, yes, the top will crack. Transfer the pan to a rack and let rest for 10 minutes, then run a table knife around the sides of the pan and unmold the cake. Turn the cake right side up and leave it on the rack to cool to room temperature.

Storing: Wrapped well, the cake will keep for at least 3 days at room temperature. It can be frozen for up to 1 month; thaw in the wrapper.

Crumble-Topped Pistachio Cake

This is *not* the crumbly-topped pistachio coffee cake I tasted when I was in Rome—the one I ate in the rain and barely shared with Michael—but it's what I had in mind when I made it. I remember that the Italian cake had abundant sweet streusel and a tender crumb, both of which are here. And because I was going for nostalgia, not verisimilitude, the cake's got dried cherries and jam, too. Also, ricotta and pistachio cream. The pistachio cream is a subtle slip-in—it tinges the cake with pale color, adds a little more flavor and softens the cake's crumb—but as much as I like it, it's not a must-have: this is a cake with built-in delectableness.

Makes about 10 servings

FOR THE CRUMBLE TOPPING

½ cup (68 grams) all-purpose flour

2 tablespoons whole wheat flour (or additional all-purpose flour)

3 tablespoons brown sugar

1 tablespoon sugar

¼ teaspoon fine sea salt

6 tablespoons (3 ounces; 85 grams) cold unsalted butter, cut into small pieces

1 teaspoon pure vanilla extract

¼ cup (40 grams) pistachios, preferably lightly toasted, coarsely chopped

FOR THE CAKE

5 tablespoons (2½ ounces; 70 grams) unsalted butter

2½ tablespoons neutral oil

1½ cups (204 grams) all-purpose flour

1¼ teaspoons baking powder

½ teaspoon fine sea salt (¼ teaspoon if the pistachios are salted)

¼ teaspoon baking soda

¾ cup (150 grams) sugar

1 lemon

¾ cup (185 grams) whole-milk ricotta, drained if necessary, at room temperature

2 tablespoons pistachio cream or pistachio butter (see above right; optional)

3 large eggs, at room temperature

1½ teaspoons pure vanilla extract

¼ teaspoon pure almond extract

½ cup (80 grams) pistachios, preferably lightly toasted, coarsely chopped

½ cup (75 grams) moist, plump dried cherries, very coarsely chopped if large

3 to 4 tablespoons thick cherry jam or store-bought lemon curd (see above)

A word on the jam: The jam adds another flavor and it also glues the crumble topping in place. For it to do its job well, it has to be thick. If you prefer, you can use lemon curd, but here, store-bought is better than homemade—I often use Bonne Maman Lemon Curd for this.

A word on the pistachio cream: You can use either pistachio cream or pistachio butter; both are available in some supermarkets and Italian specialty stores, as well as online. Choose the cream with the highest percentage of pistachio; it's the one that will give you the most flavor. (If you make this, keep the Pont-Aven Pistachio Cake, page 43, in mind—it uses pistachio cream, too.)

To make the crumble topping: Put both flours, both sugars and the salt in a large bowl and mix together with your hands. Drop in the pieces of cold butter and toss them around to coat them. Now, working with more energy, mash and press and squeeze everything together until you have a bowl full of moist clumps and curds. Squeeze some, and it will hold together. Sprinkle over the vanilla and toss to blend, then mix in the pistachios. Chill the crumble while you preheat the oven and mix the cake batter.

To make the cake: Center a rack in the oven and preheat it to 350 degrees F. Coat a 9-inch loaf pan with baker's spray or butter it, dust the interior with flour and tap out the excess. Run a piece of parchment paper over the bottom and up the long sides of the pan, leaving enough extra paper to use as lifters when the cake is baked.

Melt the butter in a saucepan or in a bowl in a microwave, then stir in the oil; set the mixture aside to cool.

Whisk together the flour, baking powder, salt and baking soda.

Put the sugar in a large bowl and grate the lemon zest over it (save the lemon for another use). Reach into the bowl and press the zest and sugar together until the mixture is fragrant. Drop in the ricotta, grab a whisk and start mixing. It will take a minute for the ricotta to yield to your efforts, but it will soften and blend with the sugar. Whisk in the pistachio cream or butter, if you're using it. One by one, whisk in the eggs, beating well after each goes in. Whisk in the butter-oil mixture, followed by the vanilla and almond extracts. You'll have a lovely, thin, satiny batter—but not for long. Continuing with the whisk (I usually do) or switching to a flexible spatula, add the flour mixture in two or three additions, stirring just enough to incorporate all of the ingredients evenly. Stir the pistachios and cherries into the batter, which will now be heavy and sticky. Scrape the batter into the pan, spreading it evenly and plunging the spatula in and out of it in several places to make sure it gets into the corners. It will only fill the pan halfway.

Dollop the top of the batter with 3 tablespoons of the jam or curd, spreading it with a silicone brush or a little offset spatula. You want a thin layer—if you can see some batter peeking out here and there, it's fine. But if you need more, add it.

Remove the crumble topping from the fridge. Grabbing bits of it and squeezing them into clumps, top the cake, pressing the crumbs gently into the jam and batter. You'll have a thick layer, and that's nice.

Bake for 55 to 60 minutes, or until the cake has risen beautifully, the crumble is deeply golden and, most important, a tester plunged into the center of the cake comes out clean. Transfer the pan to a rack and leave for 5 minutes, then use the parchment to lift the cake out of the pan and onto the rack. Gingerly peel the paper away and leave the cake on the rack to cool to room temperature.

When you're ready to cut the cake, choose a long bread knife, one with gentle serrations, and use a light sawing motion to slice—this will help keep the crumbs on top.

Storing: The crumble is crunchiest the day the cake is baked. It softens with time, but the cake remains wonderfully flavorful and a delight even as the crunch lessens. Wrapped, the cake will hold for about 3 days at room temperature.

Rosa's Chocolate-Orange Drizzle Cake

Makes 8 to 10 servings

FOR THE CAKE

- 1¼ cups (178 grams) all-purpose flour
- 1¾ teaspoons baking powder
- ¼ teaspoon baking soda
- ¼ teaspoon fine sea salt
- ¾ cup (150 grams) sugar
- 2 large, juicy oranges
- 10 tablespoons (5 ounces; 141 grams) unsalted butter, at room temperature
- 3 large eggs, at room temperature
- 1 teaspoon pure vanilla extract

FOR THE DRIZZLE SYRUP

- ¼ cup (50 grams) sugar
- ¼ cup (60 ml) freshly squeezed orange juice (from 1 to 2 oranges)

FOR THE SQUIGGLES

- 2 ounces (57 grams) semisweet or bittersweet chocolate, finely chopped

While my friend Rosa Jackson, whose cooking school Les Petits Farçis in Nice is a favorite of mine, moved to France more than twenty years ago, she, like all the expats I know, keeps a place in her heart for the foods of her childhood. For Rosa, a Canadian, that means recipes tied to England, and so I wasn't surprised when she told me that she loves one of the most British of all desserts, the drizzle cake. The drizzle is a quintessentially English bake, a golden loaf cake that's pricked and poked as soon as it's pulled from the oven and drizzled with a syrup that seeps into the cake and flavors it deeply and completely. Traditionally, the cake is lemon and so is the syrup. But Rosa, thinking about Jaffa Cakes, the soft cookies she craved as a child (we sometimes see them in America, where they're known as PiM's), makes her loaf with oranges and, mimicking the cookies, finishes the cake with chocolate squiggles. When she sent me the recipe, she included a note saying, "This was one of the first cakes I made as a child, and I've since re-created it using oranges plucked from a friend's tree in Nice." Having made the cake several times during New England winters, I can confirm that even if you or your neighbor doesn't have an orange tree to pluck, the cake will be a success.

To make the cake: Center a rack in the oven and preheat it to 350 degrees F. Butter or spray the interior of a 9-inch loaf pan and line the bottom and all four sides with parchment (either pressing one large piece of parchment into the pan or cutting two pieces to fit). Allow the paper to come up over the edges of the pan's long sides. Don't worry if the paper wrinkles in the corners—the important thing is to cover all the sides, because you're going to be pouring the syrup over the cake when it's still in the pan.

Whisk the flour, baking powder, baking soda and salt together.

Put the sugar in the bowl of a stand mixer or in a large bowl that you can use with a hand mixer. Grate the zest of the oranges over the sugar—you should have about 2 tablespoons, but if you've got more, it's a good thing. Halve the oranges and squeeze them to get ¼ cup (60 ml) juice; set the juice aside. →

Reach into the bowl and, using your fingertips, mash and mush the sugar and zest together until the sugar is fragrant and tinged orange. Add the butter to the bowl. If using a stand mixer, attach the bowl to the stand and fit the mixer with the paddle attachment. Beat the sugar and butter together on medium-high speed until creamy and well blended, about 3 minutes. Scrape the bowl and beater(s) as you go along. Add one egg and beat for a minute. Add the second egg and beat for a minute. At this point, the mixture may seem on the verge of curdling, but don't worry. Add 2 tablespoons of the dry ingredients and beat until incorporated—the mixture will come together—and then mix in the third egg. It's possible that you'll get a little curdling now, but just carry on. Working on low speed, blend in half of the flour mixture. With the mixer going, gradually pour in the orange juice and vanilla (don't be frustrated if the curdling returns). Scrape, turn the mixer to low, add the rest of the dry ingredients and mix until the flour disappears and the batter is once again smooth. Give everything a few last turns with a flexible spatula and scrape the batter into the pan.

Bake for 48 to 52 minutes, or until the cake is golden and pulls away from the sides of the pan when gently nudged. Most important, a tester inserted into the center of the cake should come out clean. Transfer the cake to a rack and immediately make the syrup—you want to soak the cake while it's hot.

To make the drizzle syrup: Put the sugar and juice in a small saucepan set over medium heat and cook, stirring, until the sugar dissolves, about 2 minutes. (You can do this in a microwave, if you prefer.)

To soak the cake: With the cake still in the pan, use a thin skewer or a toothpick to poke holes all over the top. Spoon or brush the syrup over the cake, covering the entire top. It's fine—even good—if some of the syrup slips down the sides of the cake. Let the cake cool to room temperature in the pan on the rack.

When you're ready to make the chocolate squiggle and finish the cake, use the parchment to lift the cake out of the pan and onto a serving plate. Peel away and discard the parchment, or, if you'd like, leave the cake on the paper—it makes a good drip-catcher.

To squiggle the cake: Melt the chocolate. While it's still hot and fluid, drip it over the top of the cooled cake: You can let the chocolate fall from the tip of a spoon or the tines of a fork, or you can even pipe it, if that's your style. Of course, the design is up to you—regimental stripes or wiggly-waggly squiggles.

The cake can be served as soon as it's topped with the chocolate.

Storing: Kept covered, the cake will hold for up to 4 days at room temperature. It can be wrapped well and frozen for up to 1 month; thaw in the wrapper.

Playing Around

Chocolate-Chocolate Chip Orange Drizzle Cake

It might be playing against drizzle-cake rules, but this chocolate-orange combo is good with a little more chocolate: Stir 4 to 6 ounces (113 to 170 grams) of mini chocolate chips into the batter before scraping it into the pan. Of course, you can use the same amount of chopped chocolate, and if you do, you can either chop the chocolate into chip-size morsels or give it a finer chop; incorporate the chocolate "dust" along with the pieces.

Makes 6 to 8 servings

FOR THE CAKE

About 1½ cups (about 7 ounces; about 200 grams) berries (see page 93)

1½ cups (204 grams) all-purpose flour, plus 2 teaspoons if you're using fresh berries

2 teaspoons baking powder

¼ teaspoon fine sea salt

1 cup (200 grams) sugar

1 lemon or lime (optional)

½ cup (about 115 grams) very thick plain whole-milk Greek yogurt (see page 93), at room temperature

3 large eggs, at room temperature

1 to 2 teaspoons rose water (not extract), to taste

1 teaspoon pure vanilla extract

¼ teaspoon pure almond extract

½ cup (120 ml) neutral oil

FOR THE SUGAR GLAZE (optional)

½ cup (60 grams) confectioners' sugar

A little milk (or freshly squeezed lemon or lime juice, if you've used the zest)

About 1 teaspoon strawberry powder or a drop of pink or red food coloring (optional)

Fresh berries for finishing (optional)

♥ A TREASURED FAVORITE

Berry Yogurt Cake

Very few of my French friends bake anything fancy at home. In fact, most of them don't bake at all. And with a pâtisserie on every other corner, it's easy to see why. But there's one dessert that just about every French person makes. A recipe most of them know by heart. And one that calls up memories of birthday parties and family suppers, picnics and trips to the beach: the Yogurt Cake. While it can be made in any shape, it's usually baked in a loaf pan, and it is a quintessential loaf cake: simple, golden, crowned, cracked, moist and flavorful. Mixed by hand. Sometimes flavored with a little lemon zest. Sometimes made with a combination of all-purpose and almond flours. Often undecorated, just as often covered with a slick of jam. Sometimes served with whipped cream. Sometimes with ice cream. Sometimes it's the base for berries. Most times, it's a teatime cake or a snacker.

As near as I can tell, the cake dates to the 1950s. I'm figuring that it was the creation of a yogurt company because, unlike almost every other recipe in the French repertoire, this one relies on volume measures and the original "measuring cup" for the cake was a yogurt container.

Once I learned how to make this cake, I made it over and over. I fiddled with the flavors and I fiddled with the shape. I added spices and I added herbs. I used olive oil and I used flavorless oil. I made a chocolate version. I made a cake with dried fruit and one with chunks of fresh fruit. I cut the cake into layers and filled and frosted it. Of course, I also made the cake for birthdays and added candles.

This version has fresh berries and the lightest hint of rose. It's a sophisticated combination, but not a fussy one. I like it plain or with a little glaze for everyday. And I like it with a lot of cream and a lot of berries for a celebration. Or just because.

A word on the berries: My preference is for a mix of strawberries, cut into small pieces, and whole blueberries and raspberries in the cake, but a mono-berry cake is still a thing of beauty. As is a cake made with frozen berries. If you're using frozen berries, don't thaw them.

A word on the yogurt: For years, I made yogurt cakes with regular yogurt, and I loved them. I still do. But nowadays, I prefer to make them with a very thick, very tangy Greek-style yogurt. See what you think. Whatever you use, try to pull the yogurt out of the fridge in advance—it's good to have all the ingredients as close to room temperature as you can get them.

A word on jam topping: If you'd like, bring some jam, jelly or marmalade and a spoonful of water to a boil in a small saucepan, stirring to melt the jam, and use this to shine the top of your cake instead of the sugar glaze. Or don't—the cake is perfect without a topping.

To make the cake: Center a rack in the oven and preheat it to 350 degrees F. Coat the interior of an 8½-inch loaf pan with baker's spray or butter the pan, dust it with flour and tap out the excess. Once baked, the cake releases from the pan pretty reliably, but even so, I like to run a piece of parchment over the bottom and up the two long sides of the pan. Helpful, but not critical.

If you've got big strawberries in your mix of berries, hull them and cut into ½-inch-ish chunks. Put the berries in a bowl, sprinkle 2 teaspoons of the flour on top (unless you're using frozen fruit), toss and set aside.

Whisk the remaining 1½ cups flour together with the baking powder and salt.

Put the sugar in a large bowl. If you'd like to add a bright flavor to the cake, grate the zest of 1 lemon or lime over the sugar (hold on to the fruit so that you can use the juice for the glaze, if making it); reach into the bowl and use your fingers to rub the ingredients together until the sugar is aromatic. Whisk in the yogurt. One by one, add the eggs, giving each a good whisking after it goes in and giving everything a few energetic beats at the end. Whisk in the rose water and the vanilla and almond extracts. Whisk in the dry ingredients in two additions, mixing only until they disappear into the batter. Switch to a flexible spatula and gradually fold in the oil. It will seem like a lot of oil, but it's just the right amount, and when it's fully incorporated, you'll have a thick, smooth, lovely batter with a light sheen. Add the berries and gently fold them in. Scrape the batter into the pan and, if necessary, smooth the top.

Bake for 55 to 65 minutes, or until the cake has risen and is golden, the top has cracked and, most important, a tester inserted deep into the center of the cake comes out clean. Transfer the pan to a rack and wait for 5 minutes, then run a table knife around the edges of the cake to loosen it. Turn the cake out onto the rack—or lift it onto the rack, if you've used parchment, and peel away the parchment. Allow the cake to cool to room temperature right side up.

To make the (optional) sugar glaze: It's best to make the glaze and finish the cake with berries (if you're using them) shortly before you're ready to serve. Put the sugar in a bowl and start to add milk (or lemon or lime juice) about ½ teaspoon at a time, stirring to blend. You're aiming for a glaze that falls off the tip of your spoon and can be poured or spread over the cake, so gradually add more liquid as needed. Stir in the strawberry powder or food coloring, if you're using it. Pour the glaze over the cake and just let it fall as it will, or use a small offset spatula or table knife to spread it. If you've got berries, top the cake with them. Give the glaze a little time to set before slicing the cake.

Storing: Wrapped well, the cake will keep at room temperature for about 4 days, although if you've glazed it, the glaze may weep. If you've finished it with berries, though, all bets are off—you can refrigerate the cake, but there's no guarantee that the fruit will remain fresh and bright. Unglazed, the cake can be frozen for up to 1 month; thaw in the wrapper. →

Playing Around

Classic French Yogurt Cake

The classic often includes almond flour. You can replace ½ cup all-purpose flour with ½ cup (50 grams) almond flour; omit the berries the 2 extra teaspoons flour, the rose water and almond extract. In France, the cake's made with plain regular whole-milk yogurt, but you can use Greek yogurt. Start checking for doneness at the 50-minute mark. You can top the cake with a confectioners' sugar glaze, but usually it's left plain or given a shine with a little jam or marmalade heated with a splash of water.

Berry and Herb Yogurt Cake

Keep the recipe as it is but add the grated zest of 1 lemon and some fresh herbs. I like 1 or 2 tablespoons of minced lemon balm, minced mint (lemon mint would be nice; avoid aggressive mints like peppermint or spearmint), minced lemon verbena or minced lemon thyme. Add the herbs to the sugar when you add the zest.

♥ A TREASURED FAVORITE

Grandmothers' Honey Cake

When I was very young, my grandmother used to come to our house every week, lugging brown paper shopping bags that sagged at the bottom and pulled at the handles and threatened to burst before she got to the door. Sometimes I think she feared that my brothers and I weren't being properly fed, because what she carried to us were usually jars of soup and a whole roasted chicken, a baked noodle pudding and three desserts: an apple cake, sugar cookies and a honey cake topped with almonds.

I've been chasing after those desserts ever since. I haven't given up trying to replicate the apple cake (see Sasha's Grated Apple Cake, page 5, for a cake that's reminiscent of my grandmother's). I can make cookies that are almost like hers—although I should call them "good-enough cookies." But that honey cake—it's the one that got away. I made a few that didn't measure up and then gave up. Actually, I didn't so much give up as turn my affections to French pain d'épices, a loaf that isn't really like my grandmother's but that conjured up satisfying memories of the family treat. And then, truly out of the blue, my friend Ellen Einstein sent me a recipe for honey cake. *This* honey cake. It was so like my grandmother's that it might have been hers. When I told Ellen that she'd opened a window into my childhood, she took it in stride. I could imagine her shrugging when she said, "It's the cake I grew up on." And then I thought, maybe all of us who had family that came from Russia or Eastern Europe early in the twentieth century grew up on this cake. Maybe it is every grandmother's cake.

I wonder what the cake tastes like to those whose memories haven't primed them for the first bite. I think that this kind of honey cake is unusual. It's definitely a cake, but it hovers on the edges of what defines a cake—it could almost tip over the line and be savory. In part, it's because of the honey—a sweetener that manages to have an edge and even a nip. And it doesn't have the moistness that we expect from traditional cakes. It's a bit rough, almost like bread. It rubs a little against the roof of your mouth.

Makes 12 servings

1½ cups (204 grams) all-purpose flour
1 teaspoon baking powder
½ teaspoon ground allspice
½ teaspoon ground cinnamon
¼ teaspoon baking soda
¼ teaspoon fine sea salt
½ cup (100 grams) sugar
2 large eggs, at room temperature
½ cup (120 ml) honey (see below)
¼ cup (60 ml) neutral oil
¼ cup (60 ml) strong black coffee, at room temperature, or flat cola (see below)
About ⅓ cup (33 grams) sliced almonds

A word on the honey: The honey you use is up for grabs; just know that even a mild honey will give you great flavor.

A word on the coffee: You can use either brewed coffee or make the coffee with instant. Ellen told me that the cake is often made with flat cola (I can't imagine what my grandmother would have to say about this), but not any cola—according to Ellen, it has to be Coke.

And although it's made with strong black coffee, it cries out for black tea. Perhaps tea drunk in the old Russian manner—through a sugar cube held between your teeth.

My grandmother arranged a line of whole almonds down the center of the cake. My mother, who didn't like the cake but who loved the almonds, always picked them off before we could even cut the first slice. Now that I'm making this cake myself, my preference is to scatter sliced almonds over the entire top. That coating makes for better pickings, and I think this would have amused my mom.

Center a rack in the oven and preheat it to 325 degrees F. Butter or spray an 8½-inch loaf pan and run a piece of parchment paper across the bottom and up the long sides, leaving enough of an overhang to use as lifters when the cake is baked; give the paper a swipe of butter or a spritz of spray.

Whisk together the flour, baking powder, allspice, cinnamon, baking soda and salt.

Working in the bowl of a stand mixer fitted with the paddle attachment, or in a large bowl with a hand mixer, beat the sugar, eggs and honey together on medium speed until well blended, about 2 minutes, scraping as needed. With the mixer on medium-low speed, drizzle the oil down the side of the bowl and beat until incorporated. Do the same with the coffee (or cola). Turn off the mixer, scrape the bowl and beater(s) and add the dry ingredients. Pulse the mixer on and off to get the blending started, then work on low speed, beating only until everything is worked in and the batter is homogeneous. Pour the batter into the pan, level the top if needed and scatter over the sliced almonds—I like a single(ish) layer of almonds paving the top of the cake.

Bake for 48 to 53 minutes, or until the cake feels springy to the touch and pulls away a bit from the sides when lightly tugged; a tester inserted into the center of the cake will come out clean. Transfer the pan to a rack and let the cake rest for 15 minutes, then run a table knife around the edges of the cake, lift it out of the pan and peel away the paper. Allow it to cool to room temperature on the rack.

This cake is good as soon as it's cooled, but it's even better after a day. If you can wait, wrap the cake, set it aside overnight and then treat yourself to a slice. Lovely on its own, it's also nice with butter and honey, jam or even a soft cheese like mild cream cheese or a more flavorful chèvre. And of course it's nice toasted—but wait until it's a bit stale to do that.

Storing: Wrapped well, the cake will keep at room temperature for about 5 days—it makes great toast after that. It can be wrapped airtight and frozen for up to 1 month; thaw in the wrapper.

BUNDT CAKES

Honeyed Corn Cake

I'm not the only one in my little corner of Connecticut who knows that the first ears of corn are likely to show up at the farm stand on July 4—there's always an early-morning crowd waiting to fill their baskets, and I'm always there with them. And I'm there almost every day after that. Most days we eat the corn straight from the cob with nothing other than salt, but all through the season, I'll often buy a few extra ears and freeze the kernels, knowing they'll be like sunshine on a snowy day. Or that they'll make an excellent cake. The first time I made this cake, it was with fresh farm stand corn, but happily, it's lovely with frozen or even canned corn (choose corn without added sugar). Like so many of my favorite cakes, this one's plain good looks belie its joys. The color is beautiful (yellow cornmeal keeps its warm golden hue even under heat). The texture is delightful, a little grainy, a little chewy (there are corn kernels here and there) and pleasantly substantial (that's the butter at work) with a touch of bounce (that's from the oil). And the taste is a surprise: because of the corn, sugar and honey it should be very sweet, but somehow it isn't (I haven't figured out why not). I love the cake for its balance. Because it's just off-sweet, the cake is good in the morning and awfully nice as an afternoon pick-me-up. To tip it a tad savory, cut the cake into thick slices and serve with Mary Dodd's Hot-Honey Butter (see Playing Around).

Makes about 10 servings

- 1⅔ cups (226 grams) all-purpose flour
- ¾ cup (130 grams) fine-grain cornmeal, preferably yellow (see below)
- 3 tablespoons cornstarch
- 2½ teaspoons baking powder
- ½ teaspoon fine sea salt
- 12 tablespoons (6 ounces; 170 grams) unsalted butter, at room temperature
- 1½ cups (300 grams) sugar
- ¼ cup (60 ml) olive oil
- ¼ cup (60 ml) honey
- 6 large eggs, at room temperature
- 2 teaspoons pure vanilla extract
- 1½ cups (about 8 ounces; 225 grams) corn kernels, fresh, frozen (no need to thaw) or drained canned (without sugar)

A word on the cornmeal: You need a fine-grain (or, at least, fine-ish) cornmeal. Polenta is the wrong choice for this cake because it retains too much of its grittiness even after a long bake. I like yellow cornmeal for its looks, but white makes an equally good cake.

Center a rack in the oven and preheat it to 350 degrees F. Butter the interior of a 10-cup Bundt pan, dust it with flour and tap out the excess, or coat it with baker's spray.

Whisk together the flour, cornmeal, cornstarch, baking powder and salt.

Working in the bowl of a stand mixer fitted with the paddle attachment, or in a large bowl with a hand mixer, beat the butter and sugar together on medium speed for about 4 minutes, until pale and fluffy, scraping the bowl and beater(s) as needed. Add the oil and beat on medium for a couple of minutes, then pour in the honey and beat for 2 minutes more. Add the eggs one by one, beating well after each →

egg goes in, then beat in the vanilla. The batter will be quite thin. Also, since you've got a lot of eggs and a fair amount of fat, it may look slightly curdled, but it'll be fine. Add the dry ingredients one-third at a time, mixing on low only until they're almost incorporated—there should be some visible dry spots before you add each successive batch. Add the corn, give the batter a turn or two and then finish the mixing by hand. Scrape the batter into the pan and poke it around with a spatula to make sure that it's evenly distributed. (I go around the pan, plunging the spatula into the batter and wiggling it around to guard against underground gaps.) Smooth the top.

Bake the cake for 50 to 55 minutes; take a look at it after about 30 minutes, and if you think it's browning too quickly, cover it lightly with a foil or parchment tent. When it's done, the cake will be golden brown and a tester inserted into the center will come out clean; if you tug the cake gently, it will pull away from the sides of the pan, and if you tap it lightly, it will spring back a bit. Transfer the pan to a rack and let the cake rest for 10 minutes, then unmold it onto the rack and allow the cake to cool to room temperature.

Storing: Wrapped well, the cake will keep for about 3 days at room temperature or for up to 1 month in the freezer; thaw in the wrapper.

Playing Around

Mary's Hot-Honey Butter

Mix together 8 tablespoons (4 ounces; 113 grams) soft unsalted butter with 2 to 3 tablespoons honey (start with 2), 1 tablespoon hot sauce (Mary insists that it has to be Cholula Original), a pinch of fine sea salt and a larger pinch of crushed red pepper flakes. Taste and add more of whatever you think it needs. Store it in the fridge, where it will keep for a week.

Olive Oil Dunking Bundt

I'm not sure what I did, but somehow the cake I ended up with wasn't the cake I thought I'd get. I did get the flavors I wanted—all the fragrant citrus is there, the touch of savory rosemary and the leveling green taste of fine olive oil; it was the texture that was unexpected. I thought I was headed toward a moist, traditionally substantial Bundt, but instead I baked a cake that was light and open-crumbed. The biggest surprise was how when I tugged at a slice, it stretched and pulled, just the way pannetone does. Of course, this isn't pannetone—there's no yeast—but it does have some of that sweet bread's charms, chief among them an affinity for being dunked. My accidental cake is the perfect dunker—good dipped in coffee or tea and excellent dipped in red wine or vin santo. And, yes, the cake feels so much like a pannetone that you might want to nudge it a bit closer to the Italian classic by stirring in dried fruit and candied peel; see Playing Around.

A word on the olive oil: The olive oil is not just a moisture-giving ingredient here, it's a backbone flavor, and so my preference is for an oil with character. It can be fruity, green or even peppery—what's most important is that you like its taste. If you like the idea of the cake but you're not a fan of strong olive oil, choose a mild one—it will leave more room for the citrus and rosemary flavors to show their stuff.

Makes about 10 servings

FOR THE CAKE

1¾ cups (238 grams) all-purpose flour
1½ teaspoons baking powder
½ teaspoon fine sea salt
1 cup (200 grams) sugar
2 clementines or 1 orange
1¼ teaspoons fragrant dried rosemary (or 1 tablespoon minced fresh rosemary)
4 large eggs, at room temperature
1½ tablespoons orange-blossom water
½ teaspoon pure vanilla extract
¼ cup (60 ml) whole milk, at room temperature
⅔ cup (160 ml) extra-virgin olive oil (see left)
Confectioners' sugar for dusting if not making the optional glaze

FOR THE GLAZE (optional)

1 cup (120 grams) confectioners' sugar, plus more if needed
1 to 2 tablespoons freshly squeezed clementine or orange juice

To make the cake: Center a rack in the oven and preheat it to 350 degrees F. Coat the interior of a 10-cup Bundt pan with baker's spray or butter it, dust the interior with flour and tap out the excess.

Whisk together the flour, baking powder and salt.

Put the sugar in the bowl of a stand mixer or in a large bowl that you can use with a hand mixer. Grate the zest over the sugar (hold on to the fruit so that you can use the juice for the glaze, if making it), add the rosemary and reach into the bowl and use your fingers to squish and mush the zest and rosemary into the sugar. You'll know you've done a good job when you catch a whiff of the mixture. Attach the bowl to the stand, if using a stand mixer, and fit it with the whisk attachment. Working with the mixer on medium speed, drop in the eggs one at a time, beating for a minute after each egg goes in. Scrape the bowl and beater(s) as necessary. With the mixer on low, add half of the dry ingredients, mixing only until they disappear into the batter. Stir the orange-blossom water and vanilla into the milk and, with the mixer on low, blend the milk into the batter. Add the remaining dry ingredients and mix until they're incorporated. Keeping the mixer on low, pour in the olive oil. When all of the oil is in, you might see some of it rimming the edges of the batter. If so, crank up the mixer to medium-high and give the batter a good 15-second spin—you should have a lovely, thin, satiny batter. Pour the batter into the pan.

Bake for 28 to 33 minutes, or until the cake is pale golden (the top of the cake won't get as dark as you might expect it to) and puffed. It will pull away from the sides of the pan when tugged a bit and, most important, a tester inserted into the center of the cake will come out clean. Transfer the pan to a rack and let the cake rest for 5 minutes, then unmold it onto the rack and allow the cake to cool to room temperature.

Once the cake is cooled, dust it with confectioners' sugar if you're not going to glaze it.

To make the (optional) glaze: Put the sugar in a medium bowl and add just enough juice to make a glaze that falls smoothly off the tip of a spoon. For a more opaque glaze, add more sugar; for a thinner glaze, add more juice. Drizzle the glaze over the cake; let it set at room temperature before serving.

Storing: Wrapped well, the cake will keep for about 4 days at room temperature. By nature, it's not a moist cake, so as it gets drier, it just gets better for dunking. If you'd like, toast slices and then dunk. If you haven't glazed the cake, you can wrap it well and freeze it for up to 1 month; thaw in the wrapper.

Playing Around

Pannetone-ish Dunking Cake

While you can add whatever kinds of dried and candied fruits you'd like to this batter, raisins seem traditional to me, as does candied citrus, especially peel. The "ish" in this variation's title leaves you plenty of fiddle room. Use about ½ cup finely chopped or cubed fruit (and peel). If using dried fruit, it should be soaked, then drained and patted dry before cutting it into pieces. For this cake, soaking the fruit in rum is nice. Or, if using candied fruits and peel, check that they are moist—if not, give them a very quick dunk in hot water, drain and dry. I like to add a few spoonfuls of pearl sugar (sometimes called Swedish sugar) to the batter—the sugar doesn't soften or melt in the oven, so you get great crunch every time you hit a pearl.

Simplest, Plainest, Most Old-Fashioned—and Best-Tasting—Marble Cake

A tip of the hat to the internet for teaching me that the marble cake, a cake I grew up with, can be traced to nineteenth-century Germany, where the two-tone marble effect was achieved by swirling a dark molasses or spice batter with a lighter-colored batter and baking it in a kugelhopf pan, the curvy Bundt pan's grandmother. I'm sure that the history is correct, but I prefer my take on the treat's origins: I like to think we got this cake because a baker as wise as King Solomon invented it to make peace between chocolate and vanilla partisans. Whatever the case, the truth that holds is that the cake is good, good enough to have been passed along from generation to generation, to have skipped across many borders and to have sparked the imaginations of tinkering bakers everywhere.

As much as I love to riff on recipes, I held back here and went (mostly) classic—I wanted the vanilla and chocolate flavors to be robust, both singly and together. With a marble cake, it's important that the foundation batter, a vanilla one that will also serve as the base for the chocolate batter here, stands proud on its own, and this one does. Both flavors benefit from the cake's richness and sour-cream tang and that there's less sugar than there might normally be. I think the real surprise is the chocolate, because it's a mix of dark chocolate and cocoa. I love Dutch-processed cocoa for this because its color is deeper and its flavor denser, more profound and more in contrast with the vanilla. The chocolate swirls are the marvels of the cake.

Makes about 14 servings

¼ cup (60 ml) water

⅓ cup (28 grams) unsweetened cocoa powder, preferably Dutch-processed (see headnote)

1½ cups (300 grams) sugar

2 ounces (28 grams) semisweet or bittersweet chocolate, finely chopped

2 cups (278 grams) all-purpose flour

2 teaspoons baking powder

½ teaspoon fine sea salt

16 tablespoons (8 ounces; 226 grams) unsalted butter, at room temperature

4 large eggs, at room temperature

2 teaspoons pure vanilla extract

½ cup (120 grams) full-fat sour cream, at room temperature

A word on marbling: Have fun! I like to use a cookie scoop to alternate and layer mounds of chocolate and vanilla batter. But you can be more random or more precise. The only caveat is that when you dip your knife into the batter to swirl it, don't multiswirl—one or two passes will do the trick. Too much swirling, and the flavors and colors will be overblended and you'll have defeated the work you did to make a cake with two distinctive flavors and an equally distinctive look.

Center a rack in the oven and preheat it to 325 degrees F. Coat the inside of a 10-cup Bundt pan with baker's spray or butter it, dust it with flour and tap out the excess.

Bring the water to a boil in a small saucepan. Turn off the heat but keep the pan on the hot burner. Whisk the cocoa powder into the water, followed by ¼ cup of the sugar. When the mixture is smooth, drop in the chocolate and stir until it melts. You can either move the pan to a trivet or a cool burner or scrape the mixture into a medium bowl and set aside. →

Whisk together the flour, baking powder and salt.

Working in the bowl of a stand mixer fitted with the paddle attachment, or in a large bowl with a hand mixer, beat the butter and the remaining 1¼ cups sugar together on medium speed for about 3 minutes, scraping the bowl and beater(s) often. Add the eggs one at a time, beating well after each one goes in and scraping regularly. The mixture may seem on the verge of curdling—don't be discouraged. Beat in the vanilla and then the sour cream. By now the mixture might be in full curdle, which is ugly but not fatal. Working on low speed, add half the dry ingredients, and when they're almost incorporated, add the rest, mixing to blend and scraping as needed. The batter will have regained its smoothness.

Scrape about one-third of the batter into the pan or bowl of chocolate and use a spatula to thoroughly blend the two mixtures together.

It's marbling moment! And the moment to decide if you'd like to simply make a layer of white batter topped by a layer of chocolate batter or use a cookie scoop or a soupspoon to transfer the batters to the pan before you marble them. If you're going to scoop—it's what I do—I think it's nice if you alternate mounds of chocolate and white batters. Depending on the shape and depth of your pan, you'll have enough batter for two or three layers of scoops. However you got the two batters into the pan, grab a table knife or a skewer, dip it almost to the bottom of the pan and draw it through the batter, making a full circle. You can swirl the batters again, if you'd like, but two times around is really the max—the sparer the swirling, the more striking the marble pattern will be.

Bake for 55 to 60 minutes, or until the cake has risen, is golden and pulls away from the sides of the pan when gently tugged; a tester inserted into the center of the cake will come out clean. Transfer the pan to a rack and let it rest for 5 to 10 minutes, then unmold it onto the rack and allow the cake to cool to room temperature.

Storing: Wrapped well, the cake will keep for about 4 days at room temperature. It will get a little dry, but it will still be delightful. You can freeze the cake for a month; thaw in the wrapper.

Cafuné Corn Cake

I came to this cake by accident, when I wandered into Cafuné, a Brazilian café in Paris, and spotted it on the counter under an old-fashioned glass dome. It was plain and inviting and looked as though it had come from a cozy home kitchen, and it had: Taciana, the owner, had baked it herself that morning and brought it to the café. One bite, and I was smitten, but also mystified—the cake was so different from any I'd ever had. Had I known more about Brazilian desserts, I might have immediately recognized it as a *bola de fubá*. But everything about the cake was new to me. The easily identifiable taste is corn—kernels and cornmeal—and the brilliant golden color comes from corn, too. The cake is sweetened with condensed milk and lightly flavored with coconut. The texture is exceedingly moist. And the method for making it is not the usual.

When Taciana gave me the recipe—an act of great sweetness—she said, "It's hard to believe that it makes a cake, but it does." And it did—the first time, but not the second or third. I could never understand why I couldn't get the recipe to work again, and I gave up on it. But I didn't forget it. When the memory of it tugged at me, I returned to it, changing the amount of cornmeal and the baking time, making it in a more common Bundt pan, rather than the ring pan Taciana used, and giving it a little spiff—I couldn't resist a little icing and a lot of coconut on top.

My cake is neither traditional nor exactly like the original (although I named it for the café), but it carries the distinctiveness of that cake, its satisfying but not immediately knowable flavor, unusual texture and push-button ease. And you'll still find it hard to believe that it makes a cake. But it will. Every time.

A word on the corn: Try to find a brand of canned corn that's unsweetened, and drain it well. You should have about 1¾ cups kernels (about 260 grams). Make sure to save the liquid for the glaze.

A word on the coconut: I used unsweetened shredded coconut for the cake itself, but if sweetened coconut is what you've got, carry on. And while you can use any coconut (or none at all) to top the cake, I think big curls of coconut are really pretty.

Makes 12 servings

FOR THE CAKE

Unseasoned breadcrumbs, for dusting the pan

1 can (about 15 ounces/ 430 grams) corn kernels (see below left), very well drained (save the liquid)

1 can (14 ounces; about 400 grams) sweetened condensed milk

¾ cup (180 ml) corn or neutral oil

4 large eggs, at room temperature

1½ teaspoons pure vanilla extract

¾ teaspoon fine sea salt

½ teaspoon freshly grated nutmeg

1¼ cups (180 grams) fine-ground yellow cornmeal (*not* polenta)

2½ teaspoons baking powder

¼ teaspoon baking soda

1 cup (about 50 grams) unsweetened shredded coconut or coconut flakes (see below center)

FOR THE GLAZE

1 cup (120 grams) confectioners' sugar

About 2 tablespoons reserved liquid from the canned corn (or milk or water)

Coconut flakes, toasted if you like, for scattering over the top (see below center)

To make the cake: Center a rack in the oven and preheat it to 350 degrees F. Generously butter or spray the inside of a 12-cup Bundt pan—choose a simple pan without many crannies—or a one-piece tube or ring pan. Dust the interior with breadcrumbs and tap out the excess. Since the cake is naturally gluten-free, you may want to use GF crumbs.

Working in a large blender (first choice) or a food processor, whir the drained corn, condensed milk, oil, eggs, vanilla, salt and nutmeg together until very well combined. If you've still got some discernible pieces of corn, that's fine. Actually, it's great—it's nice to get a few bits here and there. As you're working, stop to scrape and mix the ingredients with a sturdy spatula. Add the cornmeal and whir to incorporate, then blend in the baking powder and soda. Scrape and stir, then add the coconut. Give everything a few more spins, then scrape and stir again. Pour the batter into the pan and swivel the pan around to even it. Rap the pan on the counter a few times to settle the batter.

Bake for 30 to 35 minutes, or until the cake is golden, springs back to the touch, pulls away from the sides of the pan when gently tugged and, most important, doesn't leave crumbs on a tester inserted into its center. Transfer the pan to a rack and let rest for 10 minutes, then run a table knife around the edges of the cake if you're using a ring pan, or pull a little at the edges if you're using a Bundt or tube, and turn the cake out onto the rack. Let the cake cool to room temperature.

To make the glaze: Put the sugar in a medium bowl and drizzle in the corn water (or milk or water), stirring until you have a mixture that falls easily off the tip of a spoon; you may need more or less than 2 tablespoons liquid. Pour the glaze over the cake and scatter over the coconut. Give the glaze a little time to set before serving the cake.

Storing: As good as the cake is soon after it's baked, it's even better the next day, so consider wrapping the cooled cake in plastic and setting it aside overnight. If you do that, you might want to hold off on the glaze until you're ready to serve the cake. The cake will keep at room temperature for about 5 days. You can wrap the unglazed cake airtight and freeze it for up to 1 month; thaw in the wrapper. Slices of cake are scrumptious toasted and buttered, or buttered and jammed or honeyed.

Holiday Bundt

Makes 12 servings

FOR THE CAKE

2⅓ cups (320 grams) all-purpose flour

2 teaspoons baking powder

1¼ teaspoons ground cardamom

¾ teaspoon fine sea salt

¾ teaspoon ground coriander

½ teaspoon baking soda

½ teaspoon ground ginger

1½ cups (300 grams) sugar

1 orange or tangerine or 2 clementines

12 tablespoons (6 ounces; 170 grams) unsalted butter, cut into chunks, at room temperature

⅓ cup (80 ml) neutral oil

3 large eggs, at room temperature

2 teaspoons pure vanilla extract

1 cup (230 grams) plain whole-milk Greek yogurt, drained of excess liquid if necessary

2 cups (200 grams) cranberries, fresh or frozen (not thawed), coarsely chopped

FOR THE GLAZE

2¼ cups (275 grams) confectioners' sugar, sifted if lumpy

2 tablespoons cranberry or pomegranate juice, plus more if needed

This cake is proof that not every bake for the holidays has to be fancy, fussy, showy or frilly. Done right, simple works, too—and this cake is indeed simple. But charming. It's a sturdy, long-keeping Bundt with a featherlight crumb and the zing of fresh cranberries in every slice. It has the kind of easygoing sweetness and spiced warmth that beckons you back for more and a glaze as pink and gleeful as a giant flower from a fairy-tale garden. And it's the cake I make for all the end-of-year holidays. It may not be most people's idea of what a traditional festive cake should be, but it turns out to be something better: everyone's idea of comfort and joy.

The cake owes much of its tenderness to the addition of yogurt, but you can also get that delicacy from sour cream or buttermilk. And while I always turn to cranberries in fall and winter, I keep making the cake when the weather warms, replacing them with fresh (or frozen) berries. You can switch up the glaze, if you'd like, but I think you'll find it's a good match for almost every kind of soft fruit or berry you might fold into the batter.

To make the cake: Center a rack in the oven and preheat it to 350 degrees F. Butter a 12-cup Bundt pan, dust the interior with flour and tap out the excess, or lightly coat it with baker's spray.

Whisk the flour, baking powder, cardamom, salt, coriander, baking soda and ginger together.

Put the sugar in the bowl of a stand mixer or in a large bowl that you can use with a hand mixer. Grate the orange (or tangerine or clementine) zest over the sugar, then reach into the bowl and use your fingertips to smush the zest into the sugar until well blended and fragrant. Attach the bowl to the stand if using a stand mixer and fit it with the paddle attachment. Drop the butter into the bowl and mix on medium-high speed for 3 to 4 minutes, until the mixture is pale, creamy and fluffy. Scrape the bowl and beater(s) as you go along. Reduce the speed to medium, slowly pour in the oil and beat for a couple of minutes to blend well. One by one, add the eggs, beating at medium speed for a minute after each one goes in. Beat in the vanilla—the →

mixture will look like frosting—and then blend in the yogurt on low speed and scrape. With the mixer off, add half the flour mixture. Still working on low, mix until the dry ingredients are almost incorporated. Turn the mixer off, add the remaining flour mixture and, again, beat until almost blended—it's fine if you can still see speckles of flour here and there.

Working with a flexible spatula, fold in the cranberries and any flour that remains in the bottom of the bowl. Scrape the batter into the pan and even it as best as you can—I plunge my spatula in and out of the batter in a few places to help get it into the pan's curves.

Bake for 55 to 60 minutes, or until the cake is deeply golden brown and pulls away from the sides of the pan when gently tugged—a tester inserted into the center of the cake will come out clean. Transfer the pan to a rack and let rest for 5 minutes, then unmold the cake onto the rack. The cake has to be completely cool before you glaze it, so give it enough time to come to room temperature.

To make the glaze: Put the sugar in a medium bowl and sprinkle over the juice. Using a flexible spatula, stir the juice into the sugar. You're aiming for a glaze that flows easily off the side of the spatula. If it's too thick, add more juice little by little. Spoon the glaze over the cake, allowing it to run down the sides. Let dry before cutting the cake.

Storing: Covered, the cake will keep at room temperature for about 4 days. If you haven't glazed the cake, you can wrap it airtight and freeze it for up to 1 month; thaw in the wrapper. If you like, you can then glaze the cake when it's fully defrosted and at room temperature.

Playing Around

A Different Spice Bundt

If you aren't as crazy about cardamom as I am, you can swap it for cinnamon. You can also play with the spices—I think it's nice to have warm winter spices with the perky cranberries, but the choice is yours.

Dried Fruit and Nut Bundt

The batter is so good and so welcoming that you can switch up the add-ins easily. Moist, plump dried fruits—raisins or snipped apricots, pears or even mango—and chopped toasted nuts are lovely in the cake with or without the tart cranberries. And I love the cake with tiny bits of soft candied or stem ginger. If you're a fan of the sweet-and-tart combo, think about using the ginger along with the cranberries—you'll get a pack of pucker.

A Summer Bundt

When it's no longer cranberry season, use other fresh or frozen (not thawed) berries in place of the cranberries. Go light on the spices and trade the orange for a lemon or lime. If you do this, you might want to use lemon or lime juice in the glaze instead of pomegranate or cranberry juice.

Date and Walnut Bundt

Makes 10 servings

- 1½ cups (204 grams) all-purpose flour
- ½ cup (68 grams) whole wheat flour
- 2 teaspoons baking powder
- ½ teaspoon fine sea salt
- 16 tablespoons (8 ounces; 226 grams) unsalted butter, at room temperature
- 3 ounces (85 grams) full-fat cream cheese, at room temperature
- 1 cup (200 grams) sugar
- ½ cup (100 grams) brown sugar
- 4 large eggs, at room temperature
- 1½ teaspoons pure vanilla extract
- ½ teaspoon pure almond extract
- 1 cup (145 grams) snipped dates (see headnote)
- 1 cup (120 grams) walnuts, preferably toasted, coarsely chopped

Ever since I had my first cream cheese sandwich on date-nut bread at a Chock full o'Nuts coffee shop in New York City, I've loved the combination. And ever since I've been a baker, I've looked for ways to bring the team together in a cake. This is my latest, a Bundt that can claim my memory of the sandwich as its birthright. The cream cheese in the Bundt helps smooth the cake's texture, adding a bit of tenderness to the crumb. The cake is the color of pale honey, and the flavor is wholesome, with a whole wheat and brown-sugar sweetness, which is particularly nice when you come to an off-bitter walnut.

If you've got time, give the walnuts a brief toasting (see page xix)—it will intensify their flavor and help them keep their bite. As for the dates, you can chop whole pitted dates yourself—actually, it's easiest to snip them with scissors—or you can buy date pieces. What's most important is that they're soft. If they're not, give them a quick soak in some very hot water and then drain and pat dry.

Center a rack in the oven and preheat it to 350 degrees F. Coat the inside of a 10-cup Bundt pan with baker's spray, sprinkle it with granulated sugar and tap out the excess. Alternatively, you can butter the pan, then coat it with flour or sugar.

Whisk together the all-purpose and whole wheat flours, baking powder and salt.

Working in the bowl of a stand mixer fitted with the paddle attachment, or in a large bowl with a hand mixer, beat the butter and cream cheese together on medium speed for about 4 minutes, or until pale and very creamy; scrape down the bowl and beater(s) as you work. Add both sugars and beat for another 4 minutes at medium speed. One by one, add the eggs, beating on medium for about a minute after each one goes in. You'll have a thin mixture that will make a cloppity-clop sound as you beat it and it will probably look curdled—ignore that, it'll smooth out soon. Beat in the vanilla and almond extracts, stop the mixer and scrape everything down, then add the flour mixture. Pulse the mixer on and off to start blending in the dry ingredients and then mix on low just until they almost disappear.

Working with a flexible spatula, stir in the dates and walnuts. Scrape the batter into the Bundt pan, smooth the top and rap the pan on the counter a couple of times.

Bake the cake for 53 to 58 minutes, or until it is deeply golden brown and a tester inserted in the center comes out clean. Transfer the pan to a rack and let the cake rest for 10 minutes, then unmold it onto the rack and let cool to room temperature.

Storing: The cake is a very good keeper; in fact, I think it tastes better the day after it's made. Wrapped and held at room temperature, it will keep for at least 5 days. Its crumb will get tighter and a bit drier, but it will still be appealing. Wrapped well, the cake can be frozen for up to 1 month; thaw in the wrapper.

Playing Around

You can swap the dates for moist bits of dried apricots, figs or prunes, and the walnuts for almonds, hazelnuts or pistachios. You can certainly add spice if you'd like, or even herbs—some minced fresh thyme would be nice.

Jaíne's Soft and Tender Brazilian Carrot Cake

Makes 8 to 10 servings

FOR THE CAKE

1 pound (450 grams) carrots

1¾ cups (238 grams) all-purpose flour

1½ teaspoons baking powder

½ teaspoon fine sea salt

2 cups (400 grams) sugar

⅔ cup (160 ml) neutral oil

3 large eggs, at room temperature

FOR THE GLAZE (traditional but optional)

1 cup (200 grams) sugar

1 cup plus 3 tablespoons (100 grams) unsweetened cocoa powder

½ cup (120 ml) water

Jaíne Mackievicz is a wonder—a kind and generous person and an exceedingly talented baker, cook and writer. She's also a compelling ambassador for the foods of her native Brazil: as soon as Jaíne tells me about something she loves, I want it. And when I heard about this carrot cake, I wanted it immediately. For Jaíne, it was a constant in her Amazonian childhood, and she thinks it's possible that every other Brazilian grew up with the cake, too. It's simple to make and, she explains, often among the first cakes someone might learn to bake. For sure the cake is an easy bake—if you can push the button on a blender or food processor, you can make the batter. And for sure the ingredients are basic. But I'm guessing that it's the alluring flavor and sublime texture that draws bakers back to it. Unlike American cakes that call for grating carrots so they retain their roughness and chew, here the carrots are finely chopped in a blender or processor, trading their characteristic strength for a delicate nubbliness, their immediately recognizable flavor for a sweet but almost indefinable minerality. That there isn't a speck of spice in the batter marks it as different as well. And then there's the texture—soft, tender, supple and voluptuous. And the color, as orange as a sunset. It's an unexpected pleasure. As is the cake's traditional finish—a mirror-shiny chocolate glaze. (You could skip it, but that would be foolish.)

Jaíne says that in Brazil, the cake is made for every occasion from baby showers to birthdays, on weekends and on weekdays or to have as a simple snack on hand or to impress a special guest. It's a Brazilian custom that's easy to adopt no matter where you're baking.

To make the cake: Center a rack in the oven and preheat it to 350 degrees F. Coat the interior of a 10-cup Bundt pan with baker's spray or butter it, dust the inside with flour and tap out the excess. →

Peel and trim the carrots and cut them into pieces about 1 inch long. (The trimmed weight should be about 11 ounces; 300 grams.)

Put the flour, baking powder and salt in a large bowl and whisk together.

Toss the carrots, sugar, oil and eggs into a large blender or a food processor and pulse and blend until the mixture is homogeneous. Depending on the machine, it might be smooth or a tiny bit textured—either will make a great cake. Pour the carrot mixture into the bowl with the dry ingredients and, using a flexible spatula, stir the two mixtures together until there are no lumps of flour (the flour can be stubbornly clumpy here) and the batter is smooth. It will be a beautiful vibrant orange. Scrape the batter into the pan.

Bake for 43 to 48 minutes, or until the cake is golden brown, is springy to the touch and pulls away from the sides of the pan when gently tugged. Most important, a tester plunged into the center of the cake will come out clean. Transfer the cake to a rack and let it rest for 10 minutes, then unmold it onto the rack and allow it to cool to room temperature.

To make the (optional) glaze: Stir the sugar, cocoa and water together in a small saucepan set over medium heat. Stirring constantly, bring the mixture to a boil and cook for about 3 minutes, or until the glaze is glossy and has thickened enough to pour out in a ribbon. Remove from the heat.

Place the cake, still on the rack, on a baking sheet or a piece of parchment paper (drip-catchers) and pour the glaze over the cake. You can cut the cake now while the glaze is soft, but it's best to wait until it sets a bit.

Storing: Covered, the cake will keep at room temperature for about 3 days. The unglazed cake can be wrapped well and frozen for up to 1 month; thaw in the wrapper.

Poppy Seed Baby Bundts

These cakes look cute—small Bundts always do—but they're much more sophisticated than they appear. They're rich with eggs, cream and butter, a combination that gives them a delicate, moist crumb, the kind you find in fancy pâtisserie gâteaux. The spicing, although unusual for a poppy seed cake—it's a mix of coriander and ginger—is quiet, there to make the cake a little cozier. And the poppy seeds are abundant. Not a decoration. Not a speckle. Not a sprinkle. Not a dash. There are enough poppy seeds for you to taste their nut-like flavor and fruitiness, to appreciate their crunch and to feel them crack under your bite. The cake reminds me of many others: those my mother used to buy from the German bakery near our house; the cakes I'd buy from the Hungarian bakery across town from us; the cake I found at a bake sale in Paris; and the cakes I loved at coffeehouses in Vienna. These cakes take inspiration from many sweet places, but in the end, they're comfortable anywhere in the world—even if I think they're happiest sitting alongside a cup of espresso or dark tea at home in the kitchen.

I find the twin Bundts irresistibly adorable, but they're not the only way to make this cake. If you'd prefer one handsome loaf, see Playing Around.

A word on poppy seeds: The recipe needs more seeds than you get in one of the small spice jars from the supermarket, so look for larger bags and, after you've measured out what you need, seal the bag and store it in the freezer or fridge. Like other nuts and seeds, poppy seeds are oily and so they can go rancid—always smell and taste your seeds before using them.

Makes 2 cakes; 10 to 12 servings

FOR THE CAKE

4 tablespoons (2 ounces; 57 grams) unsalted butter

2 tablespoons neutral oil

1½ cups (204 grams) all-purpose flour

1 teaspoon baking powder

½ teaspoon fine sea salt

½ teaspoon ground coriander

¼ teaspoon ground ginger

1¼ cups (250 grams) sugar

2 lemons

4 large eggs, at room temperature

2 teaspoons pure vanilla extract

½ cup (120 ml) heavy cream, at room temperature

⅓ cup (47 grams) poppy seeds (see below left)

FOR THE TOPPING (optional)

Confectioners' sugar for dusting

OR

1 cup (120 grams) confectioners' sugar

About 2 tablespoons freshly squeezed lemon juice or milk

Poppy seeds for sprinkling (optional)

To make the cake: Center a rack in the oven and preheat it to 350 degrees F. Butter the insides of two 6-cup baby Bundt pans, dust with flour and tap out the excess, or coat the pans with baker's spray.

Melt the butter (you can do this in a microwave or on the stovetop) and stir in the oil; set aside while you work on the batter.

Whisk the flour, baking powder, salt, coriander and ginger together. →

Put the sugar in a large bowl and grate the zest from both lemons over it. Squeeze 2 tablespoons of juice from the lemons into a cup and set aside.

Reach into the bowl and use your fingertips to mash and mush the zest into the sugar until the sugar is moist and fragrant, and maybe even tinged yellow. Add the eggs one by one, whisking each one in energetically before adding the next. Whisk in the lemon juice, vanilla and cream.

Still working with the whisk, add the flour mixture in three additions, stirring gently and making sure that the dry ingredients are fully incorporated each time. Pour half of the butter-oil mixture over the batter and whisk it in, then add the rest and blend it in. Add the poppy seeds and either whisk them in or switch to a flexible spatula and stir them in. Divide the batter evenly between the two pans.

Bake the cakes for 28 to 32 minutes, or until they've risen, are golden brown around the edges and pull away from the sides of the pans when you tug gingerly. A tester inserted into the center of the cakes should come out clean. Transfer the cakes to racks and let them rest for 5 minutes, then unmold onto the racks and allow them to cool to room temperature. At this point, you can simply dust them with confectioners' sugar, ice them or, even more simply, just enjoy them.

To make the (optional) icing: Stir the confectioners' sugar and 1 tablespoon juice or milk together in a small bowl until smooth. If you need more liquid, add it a drop at a time until you've got an icing that falls slowly from the tip of the spoon. Spoon the icing over the cakes and let it make its way over the top and down the cakes' curves. If you'd like, sprinkle the tops of the cakes with poppy seeds.

Storing: Wrapped well, the cakes will keep at room temperature for at least 4 days. If you haven't iced them, you can wrap them and freeze for up to 1 month; thaw in the wrappers.

Playing Around

Poppy Seed Loaf Cake

If you'd prefer to make one cake rather than two small Bundts, use an 8½-inch loaf pan. Butter and flour the pan and tap out the excess flour, or coat it with baker's spray. When you're ready to slip the pan into the oven, place it on a stack of two baking sheets or on an insulated baking sheet; because the loaf needs to bake for 60 to 70 minutes, it's good to give the bottom of the pan a little cushion of air to help keep it from getting too brown. As for the top of the cake—take a look at it after it's been in the oven for about 45 minutes, and if it looks as though it's getting too dark, tent it loosely with parchment or foil. Leave the baked cake in the pan for 5 minutes before turning it out onto a rack and letting it cool to room temperature.

Makes 12 servings

FOR THE SWIRL

3 tablespoons sugar

1 tablespoon unsweetened cocoa powder

Pinch of fine sea salt

Pinch of ground cinnamon

¼ cup (43 grams) finely chopped dark chocolate or mini dark chocolate chips

FOR THE CAKE

3 cups (408 grams) all-purpose flour

2 teaspoons baking soda

1½ teaspoons ground cinnamon

1½ teaspoons ground ginger

¾ teaspoon fine sea salt

½ teaspoon ground cardamom

¼ teaspoon freshly grated nutmeg

1 cup (240 ml) neutral oil

1½ cups (300 grams) sugar

½ cup (100 grams) brown sugar

3 large eggs, at room temperature

1 tablespoon pure vanilla extract

1 can (15 ounces; 425 grams) pure pumpkin puree (see above right)

FOR THE TOPPING (optional; see headnote)

Confectioners' sugar for dusting, Cream Cheese Frosting (page 264), Glossy Chocolate Glaze (page 265) OR Confectioners' Sugar Icing (page 270)

Cocoa-Swirled Pumpkin Bundt

Everything about this cake is softer and gentler than you'd imagine—the crumb, the spice, even the pumpkin flavor. When I began thinking about the cake, I had Thanksgiving and Christmas in mind—pumpkin and spice have that effect on so many of us. But I ended up with a cake so lovely, so easy to pair with coffee, tea or even a glass of rum, that it became a year-rounder. In the cold months, glaze it with chocolate, top it with swipes of cream cheese frosting or drizzle over a sugar icing, maybe one with some booze or maple syrup (or both). In spring and summer, finish the cake with a shower of confectioners' sugar and serve it with ice cream. Whipped cream is welcome no matter when. As is the cocoa swirl that runs through the cake's middle. Because the rippling ribbon includes chopped chocolate and bakes to a comforting pudding-ish texture, it's nice in every season.

A word on pumpkin puree: Make sure that you choose pure pumpkin puree, *not* pumpkin pie filling, which is sweetened and spiced. While there are different versions of pumpkin puree available—many supermarkets have their own brands—if you can, I suggest you buy Libby's. It is the most consistent, it has a beautiful color and, most important, it's not watery—it always bakes well.

Center a rack in the oven and preheat it to 350 degrees F. Coat the interior of a 12-cup Bundt pan with baker's spray or butter it, dust with flour and tap out the excess.

To make the swirl: Mix the sugar, cocoa powder, salt, cinnamon and chocolate together in a small bowl and keep at hand.

To make the cake: Whisk the flour, baking soda, cinnamon, ginger, salt, cardamom and nutmeg together.

Working in the bowl of a stand mixer fitted with the paddle attachment, or in a large bowl with a hand mixer, beat the oil and both sugars together on medium speed for a couple of minutes to blend well—the mixture should look slushy, like wet sand. Still beating on medium, and scraping the bowl and beater(s) early and often, add the eggs one at a time, beating for about a minute after each one goes in. The mix will continue to look iffy until that last egg is in and then, as if by magic, it will become satiny. Reduce the mixer speed and blend in the vanilla and pumpkin puree.

Turn the mixer off, add one-third of the dry ingredients and pulse the mixer on and off to get the blending going and to help prevent the counter from getting showered with flour. Working on low speed, mix until the dry ingredients are almost incorporated. Turn off the mixer, scrape and add half of the remaining dry ingredients. Pulse, mix on low, stop and scrape again, then add the last of the dry ingredients, mixing on low until fully blended. Give everything a few last turns with a flexible spatula.

Scrape one-third to one-half of the batter into the pan and smooth it with the spatula. Spoon the cocoa swirl over the batter—you can try to make an even layer and prevent the swirl from touching the sides of the pan, but it's almost impossible, so relax. Add the rest of the batter—it will only half fill the pan, but it will rise considerably in the oven.

Bake for 55 to 60 minutes, or until the cake is beautifully puffed, is cracked around the top and pulls away from the sides of the pan when gently tugged. A tester poked into the center of the cake should come out clean—make sure you don't hit the gooey swirl. Transfer the pan to a rack and let the cake rest for 10 minutes, then turn it out onto the rack and allow it to cool to room temperature.

Once the cake is cool, you can dust it with confectioners' sugar, or you can glaze or ice it.

Storing: Wrapped, the cake will keep for about 4 days at room temperature. Unless you've used the icing, you can freeze the cake for up to 1 month; thaw in the wrapper. If you've covered the cake with chocolate glaze and the glaze looks smushed after it has defrosted, try hitting it with a little heat from a hair dryer—it should smooth out.

Coffee-Chocolate Chunk Bundt

Makes about 12 servings

FOR THE CAKE

1 tablespoon boiling water

1 tablespoon plus 1½ teaspoons instant espresso powder (see below)

2 cups (272 grams) all-purpose flour

1½ teaspoons baking powder

1 teaspoon ground cinnamon

½ teaspoon fine sea salt

16 tablespoons (8 ounces; 226 grams) unsalted butter, at room temperature

1 cup (200 grams) brown sugar

¼ cup (50 grams) sugar

3 large eggs, at room temperature

1 teaspoon pure vanilla extract

⅔ cup (160 ml) sweetened condensed milk (see below)

3 ounces (85 grams) milk chocolate, finely chopped

FOR THE GLAZE

½ cup (120 ml) sweetened condensed milk

1¾ teaspoons instant espresso powder

Michael cut into this cake while I was warming the icing—cake can make people impatient—and returned ten minutes later to say, "It's got a long finish!" And he was right. It's like a fine red wine—its flavor lingers. What perplexes me is how to describe the flavor. My intention was to capture the pleasure of Vietnamese coffee in a cake, but either I got carried away or the cake set its own course for deliciousness: it's a lot more complex than that rich, creamy drink. It's got coffee's depth and condensed milk's caramel sweetness—a luscious combo that turns up in the glaze, too. But then there's the cinnamon and the smattering of chopped milk chocolate. It's a substantial cake in every way. Also one that's naturally good with morning coffee, confident enough to hold its own alongside thick, full-tang yogurt, ready for ice cream and best served in thinnish slices rather than hefty chunks—it's nice to savor the big flavor in small bites.

To make the cake: Center a rack in the oven and preheat it to 325 degrees F. Coat the interior of a 10-cup Bundt pan with baker's spray or butter it, dust with flour and tap out the excess.

Mix the boiling water and 1 tablespoon of the instant espresso powder together in a small cup and set aside to cool. Put the remaining 1½ teaspoons espresso powder in the bowl of a stand mixer or a large bowl you can use with a hand mixer.

Whisk together the flour, baking powder, cinnamon and salt.

Add the butter and both sugars to the bowl with the instant espresso. If you're using a stand mixer, fit it with the paddle attachment. Working on medium speed, beat the butter and sugars together until well blended, about 3 minutes; stop often to scrape down the beater(s) and the bowl. Add the eggs one by one, beating for about a minute after each one goes in—you'll have a creamy batter that might remind you of frosting. With the mixer on low, beat in the vanilla and cooled coffee mixture. Still on low speed, alternately blend in the dry ingredients and the condensed milk—add the flour mixture in three additions and the milk in two, starting and finishing with the dry ingredients and scraping often. When the last of the flour mixture has almost disappeared, add the chocolate and mix for just a couple of turns, →

A word on the espresso powder and the sweetened condensed milk: While you can substitute instant coffee for the espresso powder (although its flavor won't be as pronounced), there is no substitute for the sweetened condensed milk. After you've measured out the milk for the cake (from a 14-ounce can), hold on to the remainder; it's just the right amount for the glaze.

then finish blending it in with a spatula, giving everything a last scraping while you're at it. Fill the pan with the batter, then plunge the spatula in and out in a few places just to settle the batter; swivel the pan to even the top.

Bake for about 55 minutes, or until the cake just starts to come away from the sides of the pan (give it a gentle tug) and, more important, a tester inserted into the center comes out clean. Transfer the pan to a rack and wait for 5 minutes, then unmold the cake onto the rack and allow it to cool to room temperature.

To get ready to glaze the cake, slip a baking sheet or a sheet of parchment under the rack to catch the excess glaze.

To make the glaze: Pour the condensed milk into a small saucepan and stir in the espresso powder. Cook, stirring, over low heat for 4 to 6 minutes, or until the glaze thickens slightly; don't allow the milk to boil. Transfer the glaze to a measuring cup or small pitcher with a spout and pour it over the cake. Allow the cake to sit for about an hour to set the glaze; although the glaze never sets fully and may remain a little sticky, it will be easier to cut and serve the cake if you wait a bit.

Storing: Covered, the cake will keep for about 4 days at room temperature. The glaze may stick to the plastic wrap, but it will still be good. Frozen, the cake, glazed or unglazed, will hold for up to 1 month; thaw in the wrapper. If you freeze the cake with the glaze, the glaze won't be perfect, but the cake will still be tasty.

First-of-Fall Apple Bundt

Every summer, I promise myself that I'll wait until the tomatoes are off the vine and the corn is no longer sweet and juicy before I turn my affection to apples. And every September, just when the farm stands start piling up pumpkins, the tug of the apples' fresh scent and crimson-and-gold-colored skins soften my resolve and I return home with a bushel of them, enough to make Sasha's Grated Apple Cake (page 5), Apple-Cheddar Corn Cake (page 231), an Apple Custard Cake (page 71) and this Bundt, my first apple bake of the season. The cake is big and welcoming, tender beneath its firm crust, dappled with chunks of soft apples and sweet with maple syrup and brown sugar. Finish it with the caramel (optional, but strongly recommended), and each slice will pack the quintessential flavors of the season.

A word on the apples: Choose the apples you like best. I usually grab one that's tart and one that's sweet. I don't think McIntoshes are right for the cake because they soften so significantly under heat. And I find Granny Smiths a bit dry for the recipe, but if you love them, use them—they'll add a touch of sharpness to the mix.

A word on the caramel: This old-time recipe makes a caramel that thickens but doesn't harden as it cools. You can use it as a drizzle to decorate the cake or as a sauce. If you choose to use it as sauce, why not go all out and top a slice of the cake with ice cream, then pour over the hot caramel sundae style?

Makes about 10 servings

FOR THE APPLES

2 large apples (about 1 pound; 455 grams; see below left), peeled and cored

1 tablespoon sugar

1 tablespoon all-purpose flour

½ teaspoon ground cinnamon

FOR THE CAKE

2¾ cups (374 grams) all-purpose flour

1 teaspoon ground cinnamon

1 teaspoon baking powder

½ teaspoon baking soda

½ teaspoon fine sea salt

1½ cups (300 grams) brown sugar

3 large eggs, at room temperature

½ cup (120 ml) pure maple syrup

1 cup (240 ml) neutral oil

1½ teaspoons pure vanilla extract

½ cup (120 ml) full-fat buttermilk (well shaken before measuring), at room temperature

Confectioners' sugar for dusting (optional)

FOR THE CARAMEL (optional; see above center)

8 tablespoons (4 ounces; 113 grams) unsalted butter

1 cup (200 grams) brown sugar

¼ cup (60 ml) evaporated milk, half-and-half or cream

1 teaspoon pure vanilla extract

Center a rack in the oven and preheat it to 350 degrees F. Choose a 10-cup Bundt pan, preferably one that doesn't have a complicated design; coat it with baker's spray or butter it, dust the interior with flour and tap out the excess.

To prep the apples: Cut the apples into small chunks. Try to keep them less than ½ inch, but don't fuss over neatness here; even a rough chop will work. You should have between 3½ and 4 cups of chunks (but again, precision's not necessary). Put the apples, sugar, flour and cinnamon in a large bowl and toss together to coat the apples; set aside. →

To make the cake: Whisk the flour, cinnamon, baking powder, baking soda and salt together.

Working in the bowl of a stand mixer fitted with the paddle attachment, or in a large bowl with a hand mixer, beat the brown sugar and eggs together on medium speed for about 3 minutes. Still working on medium, and scraping the bowl and beater(s) as needed, blend in the maple syrup, followed by the oil and then the vanilla. Turn off the mixer, add half of the flour mixture and mix on low speed until the dry ingredients are almost incorporated. Pour in the buttermilk and mix just until incorporated, then add the remainder of the dry ingredients and mix just until they disappear into the thin batter.

Give the apples a quick stir, scrape them into the batter—include any syrup that has accumulated—and mix them in with a flexible spatula. Pour the batter into the pan.

Bake for 60 to 70 minutes, or until the cake just starts to pull away from the sides of the pan and, more important, a tester inserted in the center of the cake comes out clean. The batter may have baked a bit higher than the center opening, but that's fine. Transfer the cake to a rack and let it sit for 10 minutes, then unmold it onto the rack and allow it to cool to room temperature.

If you won't be finishing the cake with the caramel glaze, dust it with confectioners' sugar, if you'd like.

To make the (optional) caramel: Put the butter, brown sugar, milk (or half-and-half or cream) and vanilla in a medium saucepan set over medium heat. Bring to a boil and keep at a bubble, stirring, for 2 minutes. Use the caramel immediately as a glaze for the cake (put the cake on a rack set over a baking sheet or a piece of parchment paper and pour over the caramel) or as a sauce over slices of cake, or over ice cream, if you're serving it. The caramel can also be covered and refrigerated—warm gently before using.

Storing: The cake can be wrapped and kept for about 3 days at room temperature. Without the caramel, it can be wrapped airtight and frozen for up to a month; thaw in the wrapper. You can make the caramel sauce up to 2 days ahead—cool to room temperature, cover and refrigerate; rewarm before using.

Playing Around

First-of-Fall Pear Bundt

Usually any apple cake can become a pear cake, and that's the case with this recipe. You can swap the cinnamon for cardamom (try ½ teaspoon), a half-and-half mix of cinnamon and allspice or a little ginger. You can add dried fruit—about ½ cup would be nice (make sure it's moist; dunk it in hot water if it's not, then pat dry) or chopped nuts (toasted is good, untoasted is fine). And you can also add the grated zest of a lemon, orange or tangerine.

♥ A TREASURED FAVORITE

Almost Maida's Heatter's Buttermilk Lemon Bundt

Makes 8 servings

FOR THE CAKE

1¾ cups (240 grams) all-purpose flour

¾ teaspoon baking powder

½ teaspoon baking soda

½ teaspoon fine sea salt

1½ cups (300 grams) sugar

2 lemons

11 tablespoons (5½ ounces; 150 grams) unsalted butter, at room temperature

2 large eggs, at room temperature

1 large egg yolk, at room temperature

⅔ cup (160 ml) full-fat buttermilk (well shaken before measuring), at room temperature

FOR THE GLAZE

¼ cup (60 ml) freshly squeezed lemon juice or a combination of lemon and lime juice

⅓ cup (67 grams) sugar

1 tablespoon water

Confectioners' sugar for dusting

Storing: Wrapped, the cake will keep for about 3 days at room temperature. You can freeze it, but the glaze may soften the cake's crust—hardly tragic. Thaw in the wrapper.

I can't remember exactly why I bought Maida Heatter's *Book of Great Desserts* when it was published in 1974—I think I'd read something about her cheesecake in the *New York Times*—but that book became my baking bible: I baked almost all of the recipes and learned something new with each one. There was just one photograph on the cover and a few line drawings here and there inside, yet it didn't matter—Maida, as we called her at home, wrote her recipes in such a precise but conversational way that I could picture how each sweet should look. My copy of the book now has a ragged cover, a broken spine and spots on every page—it would take a detective to figure out where they all came from. It also has my notes—sometimes Michael's, too—at the top of every recipe. Most of the comments are synonyms for "Delicious!"

One of my favorite recipes was the Buttermilk Lemon Cake that appeared on page 116 of the original book. Maida described the cake in five words: "light, moist, lemony and lovely." I added the word "precisely" and underlined it with a squiggle. I made this cake all the time and for everything. It was the cake I gave to Joshua's teachers for the holidays and the one I brought to friends' homes when we were invited for dinner. When, for a very short time, I was a baker in a pastry shop, I brought my version of the recipe into the kitchen—they're still making the cake today.

While I made the cake just about weekly, Maida Heatter stopped making it. She didn't include the recipe in the paperback edition of her book, and when the recipe finally reappeared in another of her books, she explained that her formerly reliable cake had stopped working. She couldn't figure it out and decided the only possible reason was that her kitchen had been invaded by demons! She recalled that that was what the writer Isaac Bashevis Singer claimed happened to his work, and she was sure she was plagued by the same witches. →

Happily, the recipe always worked for me, but that didn't stop me from tinkering with it. Over the years, I changed the original recipe in many ways—I fiddled with the size, the baking temperature, the amount of flour and sugar, the way the zest is incorporated, the leavening and the glaze. I guess that technically I could call the recipe my own at this point, but for me, it will always be Maida's Cake. Maybe that makes it "our" cake. That would make me happy.

And, yes, the cake is still "light, moist, lemony and lovely." I'd still write "precisely" in the margins, and I still marvel at its delicate buttermilk-soft texture, its deep and true lemon flavor and the way the glaze that's brushed over the hot cake adds extra spark to every bite.

To make the cake: Center a rack in the oven and preheat it to 350 degrees F. Coat the inside of a 10-cup Bundt pan with baker's spray or butter it, dust with flour and tap out the excess.

Whisk the flour, baking powder, baking soda and salt together.

Put the sugar in a small bowl and grate the zest of both lemons over it (hold on to the lemons). Reach into the bowl and, using your fingertips, smush the zest and sugar together until thoroughly blended and fragrant. Set aside briefly.

Halve the lemons and squeeze the juice into a measuring cup; you'll need 2 tablespoons for the cake and more for the glaze. Set aside.

Working in the bowl of a stand mixer fitted with the paddle attachment, or in a large bowl with a hand mixer, beat the butter on medium speed until smooth, about 2 minutes. Gradually add the lemony sugar and beat for another 2 to 3 minutes, scraping the bowl and beater(s) frequently. Working on medium-high speed, add the eggs and yolk one at a time, beating after each goes in—this batter needs air. Once the eggs and yolk are incorporated, beat for another 3 minutes; be sure to scrape. Turn the mixer off, spoon in one-third of the flour mixture and mix on low only until it disappears into the batter. Pour in half of the buttermilk and mix to blend. Your satiny batter may look slightly curdled after the buttermilk goes in—carry on. Repeat with half of the remaining flour mixture, the rest of the buttermilk and then the last of the dry ingredients. Give the bowl a good scrape, pour in 2 tablespoons of the juice and fold it into the batter, which will have returned to its original state of beauty. Scrape the batter into the pan and swivel the pan from side to side to even it. I often plunge my spatula into the pan in a few spots to make sure that there's batter in all the curves.

Slide the pan into the oven and bake the cake for 44 to 48 minutes (check it after 40 minutes), or until it is golden brown and pulls away from the sides of the pan when gently tugged; a tester inserted into the center of the cake will come out clean.

Meanwhile, make the glaze: Stir the lemon juice, granulated sugar, and water together in a small bowl. Give the glaze a stir now and then while the cake is in the oven.

When the cake is ready, transfer it to a rack and let it stand for 5 minutes. Slide a baking sheet or a piece of parchment paper under the rack—this will be your drip-catcher for the glaze—and turn the cake out onto the rack.

To glaze the cake: Working with a silicone or regular pastry brush and summoning a smidge of patience, brush the glaze over the hot cake. Make sure to cover the whole cake and use all the glaze—a feat requiring several applications. Allow the cake to cool to room temperature on the rack.

Just before serving, generously dust the cake with confectioners' sugar.

♥ A TREASURED FAVORITE

The Devil's Chocolate Cake

Makes 10 to 12 servings

FOR THE CAKE

1⅓ cups (180 grams) all-purpose flour

½ cup (42 grams) unsweetened cocoa powder, sifted if lumpy

¾ teaspoon baking soda

½ teaspoon baking powder

½ teaspoon fine sea salt

10 tablespoons (5 ounces; 140 grams) unsalted butter, at room temperature

½ cup (100 grams) sugar

½ cup (100 grams) brown sugar

3 large eggs, at room temperature

1½ teaspoons pure vanilla extract

2 ounces (57 grams) semisweet or bittersweet chocolate, melted and cooled but still fluid

½ cup (120 ml) whole milk, at room temperature

½ cup (120 ml) boiling-hot coffee (can be made with instant) or boiling water

4 ounces (113 grams) additional semisweet or bittersweet chocolate, finely chopped, or an equal amount of mini chocolate chips

FOR THE TOPPING, ONE OR A COMBINATION (optional)

Glossy Chocolate Glaze (page 265), warm and ready to pour

Whipped Cream (page 284)

Maraschino or Amarena cherries

Sprinkles or grated or shaved chocolate

In the summer of 2004, I printed out my manuscript for *Baking: From My Home to Yours* to mail to my editor. I was happy and tired. I'd worked on the book for years, and I was ready to put my cake pans on a shelf for a while and take a little time off before the edits and photo shoot would begin. But that night, Michael started reminiscing about an iconic chocolate cake from our childhoods: Ebinger's Black-Out Cake. It was a dark chocolate layer cake, sandwiched with a kind of pudding-ish chocolate cream, frosted with chocolate and covered with crumbled cake. Then came the question: Do you think you could make it? So much for stowing the pans. I pulled a couple down and set to work. I made a few cakes, but none matched our memory. And then I made a cake that was so good that neither of us cared that it wasn't *the* cake. Mine was close, but because I couldn't ace the frosting or the filling, I turned everything around and went from chocolate filling and frosting to vanilla meringue. I kept the crumb coating and called it Devil's Food White-Out Cake. We loved it! We loved it so much that I sent it to my editor asking if she could squeeze it into the book. The latecomer made it into the book and then ended up on the cover! A better-late-than-never story with a surprise ending.

I baked that cake a few more times, but eventually stopped thinking about it because I was working on other recipes. Then, just as I was closing in on the finish line for this book, a friend wrote to tell me how much she liked the White-Out Cake and how often she made it. It was enough encouragement for me to revisit it: the cake was just as good as I'd remembered it. And, unexpectedly, it was excellent without filling, frosting or crumbs. I made it in a Bundt pan and only wished I'd thought to do it sooner.

Because there are no layers and no thick cushions of sweet frosting, all of devil's food's delights are amplified—the chocolate flavor is so full that it's almost demonic, and the texture is bold. That it looks like your

everyday Bundt, that it's made like any old cake and that it uses the basic ingredients of so many chocolate cakes just makes the fact that it's outstanding more remarkable. Bedeviling, really.

A cake this good is good plain, great with chocolate glaze (page 265), a bit greater with glaze and pufflets of whipped cream and greatest with glaze, whipped cream and cherries on top. Or sprinkles. Or berries. Or shaved chocolate. Go wild. It's what the devil would want you to do.

To make the cake: Center a rack in the oven and preheat it to 350 degrees F. Coat the inside of a 10-cup Bundt pan with baker's spray or butter the pan, dust it with flour and tap out the excess.

Whisk together the flour, cocoa, baking soda, baking powder and salt.

Put the butter in the bowl of a stand mixer fitted with the paddle attachment, or in a large bowl if you're using a hand mixer. Add both sugars and beat on medium speed until soft and creamy, about 4 minutes, stopping often to scrape the bowl and beater(s). One by one, drop in the eggs, beating for a minute after each is incorporated. Beat in the vanilla, scrape and don't be upset if your batter looks curdled—it may not be pretty now, but it will be beautiful soon. Turn the mixer to low and blend in the melted chocolate. Beat in the flour-cocoa mixture in three additions and the milk in two, beginning and ending with the dry ingredients and scraping often. When everything's incorporated, and with the mixer still on low, slowly pour in the boiling coffee or water—the neatest way to do this is to pour it down the side of the bowl; the liquid will thin the batter dramatically. Switch to a flexible spatula and stir in the chopped chocolate. Pour the batter into the pan—it is so thin that it will level itself.

Bake for 33 to 38 minutes, or until the cake has risen—it will rise in the center around the pan's hole—and a tester inserted into the center of the cake comes out clean; gently tug, and the cake will pull a little from the sides of the pan. Transfer the cake to a rack and wait for 5 minutes, then unmold the cake onto the rack and allow it to cool to room temperature.

To finish the cake (optional): If you'd like to glaze the cake, put the rack on a piece of parchment paper or a lined baking sheet (you need a drip-catcher) and pour the glaze over the cake. If you want to add whipped cream and fruit, do that just before serving. It's easiest and prettiest to fill a pastry bag (or use a plastic bag with a bottom corner snipped off) with the cream and pipe puffs or swirls on the cake's curves. And, if you want to go all out, put a cherry on top of each cushion of cream. To go all out-er, shower the cake with sprinkles or grated or shaved chocolate.

Storing: Wrapped, the plain cake will keep for about 3 days at room temperature or for up to 1 month in the freezer; thaw in the wrapper. If you want to freeze the glazed cake, put it in the freezer to firm and then wrap it; thaw in the wrapper. Just before serving, warm the glaze with a few puffs of air from a hair dryer—the gloss will return. Since whipped cream won't keep, add it just before serving.

CAKES with CORNERS

Buttermilk Plum Cake

Nature has so many ways to tell us that fall's at our doorstep. Leaves turn color. Days get shorter. Hard-shell squash nudge zucchini off center stage. And Italian prune plums arrive for their short, jubilant stay. Those plums, with their blue-black skins and green flesh, are my favorite signifiers, the ones that tell me that sweater weather is on the way and that it's time to bake. But as good as the plums are eaten out of hand, I think they're better by lots when baked—when they soften, their fragrance intensifies and their sweetness is magnified and becomes almost honeyed. And I think they're perfect in this simple cake, which is buttermilk-tender and gently flavored with almond extract, cinnamon and coriander, ingredients that shine a spotlight on the flavor of the plums. It's the first cake I make when these small plums turn up, and although I happily make it throughout the season with other fruits (see Playing Around), in my heart, it's a plum cake.

Makes 8 servings

FOR THE CAKE

1½ cups (204 grams) all-purpose flour

2 teaspoons baking powder

½ teaspoon ground coriander

¼ teaspoon baking soda

¼ teaspoon fine sea salt

¼ teaspoon ground cinnamon

8 tablespoons (4 ounces; 113 grams) unsalted butter, at room temperature

¾ cup (150 grams) sugar

2 large eggs, at room temperature

½ teaspoon pure vanilla extract

½ teaspoon pure almond extract

½ cup (120 ml) buttermilk (well shaken before measuring), at room temperature

8 to 10 smallish Italian prune plums, quartered

FOR THE GLAZE (optional)

2 tablespoons jam or jelly (see below)

A word on the glaze: The glaze is optional, but I hope you'll make it. Choose a light-colored jam—I often use Korean yuzu-ginger jam, called tea jam (because you can dissolve it in hot water and drink it), but apple jelly or apricot jam would be nice, too.

To make the cake: Center a rack in the oven and preheat it to 350 degrees F. Butter a 9-x-9-inch baking pan, dust the inside with flour and tap out the excess, or coat the pan with baker's spray.

Whisk together the flour, baking powder, coriander, baking soda, salt and cinnamon.

Working in the bowl of a stand mixer fitted with the paddle attachment, or in a large bowl with a hand mixer, beat the butter and sugar together on medium speed until light, pale and fluffy, about 4 minutes. Add the eggs one at a time, beating for a minute after each one goes in. Pour in the vanilla and almond extracts and beat to blend—you'll have a lovely, creamy mixture. Spoon half the dry ingredients into the bowl and, with the mixer on low, beat just until they're no longer visible. Scrape down the bowl and beater(s), return the mixer to low speed, pour in the buttermilk and mix until blended. Don't be discouraged when your pretty batter threatens to (or even does) curdle—it'll be fine. Scrape the bowl and beater(s) again, add the rest of the flour mixture and beat on low just until incorporated. Scrape the batter into the pan and use a spatula to smooth and even it—make sure the corners of the pan are filled with batter.

Arrange the plums over the batter. You don't have to press on them, and you don't have to be neat or formal—as beautiful a design as you create, the batter will rise up and make its own pattern, so don't fuss with this. It's hard to say exactly how many plums you'll need—you want to be generous, but you don't want to pave the top with fruit: you're looking for a nice balance between cake and plums. Slide the pan into the oven.

Bake the cake for 38 to 43 minutes, or until it is puffed and golden brown; the edges will be more deeply browned and will have started to pull away from the sides of the pan. Most important, a tester inserted into the center of the cake will come out clean. Transfer the pan to a rack and let it rest for 10 minutes, then place a piece of parchment over the top of the pan (this will protect the plums) and turn the cake out onto a rack (or a cutting board). Lift off the pan, carefully flip the cake over onto another rack and leave it until it is only just warm or has reached room temperature before glazing or serving it. Be careful when you transfer the cake from the rack to a platter—it's a softie.

To glaze the cake (optional): Put the jam in a small saucepan with a splash of water—a couple of teaspoons is enough—and bring to a boil over medium heat, stirring. When the jam falls slowly off the spoon (or spatula) that you're using to stir, remove it from the heat. (Of course you could do this in a microwave—figure on 20 to 30 seconds.) Using a pastry brush and a gentle touch, coat the cake and fruit with the glaze. Let the glaze cool before cutting and serving.

Storing: The cake is best the day it is made, when the crumb is tender and the fruit soft and juicy. If you do need to keep the cake, cover it and leave it at room temperature. A day later, some of the fruits' juice will have melded with the cake, softening it, but it will still be a treat.

Playing Around

Other Fruits

Try the cake with pitted cherries, halved or whole; keep the cinnamon and coriander or swap the coriander for a pinch of ground cloves. If you want to use berries, you can omit the coriander. For apples, I might add a little ground allspice to the cinnamon and coriander. And for pears, I'd up the vanilla extract to 1 teaspoon.

Black Sesame Bars

Makes 9 servings

- ¼ cup (40 grams) black sesame seeds
- 1 cup (200 grams) sugar
- 1 cup (136 grams) all-purpose flour
- ½ teaspoon baking powder
- ½ teaspoon fine sea salt
- 2 large eggs, at room temperature
- 1 large egg white, at room temperature
- ¼ cup (65 grams) black sesame paste (see below left)
- ¼ to ½ teaspoon Asian roasted sesame oil (see below left)
- ½ cup (120 ml) neutral oil
- ¾ cup (128 grams) mini semisweet chocolate chips (see below center)
- Cocoa Crumbs (page 261) for topping (see below; optional)

Black sesame is an if-you-know-you-know kind of flavor, and most of us know it when we see the seeds on top of an everything bagel, flecking a loaf of rye bread or sprinkled over a rice bowl. But whir the seeds into a fluffy flour, mix them with black sesame paste (think tahini) and make them the main attraction in a cake, and they go from a little something to a big, luscious surprise. And that's the story with these easygoing bars—foolers for those new to black sesame, delights to those familiar with its charms. The bars, made with basic ingredients that let the full, slightly nutty flavor of black sesame shine, are tender and soft. I added just a splash of toasted sesame oil to the mix, mostly for its haunting fragrance, and chocolate chips for a bunch of reasons: chocolate and black sesame are like good friends—they accentuate each other's best qualities; chips hold a bit of their shape, so they add some texture to each bite; and they're playful: since the cake looks like devil's food, the chips are an impish way to keep up the ruse. Just for fun—flavor and additional enticement—I scatter a handful of chips over the just-baked cake and then spread the melted chocolate over the surface for the quickest icing ever.

The bars are excellent glossed with the icing, but if you top the icing with crunchy baked Cocoa Crumbs, you'll have something memorable. Consider it. Seriously.

A word on black sesame paste and sesame oil: Black sesame paste—sometimes called black sesame sauce or tahini—is most easily found in Asian markets and, of course, online. Regardless of the name, the ingredient list should be simple—opt for pastes that contain just black sesame seeds. (Some pastes have 0.5% emulsifiers—don't shun them.) Whether it's paste, sauce or tahini, you'll need to give the jar a good stir to blend the ground seeds with the oil that rises to the top. As for the sesame oil—it's another product that's easily found in Asian markets or the Asian section of your grocery store. Look for roasted or toasted sesame oil, which will be a rich nut brown (don't use clear sesame cooking oil). The oil is very fragrant and boldly flavored—a little goes a long way.

A word on the chocolate chips: They're here as much for texture as flavor. Although you could use an equal amount of finely chopped chocolate, I like to use chips because they hold their shape under heat and offer the pleasure of melting in your mouth.

A word on the crumbs: The recipe for Cocoa Crumbs makes about 2 cups, but you'll need only about ½ cup here. Either halve the recipe or, better yet, make the full recipe and freeze the leftovers.

Center a rack in the oven and preheat it to 350 degrees F. Coat a 9-x-9-inch baking pan with baker's spray; line it with a piece of parchment, running the paper over the bottom of the pan and up two opposite sides, leaving enough overhang on the sides to use as lifters. Alternatively, you can butter the pan, dust with flour, tap out the excess and line it with the parchment.

Put the sesame seeds and a teaspoon or two of the sugar in a food processor—a mini's perfect here—or a coffee grinder and whir, stopping to scrape the sides, until you've got a fluffy flour. If there are a couple of stray seeds here or there, leave them.

Whisk the all-purpose flour, baking powder, salt and the remaining sugar together in a large bowl. Add the black sesame flour and whisk to blend. Whisk the eggs and white together in a small bowl until they're well blended, then pour them into the bowl. Switch to a flexible spatula and stir the eggs into the dry ingredients. This is a case of easier-said-than-done—you've got a lot of dry stuff and not much liquid, so you've got to stir a little longer than usual and perhaps with a tad more vigor. The mixture will look more like a dough than a batter, but that's fine. When you've got nearly all of the dry ingredients in—you might still see some specks and streaks—scrape the black sesame paste into the bowl and stir, stir, stir to incorporate it. Add the oil in three additions, mixing it in with a motion that's a mash-up of stirring and folding, not beating. Be gentle but persistent, and you'll be rewarded with a thick batter that flows languidly from your spatula. Stir in ¼ cup of the chips, and when they're evenly distributed, scrape the batter into the pan. You'll need to spread it to get it evenly distributed and into the corners—I use an offset icing spatula for this.

Bake for 18 to 20 minutes, or until the cake can be gently tugged away from the sides of the pan and, more important, a tester inserted into the center of the cake comes out clean. Transfer the pan to a rack and turn off the oven.

Immediately scatter the remaining ½ cup chips over the top of the cake. Slide the pan back into the oven, leave the door open and let the oven's heat melt the chips. After 3 minutes, press on some of the chips with an offset spatula to see if they're spreadable—if they're not, give them another minute. Put the pan back on the rack and use the spatula to spread the melted chocolate evenly over the top of the cake. If you're using the cocoa crumbs, scatter them over the top and lightly press them into the chocolate.

Let the cake cool to room temperature. Unless your kitchen is chilly, it's likely that the chocolate will still be wet. Slip the cake into the refrigerator for about 10 minutes to set the chocolate. (Don't keep it in the fridge too long—the cake's texture is nicest when it's at room temperature.)

Run a table knife between the paper and the sides of the pan and then use the parchment overhangs to lift the cake out of the pan and onto a platter or cutting board. Peel away the paper.

Storing: Wrapped well, the cake will keep at room temperature for about 2 days. You can wrap the finished cake, melted chocolate and crumbs included, and freeze it for up to 1 month; thaw in the wrapper.

Blueberry Jam Cakes

I'm betting that there are hundreds of different recipes for jam cakes, those delectable stacks of crust, jam and chunky crumble that are eaten like a cookie. I'm also betting that the lion's share of them are good: with these types of cakes, good is a built-in. Easy-to-make is, too. Certainly that's true of these blueberry beauties, which end up right every time, no matter whose hands form them. And they're a job for hands. A job for fingers to mash and mush the ingredients together to make the press-in crust and the from-the-same-mixture crumble topping (and maybe even to dip into the pan of ten-minute jam to see if it's cool enough to spread). I'm giving you a recipe to make these with homemade blueberry jam, but the fruit is a variable and a jar of jam from the supermarket an option. Take a look at Playing Around for next-time inspiration.

Makes 8 servings

FOR THE JAM

2 tablespoons cornstarch

¼ cup (60 ml) water

2½ pints (about 750 grams) blueberries

⅓ cup (67 grams) sugar

Freshly squeezed lemon or lime juice to taste (optional)

FOR THE CRUST AND CRUMBLE

2 cups (272 grams) all-purpose flour

½ cup (50 grams) almond flour

½ cup (100 grams) sugar

3 tablespoons brown sugar

½ teaspoon fine sea salt

12 tablespoons (6 ounces; 170 grams) cold unsalted butter, cut into small pieces

Confectioners' sugar for dusting (optional)

A word on the jam: It's fine to substitute store-bought jam or a different kind of homemade jam, but just make sure that it's not too sweet and that it's thick. If yours is a bit loose, spoon it into a saucepan with a splash of water and cook it, stirring, for a few minutes to thicken. You need about 2¾ cups jam for the cakes.

To make the jam: Put the cornstarch in a small bowl and add 2 tablespoons of the water. Stir until the mixture is smooth; set this slurry aside.

Working in a medium saucepan, stir the berries, sugar and the remaining 2 tablespoons water together and set the pan over medium heat. Bring to a boil, stirring frequently, then lower the heat just enough to keep the mixture at a steady burble. Cook for about 5 minutes, stirring often, until the mixture thickens noticeably. Give the cornstarch slurry a stir, add it to the jam and cook, stirring, for 2 minutes more. Scrape the jam into a bowl and leave it to cool to room temperature. Taste and add a squirt or two of juice, if you'd like. (*The jam can be packed into a covered container and refrigerated for up to 1 week.*)

When you're ready to bake: Center a rack in the oven and preheat it to 350 degrees F. Butter a 9-x-9-inch baking pan or coat it with baker's spray.

To make the crust and crumble: Put all of the ingredients *except* the butter in a large bowl and use your hands to mix everything together. Drop in the pieces of cold butter and toss them around to coat them with the flour mixture. Reach in and, using your fingertips, pinch, press, mash and squeeze everything together until you've got a bowl full of moist clumps and curds. This will take a few minutes, so enjoy it. →

Spoon one-half to two-thirds of the mixture into the buttered pan and press it evenly over the bottom. It's not necessary, but I sometimes use the bottom of a glass or a measuring cup to tamp down and smooth the base. Spread the jam over it.

Squeeze the remainder of the mixture into crumbs of different sizes and scatter them over the jam. You might have enough to almost cover the jam completely or you might have less, so the jam will peek through in more places—there aren't any rules for this.

Bake the cake for 48 to 53 minutes, or until the top is golden brown. The jam will bubble and puff, and that's what you want. Transfer the pan to a rack and allow the cake to cool to room temperature before cutting. Cutting the cake can be tricky because you don't want to use a sharp knife and scratch your pan. You can run a table knife around the edges of the pan, cut the cake into large blocks and transfer the blocks with a wide offset spatula to a cutting board, then do the serious cutting on that. Or you can cover a cutting board with parchment, loosen the cake with a table knife, turn it out onto the covered board and then flip it again onto another cutting board or a platter for cutting and serving. Dust with sugar, if you'd like, and serve.

Storing: Wrapped well, the jam cakes will keep at room temperature for up to a day, if it's not too hot and humid, or in the refrigerator for about 2 days. They can be frozen for up to 1 month; thaw in their wrapper.

Playing Around

It's easy to substitute a different berry jam for the blueberry, and you can also use apricot jam (in which case it would be nice to swap the almond flour for ground pistachios) or plum jam (nice with almonds, also nice with walnuts or pistachios). You could use citrus curd instead of berry jam (I love the curd on page 275, but it isn't thick enough for this cake, so it would be better to use a commercial curd) or even a fruit butter, like apple or pumpkin.

Beggars' Bars

Makes 12 servings

FOR THE CAKE

- ½ cup (80 grams) moist, plump raisins (see below left)
- ¼ cup (40 grams) moist, plump crystallized (or stem) ginger (see below center), cut into bits
- ⅔ cup (90 grams) all-purpose flour
- 2 tablespoons unsweetened cocoa powder
- ½ teaspoon fine sea salt
- ¼ teaspoon freshly ground black pepper
- 8 tablespoons (4 ounces; 113 grams) unsalted butter, cut into 8 pieces
- 2 tablespoons neutral oil
- 5 ounces (142 grams) semisweet or bittersweet chocolate, coarsely chopped
- ⅔ cup (133 grams) sugar
- 3 cold large eggs
- 1 teaspoon pure vanilla extract

FOR THE TOPPING

- ½ cup (85 grams) chocolate chips
- 3 to 5 tablespoons chopped nuts (see below), preferably lightly toasted
- 6 to 8 moist, plump dried figs
- 1 or 2 chunks crystallized ginger
- 1 or 2 tablespoons moist, plump raisins

These soft chocolaty bars were inspired by one of the simplest French bonbons I know, the mendiant. *Mendiant* means *beggar* in French, and the candy—a small round of chocolate sparingly topped with dried fruits and nuts—is bound up with the practices of four religious orders whose communities take vows of poverty and depend on alms to sustain them. Traditionally the chocolates have had raisins for the Augustinians, hazelnuts for the Carmelites, figs for the Franciscans and almonds for the Dominicans. But as is often true in the kitchen, tradition gets bent—sometimes out of necessity, often out of restless creativity—and today it's common to find mendiants with pistachios or walnuts, apricots or even pineapple, and any combination of toppers perked up with candied citrus peel. In the French tradition of breaking tradition, I was inspired by mendiants but not tied to them when I made this cake.

You can think of the base as a brownie, but if you do, please think of it as a maximal brownie—there's nothing in the batter except a bit of enlivening black pepper to interrupt the pleasure of full-on dark chocolate. For the fruits and nuts, I've gone with custom and chosen raisins and figs, but I added crystallized ginger. Aside from the obvious surprise and zip of the ginger, the morsels (I kept them tiny) perfume the cake. For the nuts, I often use almonds and walnuts, because that's what I've always got in the house, but, of course, they're up for grabs.

A word on dried fruit: For this cake to be truly delicious, the fruit has to be truly moist. To get the right texture, soak the fruit in a bowl of very hot water for a minute or two (the crystallized ginger and figs might need longer). Drain and pat dry. If you're going to cut up the fruit, do it after you've soaked it. For more flavor, you can add a tablespoon or so of brandy or another alcohol to the water, or soak the fruit in hot tea.

A word on the ginger: Crystallized ginger is sugar-coated dried ginger. Sometimes the ginger is thin and oddly shaped and sometimes you can find it diced or in squares. For this recipe, I prefer chunkier pieces. If the pieces are hard, soak them before you cut them down to size. If you have stem ginger—cubes of ginger packed in sugar syrup—you can use it. Rinse it quickly, pat dry and cut.

A word on choices: You can choose whatever fruit you like for the cake and the topping. No matter what I use in the cake—I usually use raisins, cherries or snipped apricots—I always use crystallized ginger. Similarly, you can use whatever nuts you like—almonds, hazelnuts, walnuts, pistachios and even pine nuts are all good choices.

To make the cake: Center a rack in the oven and preheat it to 325 degrees F. Coat an 8-x-8-inch baking pan with baker's spray or butter it, dust with flour and tap out the excess. Run a sheet of parchment paper over the bottom and up two opposite sides of the pan, leaving enough paper to use as handles for unmolding the cake.

If you haven't already soaked the raisins and ginger (or whatever fruit you've chosen), give them a soak now, drain and pat dry.

Whisk the flour, cocoa powder, salt and pepper together.

Put the pieces of butter in a medium saucepan, pour in the oil and scatter over the chocolate. Place the pan over the lowest heat and cook, stirring often, until the butter and chocolate have melted. Take care not to use too much heat, or the mixture will separate. Alternatively—and requiring less vigilance—put the ingredients in a heatproof bowl set over a pan of gently simmering water (the bottom of the bowl should not touch the water) and heat, stirring occasionally, until the butter and chocolate have melted.

Remove the pan (or bowl) from the heat and whisk in the sugar—the mixture may turn grainy, but that's fine. Wait a minute or two, then beat in the cold eggs one by one. By the time the third egg is in, the mixture should be beautiful—thick and shiny. Give it a few brisk beats with the whisk and then beat in the vanilla. Still working with the whisk, or switching to a flexible spatula if you prefer, gradually and gently stir in the flour-cocoa mixture until almost completely incorporated. Drop in the raisins and ginger and stir to mix them in evenly. Scrape the batter into the pan and smooth the top.

Bake the cake for 22 minutes; it's hard to test these bars—better to go by time and faith. (As soon as the cake goes in, make sure that everything that you need for the topping is at hand.)

Remove the pan from the oven (turn off the oven) and sprinkle the chips as evenly as you can over the top of the cake. Slide the pan back into the oven and leave it for 2 minutes. Remove the pan from the oven and transfer it to a rack, then grab an offset spatula and "ice" the cake with the melted chocolate. Don't worry about getting a perfectly smooth finish here—it will be covered. Working quickly—you want the chocolate to still be wet—press the fruit and nuts into the top of the cake. I usually add the fruit first and press it down lightly, then scatter over the nuts—but there's no right way here. If the chocolate has set—unlikely, but possible—slip the pan back into the oven and let it sit with the door open for another minute or so, then remove and give the topping a couple of love pats to make sure it's nestled into the chocolate.

Leave the cake on the rack for 5 minutes, then run a table knife around the sides and, using the parchment handles, lift the cake out of the pan and onto the rack. This is a very soft cake, so work deliberately, and don't try to remove the parchment until the cake has cooled. (The cake is never easy to cut because it's got so much good fruit in and on top of it, but it's more difficult to cut when it's still the slightest bit warm.) If the chocolate is still wet when you're ready to cut and serve the cake, you can give it about 10 minutes in the fridge.

Storing: Wrapped well, the cake will keep for up to 4 days at room temperature and for up to 1 month in the freezer; thaw in the wrapper.

Cookie-Butter Blondies

Makes about 16 servings

- 1½ cups (204 grams) all-purpose flour
- ½ teaspoon baking powder
- ½ teaspoon fine sea salt
- ½ teaspoon ground cinnamon
- ¼ teaspoon baking soda
- ½ cup (140 grams) cookie butter (see below)
- 8 tablespoons (4 ounces; 113 grams) unsalted butter, at room temperature
- ½ cup (100 grams) sugar
- ½ cup (100 grams) brown sugar
- 2 large eggs, at room temperature
- 1 large egg yolk, at room temperature
- 1 teaspoon pure vanilla extract
- 3 ounces (85 grams) milk or semisweet chocolate, chopped into chip-size pieces, or about ½ cup (85 grams) chocolate chips
- 6 speculoos cookies (about 75 grams), coarsely chopped (see below)

A word on the cookie butter and cookies: Biscoff is my go-to, but if you have a favorite cookie butter, use it. Ditto the cookies.

Here's how I saw it: if speculoos cookies, those crisp cinnamon and Christmas-spice cookies that are the ideal go-along with coffee, are good, and if cookie butter made from speculoos is two good things in one, or doubly good, then putting them together in a blondie could only be the best. I loved the idea for its logic and its irresistibility, and then I loved the blondies for their taste and texture. The cookie butter gets worked in with the regular butter and, to make sure that there's layer on layer of flavor, a handful of chopped cookies is stirred into the batter along with some chocolate. The blondies bake up golden and have that characteristic blondie chew. The surprise is the edges—they're like chocolate-chip cookies! Although the blondies have plenty of flavor, they are happily companionable—as good with coffee as the little speculoos cookies are. Also good with ice cream. Also good cut into triangles, and just as good cut into small cubes and nibbled on the way to anywhere.

Center a rack in the oven and preheat it to 325 degrees F. Spray a 9-x-9-inch baking pan with baker's spray, line the bottom with a piece of parchment paper, lightly spray the paper and smooth the spray over the surface with a pastry brush—a silicone brush makes the job easier. (Although you could butter and flour the pan, I find that baker's spray works best here.)

Whisk the flour, baking powder, salt, cinnamon and baking soda together.

Working in the bowl of a stand mixer fitted with the paddle attachment, or in a large bowl with a hand mixer, beat the cookie butter, butter and both sugars together on medium speed until light and smooth, about 2 minutes. Add the eggs one by one, beating for a minute after each egg goes in. Add the yolk and beat for a minute, then beat in the vanilla—be sure to scrape down the bowl and beater(s) as you go. Turn the mixer off, add the flour mixture and pulse the machine on and off to start the blending. With the mixer on low, beat just until the dry ingredients are almost incorporated and the batter is light and silky—you don't need to be thorough now. Add the chocolate and cookie pieces and spin the mixer on low a couple of times, then stop and finish the blending by hand with a sturdy spatula. Scrape the batter into the pan and smush it around to even it; pay special attention to the corners—you want to make sure they get their fair share of batter.

Bake the blondies for 32 to 35 minutes, or until the top is golden and feels dry; a tester inserted into the center of the cake should come out clean. Transfer the pan to a rack and wait for 5 minutes, then run a table knife around the edges of the cake and carefully turn it out onto the rack. Peel away the parchment, flip the cake over onto another rack and let it cool to room temperature.

How you cut the blondies is up to you: large squares, slender rectangles, pointy triangles or bite-size bits.

Storing: Tightly wrapped, the blondies will keep at room temperature for about 3 days. Wrapped airtight, they can be frozen for up to 1 month; thaw in the wrapper.

Makes 9 to 12 servings

FOR THE CRUNCH

¼ cup (50 grams) sugar

¼ cup (about 40 grams) mini chocolate chips or chopped semisweet or bittersweet chocolate

¼ cup (about 30 grams) chopped or sliced nuts, toasted if you'd like

1½ teaspoons unsweetened cocoa powder

Pinch of ground cinnamon

Pinch of fine sea salt

FOR THE CAKE

1½ tablespoons instant espresso powder (or instant coffee)

1 tablespoon boiling water

1¾ cups (238 grams) all-purpose flour

1¼ teaspoons baking powder

1 teaspoon ground cinnamon

½ teaspoon fine sea salt

7 tablespoons (3½ ounces; 99 grams) unsalted butter, at room temperature

¾ cup (150 grams) sugar

¼ cup (50 grams) brown sugar

3 large eggs, at room temperature

3 tablespoons neutral oil

1 teaspoon pure vanilla extract

½ cup (120 ml) full-fat coconut milk, well stirred before measuring (see above center)

½ recipe Cocoa Crumbs (see above right; page 279), chilled

Confectioners' sugar for dusting (optional)

Coffee-Crunch Coffee Cake

The full name of this recipe should be something like "The Coffee Cake That I Made Especially for Michael Because He Likes Soft Snacking Cakes with Lots of Flavor That Have a Crunchy Chocolate Ripple Running Through Them and Also Crumbs on Top." The cake started life as a simple coffee-flavored cake—a nibbler. But when Michael walked into the kitchen and asked if I'd planned to put crumbs on it—less a question than a request—I went all in and added the crumbs as well as a mid-level crunch. It's an easy ripple made with chocolate chips and nuts, and it's awfully nice with the crumb topping.

A word on coconut milk: Please look for full-fat coconut milk—it's an important part of what makes the texture of this cake so lovely.

A word on the crumb topping: Even though you need only a half recipe of the cocoa crumbs for the cake, I urge you to make the full recipe—you can freeze the leftovers, and the next time anyone walks into your kitchen wanting this cake, the Black Sesame Bars (page 143) or any other cocoa crumb-topped sweet, you'll be ready.

Center a rack in the oven and preheat it to 350 degrees F. Coat a 9-x-9-inch baking pan with baker's spray and run a sheet of parchment paper over the bottom and up two opposite sides, leaving enough overhanging paper to grab and lift the baked cake out of the pan. Or butter the pan, dust the interior with flour, tap out the excess and line it with the paper.

To make the crunch: Toss all the ingredients together; set aside.

To make the cake: Stir the espresso powder and boiling water together in a small cup; set aside.

Whisk the flour, baking powder, cinnamon and salt together.

Working in the bowl of a stand mixer fitted with the paddle attachment, or in a large bowl with a hand mixer, beat the butter and both sugars together on medium speed until well blended, about 3 minutes; scrape the bowl and beater(s) early →

and often. The mix will seem pasty, and that's fine. One by one, add the eggs, beating for a minute after each one goes in. Don't be concerned if the mixture looks as though it's on the verge of curdling or even if it curdles—it'll smooth out soon. With the mixer running, beat in the oil, followed by the espresso mixture and vanilla. Turn off the mixer, add one-third of the dry ingredients and mix on low until they almost disappear. With the mixer running, gradually pour in half of the coconut milk. Scrape, add half of the remaining dry ingredients and mix on low until they almost disappear, then blend in the rest of the coconut milk. Scrape, and mix in the rest of the dry ingredients. You'll have a thick, creamy, easily spreadable batter.

Scrape half of the batter into the pan, then use an icing spatula or a knife to nudge it into the corners and to smooth the surface. Scatter the crunch mixture evenly over the batter—don't miss the edges—and top with the remaining batter, taking care to again smooth the top. Take the crumbs out of the refrigerator and, if they need it, smush and press them into curds or clumps before topping the cake with them.

Bake for 38 to 43 minutes, or until the cake is risen and richly browned and can be pulled from the sides of the pan when gently nudged; a tester inserted into the center of the cake will come out clean. Transfer the pan to a rack and let it rest for 10 minutes, then use the parchment handles to lift the cake out of the pan and onto the rack. Turn the cake over onto another rack, carefully peel away the paper and then invert back onto the rack to cool until just warm or at room temperature.

When ready to serve, give the top of the cake a light dusting of confectioners' sugar, if you'd like.

Storing: You can make the crunch up to 1 week ahead and keep it, covered, on the counter. Wrapped, the cake will keep for about 4 days at room temperature or for up to 1 month in the freezer; thaw in the wrapper.

Crunchy-Topped Almond Cake

Makes about 12 servings

FOR THE TOPPING

1 large egg white

1½ cups (150 grams) sliced almonds (blanched or unblanched)

FOR THE CAKE

1¾ cups (238 grams) all-purpose flour

1¾ teaspoons baking powder

½ teaspoon fine sea salt

¼ teaspoon baking soda

¼ teaspoon freshly grated nutmeg

¾ cup (75 grams) almond flour

2 large egg whites, at room temperature

1 large egg, at room temperature

1 cup (200 grams) sugar

¾ cup (150 grams) brown sugar

12 tablespoons (6 ounces; 170 grams) unsalted butter, at room temperature

¼ cup (60 ml) neutral oil

2 teaspoons pure vanilla extract

½ teaspoon pure almond extract

1 cup (240 ml) full-fat buttermilk (well shaken before measuring), at room temperature

A couple pinches of fleur de sel or flaky salt for finishing

Sanding sugar for finishing

For all the years that I've been baking, you'd think that I could pull a cake out of the oven, smile because the recipe worked and move on until it's time to cut and share it. But nope—I still coo over cakes. Still want to pat the pretty ones as though they're kindergartners who deserve a gold star. This cake is a coo-er—it was from the start, and it continues to be. Seeing the pavé of polished, golden, crunchy and sugar-sparkled almonds across the cake's top makes me feel like a sorcerer, even if all I did was swish some nuts around in beaten egg white. But the real magic is the cake. Because it's made with buttermilk, both butter and oil, all-purpose and almond flour and granulated and brown sugar, it's cushiony soft-crumbed and just a smidge chewy. Crunch on top, tenderness beneath and the deep, comforting flavor of almond everywhere.

Center a rack in the oven and preheat it to 350 degrees F. Coat a 9-x-13-inch baking pan, one with sides that are at least 2 inches high, with baker's spray, or butter and flour it, tapping out the excess flour. Run a piece of parchment paper over the bottom of the pan and up the two long sides.

To make the topping: Put the egg white in a medium bowl and beat it lightly with a fork, just to break it up. Add the sliced almonds, then reach in and use your fingers to toss the ingredients together for a minute or two—you want the nuts to be evenly coated with the white. It's a messy job, but a quick one. Set aside.

To make the cake: Whisk the all-purpose flour, baking powder, salt, baking soda and nutmeg together, then whisk in the almond flour.

Lightly whisk the whites and whole egg together in a small bowl, just to bring them together a bit.

Working in the bowl of a stand mixer fitted with the paddle attachment, or in a large bowl with a hand mixer, beat both sugars and the butter together on medium speed until creamy and light, about 3 minutes. Scrape the bowl and beater(s) now, and intermittently forever more—there'll soon be a lot of batter, and you want to make sure you're mixing it evenly. Slowly pour in the oil and beat for 2 minutes. Lower the mixer speed and gradually pour in the eggs, then increase the speed to medium →

and beat for about 3 minutes—you'll have a lovely frosting-like mixture. Beat in the vanilla and almond extracts. Turn the mixer off, spoon in one-third of the dry ingredients and mix on low just until they disappear. With the mixer on low, pour in half of the buttermilk. When it's in, stop the mixer, scrape and add half of the remaining dry ingredients. Mix to incorporate, then add the remaining buttermilk and blend. Stop the mixer, scrape, add the last of the dry ingredients and mix on low until thoroughly blended. Give the batter one last stir with a spatula, then scrape it—it will be beautiful—into the pan. Use a small offset icing spatula or a table knife to spread the batter in the pan, taking care to get it into the corners. Use the spatula to smooth the top.

Give the nut topping a quick toss to catch some of the egg white that might have settled in the bottom of the bowl, and then, using your fingers, drop the nuts over the top of the batter. I find it's easiest to dollop the top with the nuts and then to use my fingers to spread them as evenly as possible over the batter—imagine you're shingling the cake. Perfection is impossible here, so don't fuss over it. Dust the nuts lightly with a pinch or two of fleur de sel or flaky salt (don't use too much, and don't try to distribute it evenly—you want here-and-there surprises) and then sprinkle over sanding sugar (be more generous and more evenhanded with it).

Bake the cake for 34 to 37 minutes, or until it has risen evenly (it's important for the center to have risen as much as the sides), the topping is golden (it may be darker around the sides) and the cake pulls away from the pan when gently tugged; a tester inserted into the center will come out clean. Transfer the pan to a rack and leave it to rest for 5 minutes. Turn the cake over onto the rack, carefully peel away the paper and gently turn the cake over onto another rack. As tempting as it is to grab a slice when the cake is warm, resist: the cake is exceedingly tender, and you'll mash its lovely crumb if you try to cut it before it cools to room temperature.

Storing: Wrapped well, the cake will keep for about 3 days at room temperature. You can freeze it for up to 1 month and thaw it in its wrapper, but while the cake will be fine, the topping will lose some of its crunch. Alas.

Semolina-Chocolate Cake

Makes 9 servings

- 1 cup (180 grams) semolina flour
- 2 tablespoons unsweetened cocoa powder, preferably Dutch-processed
- 2 teaspoons baking powder
- ½ teaspoon baking soda
- ½ teaspoon fine sea salt
- 3 large eggs, at room temperature
- ¾ cup (150 grams) sugar
- ⅓ cup (80 ml) neutral oil
- ¾ cup (170 grams) thick plain whole-milk Greek yogurt, at room temperature
- ¼ cup (60 ml) whole milk, at room temperature
- About 1 cup (170 grams) mini chocolate chips (see headnote)

Even if you know, love and bake with semolina, you might not immediately recognize it in this cake. Here it's the stealth ingredient that bolsters the cake's moistness and makes it a standout. Semolina's beautiful golden color is invisible in the cake and its flavor isn't strong, but you'll catch a tiny touch of its sandiness that makes you pay attention to the surprise star: cocoa. There's not much cocoa, but somehow, almost magically, the cake tastes fully chocolaty. To play that up, I use dark Dutch-processed cocoa and fold chocolate chips into the batter. My usual preference is for chopped chocolate, but chips are better here. Because chips don't melt completely during baking, you'll notice them with each bite, and I wanted that. Also, chips have a way of falling to the bottom of a batter, and I actually think of that as a plus here: they build another texture at the base of the cake. If you want to substitute an equal amount of chopped chocolate, of course you can—it will melt more completely than chips and you'll have a more uniformly chocolaty cake.

Center a rack in the oven and preheat it to 350 degrees F. Butter the interior of an 8-x-8-inch baking pan or coat it with baker's spray. Line the pan with parchment and butter or spray the paper.

Whisk together the semolina, cocoa, baking powder, baking soda and salt.

Working in the bowl of a stand mixer fitted with the whisk attachment, or in a large bowl with a hand mixer, beat the eggs and sugar on medium speed for about 4 minutes, until the mixture pales and the whisk leaves tracks when lifted. Turn the mixer to low and add the oil in a steady stream, then increase the speed to medium and beat for 1 minute. Do the same with the yogurt and then with the milk. Add half of the semolina mixture and mix on low only until mostly incorporated. Add the remaining dry ingredients and beat just to combine. Finish blending the dry ingredients in by hand with a flexible spatula. Set the bowl aside for 5 minutes to allow the semolina to absorb some of the liquid. Use the spatula to stir in the chocolate chips.

Even after this rest, the batter will be thin. Pour it into the pan and slide it into the oven.

Bake the cake for 35 to 38 minutes, or until it is uniformly risen (it bakes up beautifully), springs back when lightly poked and is starting to come away from the sides of the pan; a tester inserted into the center of the cake will come out clean. Place the pan on a rack and wait for 5 minutes, then carefully run a table knife around the edges of the cake and turn it out onto the rack. Invert onto another rack and allow the cake to cool to room temperature.

Storing: Wrapped well, the cake will keep for about 3 days at room temperature or for up to 1 month in the freezer; thaw in the wrapper.

Greek Orange Cake

Makes 12 servings

FOR THE CRUMBLED PHYLLO

1 pound (454 grams) phyllo dough (see below)

FOR THE ORANGES

2 medium oranges or 3 clementines (total weight about 12 ounces; about 340 grams), preferably unwaxed and organic

FOR THE SYRUP

⅔ cup (160 ml) freshly squeezed orange juice

⅔ cup (160 ml) water

⅔ cup (133 grams) sugar

1 cinnamon stick

FOR THE CAKE

1¼ cups (250 grams) sugar

4 large eggs, at room temperature

1 cup (230 grams) thick plain whole-milk Greek yogurt, at room temperature

1 cup (240 ml) neutral oil

1½ teaspoons pure vanilla extract

1¼ teaspoons baking powder

½ teaspoon baking soda

½ teaspoon ground cinnamon

¼ teaspoon fine sea salt

Thick plain whole-milk Greek yogurt or vanilla ice cream for serving (optional)

A word on phyllo dough: You want thin sheets for the cake—they're often labeled #4, and they're what you commonly find in a supermarket. Specialty stores may have other thicknesses—stick to the thin ones.

Michael and I were frantically packing, hoping not to miss the ferry back to Athens, when our host in Sifnos handed me a piece of cake for the voyage. "It's orange," she said, and then we were off. It was most assuredly orange—the cake itself tasted full of orange and every bit of it was soaked through with orange syrup. It was so moist that when you pressed on it, a bit of syrup bubbled around your finger, and firm, like a set pudding. It was deeply satisfying and mystifying—there was a flavor that fluttered in the background of every bite, and I couldn't place it.

I enjoyed the cake but then didn't think about it again until my Parisian friend Hélène Samuel, who spends part of every year in Greece, told me she had a recipe for an orange cake that I absolutely had to try: portokalopita. And yes, it was *the* cake. It was also the key that solved the mystery: that unidentifiable flavor was oven-dried, crushed phyllo dough. The cake has no flour and, until you stir in the phyllo shards, no resemblance to anything other than scrambled eggs. That it bakes to a golden cake seems like magic. Even more magical is that, after absorbing the eggs, oil and yogurt—of course there's Greek yogurt in this cake!—the phyllo can still welcome an abundance of syrup.

Making the cake is simple (especially since the batter is mixed in a food processor), but there's a lot of waiting around. You have to dry the phyllo, which takes about an hour (crumbling it is a quick job that I wish went on longer—it's exceptionally relaxing); boil the oranges (a lovely technique used often in Mediterranean cooking); and then wait, and wait, and wait until the syrup soaks into the cake. When I make the cake, I never plan on serving it until the next day. Happily, it's great the day after it's made and just as good for four more days.

To dry the phyllo: Position the racks to divide the oven into thirds and preheat it to 200 degrees F. Have two baking sheets at hand.

I think the easiest way to get all the dough dried evenly at once is to accordion the sheets. Place one sheet of dough on a work surface—don't worry if it tears, because you'll eventually be shredding it—position it so that a long side is parallel to you, hook your thumbs under the dough close to each of the edges and use your fingers to pull the dough up into soft folds, like a scarf. Transfer the scrunched-up dough to the baking sheet. Repeat with the remaining phyllo, lining up the accordioned sheets as you place them on the pans and squeezing them close together—fill each sheet with half of the dough.

Slide the pans into the oven and bake for 30 minutes, then turn each sheet of phyllo over and bake for about 30 minutes more. The dough should be dry but not colored.

Remove the pans from the oven and allow the sheets to cool, then squeeze, pinch, crumble and tear each sheet of dough until it shatters into small pieces. Like so many messy jobs, this one's fun. I think the mess is best contained if you leave the dough on the baking sheets and break it up there, keeping the dough as low to the pan as possible as you work—lift one up, and you'll be finding phyllo shards all over your kitchen for days. Leave the crushed phyllo at room temperature until needed, or for as long as overnight. If your room isn't humid, you can leave it uncovered.

While the phyllo is baking, cook the oranges: Scrub the fruit and place them in a medium saucepan, one that has a lid. Cover the oranges with water and bring to a boil, then cover the pan, lower the heat to a simmer and let the fruit bob away for an hour, at which point they will be very soft. (Turn the oranges a couple of times, so that they cook evenly.) With a slotted spoon, lift the oranges out of the pan and into a bowl and let cool; they can be slightly warm when you use them, but you don't want them to be hot.

To make the syrup: Put the orange juice, water, sugar and cinnamon stick in a medium saucepan set over medium heat. Bring just to a boil, stirring until the sugar is dissolved, then remove the pan from the heat; transfer it to a bowl, jar or pitcher and set aside. (*You can make the syrup up to 3 days ahead and keep it in the refrigerator—if you make it in advance, remove the cinnamon stick before storing.*)

To make the cake: Center a rack in the oven and preheat it to 350 degrees F. Coat the interior of a 9-x-13-inch baking pan with baker's spray.

The batter is best made in a food processor. You can make it with an immersion blender or in a stand blender; just work on low and bang the container insistently against the counter to de-bubble the mixture before adding the phyllo.

Cut the boiled oranges or clementines in half—wear an apron and stand away, because the juice will sputter. Squeeze out all of the juice and discard (it's bitter); pick out all of the seeds and discard. Cut the rind and pulp into chunks and toss them into the food processor. Add the sugar and pulse a few times, just to start chopping the oranges. Add the eggs, yogurt, oil, vanilla, baking powder, baking soda, cinnamon and salt and pulse and process until the mixture is smooth; scrape down the bowl once or twice as you work. Remove the bowl and rap it on the counter a couple of times—you'll never get rid of all the bubbles, but you can cut down on them a bit. Pour the batter into a large bowl.

Grab a handful of the phyllo pieces and drop them into the bowl. Stir with a flexible spatula until the pieces are moistened, then repeat with another handful. Don't be tempted to add all of the phyllo at once—this is a slow-and-steady process. When all the phyllo is in and evenly moistened, pour the batter into the pan and push it around a little with the spatula to settle it into the corners. →

Bake for 40 to 45 minutes, or until the cake is a lovely honey brown. It will start to pull away from the sides of the pan and a tester inserted into the cake will come out clean. Transfer the pan to a rack. Poke a bunch of holes in the top of the cake with a skewer or toothpick and slowly pour the cooled syrup over the hot cake—it's a lot of syrup. The syrup will slip down the sides of the pan and it may pool on top—it's all okay. Let the cake sit until all of the syrup is absorbed—this might take a couple of hours.

When all the syrup has soaked into the cake, it's ready to cut and serve. The cake is too wet to easily remove it whole from the pan, so use a table knife to cut it into square, rectangular or diamond-shaped portions (the trimmings from diamond shapes are the baker's treat). A blunt knife and a soft touch will keep your pan out of harm's way.

If you like, top each serving with a dollop of yogurt or a scoop of ice cream.

Storing: Covered, the cake will keep at room temperature or in the refrigerator for at least 4 days—it's nice that the cake is good cold. Because of the syrup, it's not a good candidate for freezing.

Makes about 9 to 12 servings

FOR THE NUT LAYER

½ cup (100 grams) brown sugar

3 tablespoons (1½ ounces; 42 grams) unsalted butter

¼ cup (60 ml) heavy cream

½ teaspoon fine sea salt

¼ teaspoon ground cinnamon

About 1½ cups (6 ounces; 170 grams) pecans or walnuts, coarsely chopped, at room temperature

FOR THE CAKE

12 tablespoons (6 ounces; 170 grams) unsalted butter, cut into chunks

6 ounces (170 grams) semisweet or bittersweet chocolate, coarsely chopped

¾ cup (102 grams) all-purpose flour

1 teaspoon instant espresso powder

½ teaspoon baking powder

½ teaspoon fine sea salt

¼ teaspoon ground cinnamon

⅔ cup (134 grams) sugar

2 large eggs, at room temperature

Caramel-Nut Chocolate Upside-Down Cake

Put on your dreaming cap and imagine celebrating the marriage of a pecan pie and a soft, moist chocolate cake. Actually, imagine the very top of the pecan pie, the part where the caramel is most flavorful—where it's still soft, but a little like candy—and where the nuts are the most caramel-coated. And then picture the sweet nuts skimming the top of a rich chocolate cake made with dark chocolate lightly underscored with espresso powder and a touch of cinnamon. I imagined this cake for a long time, but I kept imagining it wrong and I kept being frustrated, until I realized that the way to get the perfect meld of caramel nuts and cake was to build this treat upside down. It not only made a better dessert—it was easy. The caramel is simple—no candy thermometer needed—and the batter is whisked together quickly. Since I imagined this cake as a riff on my husband's favorite chocolate-chip pecan pie, I usually turn to pecans, but it's just as good with walnuts.

Center a rack in the oven and preheat it to 325 degrees F. Coat the inside of an 8-x-8-inch baking pan, one with at least 2-inch-high sides, with baker's spray (it's better than butter and flour for this cake) and then line the bottom and sides of the pan with two pieces of parchment, crisscrossing them so that all four sides are covered with paper; spray the parchment.

To make the nut layer: Put the sugar and butter in a saucepan over medium heat and cook, stirring, until the sugar dissolves, the butter melts and the mixture boils. Cook, stirring, for a minute or two, then add the cream, salt and cinnamon, bring back to a boil and cook and stir for another 2 minutes. Add the nuts and stir until they are coated with the caramel.

Turn the mixture out into the baking pan and use a flexible spatula to spread it into the corners and to even the layer. Set aside. →

To make the cake: Put the butter and chocolate in a small saucepan and set it over very low heat. You want to melt the butter and chocolate slowly so that they blend beautifully and don't get so hot that they separate. (If your stovetop doesn't have a very low setting, melt the butter and chocolate in a heatproof bowl set over a pan of gently simmering water—the bottom of the bowl should not touch the water—or do this in a microwave.)

Whisk the flour, espresso powder, baking powder, salt and cinnamon together.

Put the sugar in a large bowl, drop in the eggs and immediately start whisking, then continue to whisk energetically for a couple of minutes. Pour in the melted chocolate-butter—it might still be a little warm, and that's fine—and whisk to incorporate completely. Add the dry ingredients and, continuing with the whisk or trading it for a flexible spatula, mix them in until there's no trace of flour. Scrape the batter into the pan and smooth the top.

Bake for 34 to 37 minutes, or until the top looks dry, the cake starts to pull away from the sides of the pan and, most important, a tester poked into the center of the cake comes out clean or with a few dry crumbs. Transfer the pan to a rack and let it sit for 10 minutes.

Very carefully—the caramel will be superhot—turn the cake out onto another rack and peel away the parchment. If a few nuts and some caramel have stuck to the paper, use a table knife to scrape them off and onto the cake. Let the cake cool to room temperature. It's tempting to eat the cake when it's only just warm—and I wouldn't stop you—but the texture of both the nuts and the cake is better after a few hours. In fact, I think this cake really comes into its own the next day.

Storing: You can't freeze this cake, but it keeps surprisingly well at room temperature. Wrap it well, and it will be good for about 4 days.

Fall Harvest Cake

There's nothing especially French about this cake, but because I made it for the first time in my small Paris kitchen, I'll always think of it as the cake to make after shopping at my local outdoor market there on a chilly fall day. As I mixed the batter, I found myself adding more fruits and flavors, wondering if I'd gone a little overboard, and then was delighted to discover that I'd made a cake with so many textures and pleasures: there's no telling what combination of fruits and nuts will turn up in each bite. There's plump dried fruit stirred into the batter—choose your favorite, knowing that any fruit you pick will be a nice match to the cake's tender olive oil–rich crumb and yogurt tang. Top the cake with slices of apple or pear—fall's darlings—and dot it with grapes, the surprise addition and the fruit that just about defines the word *harvest* for the French. Baked grapes are a treat—heat sweetens and softens them. Finish with a generous handful of nuts, slip the cake into the oven and spend the next hour or so deciding whether you'll have your first slice with tea, coffee or a glass of warming sherry.

A word on the dried fruit: It's nice to add small bits of dried fruit to the batter for surprise, color, flavor and texture, but the fruit's got to be soft and the pieces have to be very small. So take scissors to the chunky bits and then give all of the fruit a quick soak in hot water and a pat dry. I like dried cranberries, raisins and apricots here, but choose your own mix or go with just one kind of fruit.

Makes 9 to 12 servings

- 1 cup (200 grams) sugar
- 1 lemon
- 1 medium pear or apple
- 1½ cups (204 grams) all-purpose flour
- 2 teaspoons baking powder
- ½ teaspoon fine sea salt
- ½ cup (50 grams) almond or hazelnut flour
- 3 large eggs, at room temperature
- 1 large egg yolk, at room temperature
- ¾ cup (170 grams) thick plain whole-milk Greek yogurt, at room temperature
- 1 teaspoon pure vanilla extract
- ¼ teaspoon pure almond extract
- ¾ cup (180 ml) extra-virgin olive oil
- 1 cup (about 150 grams) moist, plump dried fruit, cut into small pieces if necessary (see left)
- A small bunch of seedless grapes, stemmed (about 1 cup; 170 grams) and left whole or halved
- A small handful of nuts (about ¼ cup; 30 grams), such as sliced almonds, chopped pistachios, broken walnuts and/or pecans
- About ½ cup (160 grams) lemon or orange marmalade or apricot jam for glazing (optional)

Center a rack in the oven and preheat it to 350 degrees F. Coat the interior of a 9-x-9-inch baking pan that has at least 2-inch-high sides—this cake has a glorious rise—with baker's spray and run a piece of parchment paper over the bottom and up two opposite sides. If you prefer, you can butter the pan, flour it, tap out the excess and line it with parchment.

Put the sugar in a large bowl and grate the lemon zest over it (hold on to the lemon for squeezing over the fruit). Reach into the bowl and use your fingers to squish and squeeze the mixture until it's fragrant. →

Peel the pear or apple, cut it in half from top to bottom, remove the core and trim the top and bottom. Place the halves cut side down on a cutting board and slice each one crosswise into scant-¼-inch-thick slices. Then cut each half in half down the center from top to bottom. Squeeze some lemon juice over the fruit to help keep it from browning.

Whisk the flour, baking powder and salt together in another large bowl, then whisk in the nut flour.

One by one, whisk the eggs and the yolk into the lemon sugar. You want to give the whisking a bit of energy and keep at it for a minute or two—you'll feel the mixture thickening a bit. Whisk in the yogurt, followed by the vanilla and almond extracts. Whisking all the while, gradually pour in the olive oil and continue to whisk until it's thoroughly incorporated—you'll have a thick, shiny, kind of lava-ish batter. Pour it into the bowl with the dry ingredients and, still working with the whisk, gently stir until the mixture is smooth and homogenous. Switch to a flexible spatula and stir in the dried fruit. Scrape the batter into the pan and smooth the top.

Top the batter with the sliced pear (or apple) and grapes—arrange the fruit any which way or in whatever pattern you like, lightly pressing each piece into the batter to anchor but not submerge it. Scatter over the nuts and pat them down gently.

Bake for 55 to 65 minutes, or until the cake is deeply golden and pulls away from the sides of the pan when gently tugged; most important, a tester inserted into the center of the cake (find a fruitless spot to test) should emerge clean. Transfer the pan to a rack and let the cake rest for 30 minutes before unmolding.

Place a cutting board or a platter over the top of the cake, flip it over, remove the pan and peel away the parchment, then turn the cake over onto the rack. While it's best to wait until the cake cools to room temperature to serve it, if you're going to glaze it, now's a good time.

To make the (optional) glaze: Heat the marmalade or jam with a few splashes of water in a saucepan over medium heat, stirring, or heat in short spurts in a small bowl in a microwave. Stir and add more water as needed to get a mixture that's thin enough to brush on the cake. Using a silicone brush or a regular pastry brush, coat the top of the cake with a thin layer of glaze—I use a combination of brushing and dabbing to cover the bumpy nuts as well as the cake. Let the cake cool completely

Storing: Wrapped well, the cake will keep at room temperature for 2 to 3 days—it's the fruit that makes it somewhat fragile and not a prime candidate for freezing.

Playing Around

Later-in-Fall Harvest Cake

As it gets closer to Thanksgiving, you might want to change up the fruit a bit. Keep the pear or apple, but add some very thin slices of butternut squash. Keep the grapes—they're such a terrific part of the cake—but add some fresh cranberries to the top of the cake. And, if you'd like, add a small handful of both fresh and plump dried cranberries to the batter.

Makes 9 servings

- 8 tablespoons (4 ounces; 113 grams) unsalted butter, cut into chunks
- ½ cup (42 grams) unsweetened cocoa powder, preferably Dutch-processed, sifted if lumpy
- ½ teaspoon fine sea salt
- 2 large eggs
- ½ cup (100 grams) sugar
- ¼ cup (34 grams) all-purpose flour
- 16 thin dark-chocolate-covered peppermint patties (5 ounces; 140 grams), preferably York, chopped into approximately ½-inch pieces (if you've got regular patties, you'll need only 10 to 11 to get about the same weight)

Very Cool Brownies

These are so cool they're cold. Take-a-breath-through-your-teeth-and-shiver cold. Also dark, deeply chocolaty and delicious. Slender and chewy, the way some of the best brownies are. And completely lovable . . . if you love York Peppermint Patties. The patties are chopped up, stirred into the batter and baked until they melt, look like nebula and waft the fragrance of the freshest winter wind through your kitchen.

York is my favorite brand of peppermint patties and I like the "thin" dark chocolate ones for this recipe (although the regular ones work, too). Since I keep a stash in the freezer—everyone in my family loves snacking on them—and since the brownies are based on cocoa rather than chocolate (it's what makes them so full flavored) and use melted butter (no waiting for sticks to come to room temp), they're the stuff of spur-of-the-moment baking.

Center a rack in the oven and preheat it to 325 degrees F.

Melt the butter in a medium saucepan over low heat, then add the cocoa powder and salt and stir to blend. Take the pan off the heat and set it aside for a few minutes while you prep the baking pan.

Coat an 8-x-8-inch baking pan with baker's spray, then run a piece of parchment over the bottom and up two opposite sides, leaving enough overhang to create handles you can use to unmold the brownies once they're baked. Give the paper a light spray. Alternatively, you can butter and flour the pan—tap out the excess flour—and butter the paper.

Whether you continue to work in the saucepan or scrape the butter-cocoa mixture into a medium bowl, grab a whisk and add the eggs one at a time, whisking with a bit of vigor so you get a smooth, shiny mixture. Add the sugar and blend it in well. Continuing with the whisk or switching to a flexible spatula, gently stir in the flour and then the peppermint patty chunks. Scrape the batter into the pan—you'll have a thin layer—and smooth the top as best as you can. →

Slide the pan into the oven and bake for 19 to 22 minutes, or until the top of the brownies is dull and feels set—the cake will test done-ish, meaning that when you stick a toothpick into the center, it may emerge slightly streaked. (Don't be alarmed when, as the batter bakes, it bubbles and seethes and looks like the dark side of the moon.) With these brownies, underbaked is better than overbaked—keep in mind that they will set more as they cool. Transfer the pan to a rack and let rest for 15 minutes.

Run a table knife between the cake and the sides of the pan. Use the parchment handles to gingerly lift the cake onto the rack, turn the cake over onto another rack, peel away the paper and carefully flip the brownies over. Resist cutting into them now—let them cool until they're only just warm or reach room temperature.

Storing: You can wrap the cooled brownies well and keep them at room temperature for about 3 days or freeze them for up to a month; thaw in the wrapper.

Honey-Ricotta Cheesecake from Sifnos

Is this cake only made on the Greek island of Sifnos? I'm not sure, but I'm going with what I was told by the server at our guesthouse there, who insisted that I have a slice with my breakfast. Calling it melopita—*melo* means *honey* in Greek and *pita* translates as *cake*—she explained that once upon a time, the hometown specialty was served exclusively at Easter, but now it is so beloved that it has no season. She might also have added that it has no right time to be eaten—I liked it for breakfast, but then, when I began making it at home, I liked it as a dessert after dinner and as an anytime snack, too: unlike many American cheesecakes, this one is firm enough to be eaten out of hand.

The list of ingredients is spare, essentially cheese, eggs, honey, sugar and cinnamon for topping. Authentically, the cheese would be fresh anthotyro, made from either sheep's or goat's milk, or a combination of the two. Milder, less salty fresh ricotta was suggested as a substitute, and I later learned that many Greek bakers use it. As for the honey, there's a reason it appears in the name: it's the ingredient that carries the cake. If you can find Greek honey, use it; if you can find thyme honey from Greece, grab it; but if all you can find is ordinary honey from your local supermarket, don't let that stop you. The first time I made this cake, all I had was a run-of-the-mill mixed-flower honey, and still the cake was a delightful surprise—it reminded me of crème caramel or a caramel flan. The flavor was immediately recognizable as honey, of course, but the heat of the oven had added that baked caramel-sugar taste. That first time, I didn't finish the cake with the traditional shower of cinnamon for two reasons: (1) I was, perhaps for the first time in my life, out of cinnamon; and (2) I loved how the top of the cake baked to a burnished mahogany brown and I was happy not to cover it up. Later I was admonished for the pass by a Greek friend who insisted that, without the cinnamon, it wasn't truly Greek.

I have that lovely woman from Sifnos to thank for sparking my interest in this cake and the island's magazine, *You Are Here*, for providing the recipe that began my melopita adventure.

Makes 9 servings

- 1⅓ pounds (600 grams) whole-milk ricotta, drained of excess liquid (see below), at room temperature
- 5 large eggs, at room temperature
- ⅔ cup (180 ml) honey
- ¾ cup (150 grams) sugar
- 1 tablespoon cornstarch
- Finely grated zest of 1 lemon or ½ orange (optional)
- Cinnamon for sprinkling

A word on the ricotta: If you have time, line a strainer with a piece of damp cheesecloth (or even a damp paper towel or two), place it over a bowl and spoon in the ricotta. Leave it to drain for 30 to 60 minutes, then discard the liquid and proceed with the recipe. If you're short on time, just make sure to pour off as much of the liquid that may have pooled in the container as possible.

Center a rack in the oven and preheat it to 350 degrees F. Butter or oil the interior of a 9-x-9-inch baking pan. Fit a piece of parchment into the pan, pressing it over the bottom and up and above all four sides—the paper will pleat, and that's fine. (If your parchment isn't wide enough to cover the pan, use two crisscrossed sheets.)

Put the cheese, eggs, honey, sugar, cornstarch and zest, if you're using it, into a food processor or blender. Process or blend on low speed, scraping the bowl or blender jar as needed, until the mixture is smooth, velvety and liquid. Rap the container against the counter a few times to de-bubble the batter and then pour it into the pan.

The cake will probably need a full 60 minutes in the oven, but start checking after 45 minutes. You want the top of the cake to be deeply golden brown; it should pull away from the paper easily, and a tester inserted into the center should come out clean. The cake will puff as it bakes, and you want to be sure that the center puffs just as fully as the sides. Transfer the pan to a rack and let sit for 20 minutes.

To unmold the cake, carefully grab the parchment overhang and lift the cake out of the pan and onto the rack; leave the cake on the paper until you're ready to serve. Sprinkle the top generously with cinnamon and allow the cake to come to room temperature—you want the cake to be completely cool before cutting and serving.

If the cinnamon has been absorbed by the cake or if it's spotty, give it a fresh sprinkling before serving.

Storing: Wrapped well, the cake will keep in the refrigerator for about 3 days. Bonus: It's really nice served cold.

PB and Chocolate Squares

The bottom line on this cake is that it's both fun and seriously delicious, but the backstory's a little more complicated: it took cake math, sugar chemistry, a bunch of trials and a handful of chocolate to make the cake, which looks as simple as sunshine. It took doubling up on the original amount of peanut butter and cutting down on the butter-butter to get a seductively soft crumb. And it took a hard-to-pin-down blend of cinnamon, nutmeg and instant espresso to give the peanut butter character and to make the cake beguiling. Adding chocolate chips to the mix was the fun part, the way I got a bit of kid-like delight into every square. You could use chopped bar chocolate in the batter—it's my usual—but you'd be cutting back on the fun factor: it's nice to find the chocolate buttons dotting the cake and nice that they retain a touch of their texture. Chocolate chips were also how I got a great topping—nothing beats the ease of scattering chips over the top of the hot cake, popping the pan back into the oven for a couple of minutes and then swirling the melted chocolate around. Oh, and finishing the whole thing off with chopped honey-roasted nuts from the supermarket. Even if you serve the cake with on-the-edge-of-bitter coffee ice cream (as I do) and chase it with a double espresso (as I have), it'll still be fun and maybe even still reminiscent of childhood.

Makes about 9 squares

FOR THE CAKE

1 cup (136 grams) all-purpose flour

½ cup (68 grams) whole wheat flour

2 teaspoons baking powder

1 teaspoon ground cinnamon

½ teaspoon freshly grated nutmeg

½ teaspoon fine sea salt

½ cup (128 grams) creamy peanut butter (see below)

4 tablespoons (2 ounces; 56 grams) unsalted butter, at room temperature

¾ cup (150 grams) sugar

2 teaspoons instant espresso powder

2 large eggs, at room temperature

1 teaspoon pure vanilla extract

½ cup (120 ml) whole milk, at room temperature

½ cup (85 grams) semisweet chocolate chips

FOR THE TOPPING

½ cup (85 grams) semisweet chocolate chips

½ cup (75 grams) honey-roasted peanuts, coarsely chopped

Ice cream, preferably coffee, for serving (optional)

A word on the peanut butter: Save the expensive all-natural peanut butter for sandwiches and snacks—you want a commercial butter, like creamy Skippy or Jif, for this cake.

To make the cake: Center a rack in the oven and preheat it to 350 degrees F. Butter an 8-x-8-inch baking pan, dust the interior with flour and tap out the excess, or coat the pan with baker's spray. Run a piece of parchment paper over the bottom of the pan and up two opposite sides, leaving enough paper hanging over the rim to use as lifters when the cake is baked and topped.

Whisk together the all-purpose and whole wheat flours, baking powder, cinnamon, nutmeg and salt.

Working in the bowl of a stand mixer fitted with the paddle attachment, or in a large bowl with a hand mixer, beat the peanut butter, butter, sugar and espresso powder together on medium speed for about 3 minutes. One by one, add the eggs, beating for a minute after each goes in; scrape the bowl and beater(s) as you work. Beat in the vanilla. Turn off the mixer, add half of the dry ingredients and beat on low speed until just incorporated. Still on low, pour in the milk and mix to blend. Turn off the mixer, add the remainder of the dry ingredients and mix on low just until they almost disappear. Beat in the chips. There's a chance that your batter may look as though it's on the verge of curdling—if so, try giving it a few beats with your spatula. Scrape the batter into the pan, making sure to push it into the corners, and smooth the top.

Bake the cake for 32 to 35 minutes, or until it has risen—it may have a few cracks in the top, and that's fine—and pulls away from the sides of the pan when gently tugged; a tester inserted into the center of the cake will come out clean. Transfer the pan to a rack.

Make the topping: Scatter the chocolate chips over the top of the cake and slide the pan back into the oven for 3 minutes. Return the pan to the rack and spread the melted chips over the top of the cake with a small offset spatula, the back of a spoon or a table knife. Swirl the chocolate around or smooth it—your choice—and then top with the chopped nuts. If you think they need it, give the nuts a gentle pat to glue them to the chocolate.

Let the cake rest on the rack for about 10 minutes, then run a table knife around the edges of the pan and, using the parchment handles, carefully lift the cake onto the rack. Slide a cake lifter or two wide spatulas under the cake and pull away the parchment, then set the cake back on the rack and let it cool to room temperature.

If the chocolate hasn't firmed, you can pop the cake into the refrigerator for 10 minutes to set it. But don't leave it in the fridge for too long—the pleasure of the tender crumb diminishes when the cake is cold. That said, everything about the cake is enhanced by being served with ice cream.

Storing: Once the chocolate has set, you can wrap the cake and keep it for 3 days at room temperature or for up to a month in the freezer; thaw in the wrapper.

Texas Sheet Cake, At Last

I'd been baking for a very long time before I learned about the Texas Sheet Cake. Yes, I regret my decades of ignorance. News of the legendary treat came to me from an unlikely source: my friend Zanne Stewart, the longtime food editor of *Gourmet*, the gone and greatly missed food magazine. We were having a catch-up lunch and talking about, of course, what we love best, making food. That's when she told me, in a slightly conspiratorial voice, that she had been enjoying two decidedly un-*Gourmet* cakes: a vanilla box cake from Trader Joe's and Texas Sheet Cake. The Lone Star favorite, which Zanne said had become her dinner-party go-to, is a thin, surprisingly light and deeply flavorful chocolate cake—I'm convinced it's devil's food's next of kin—topped with a very dark and unabashedly sweet chocolate icing that hides bits of toasted pecans. The cake is easy to make (even if it uses a stack of bowls) and deliciously quirky—the quickly made boiled topping is poured over the cake as soon as it comes out of the oven. Pouring hot icing over a hot cake has a couple of practical benefits: there's no waiting around to finish the cake and, even better, a little of the icing seeps into the cake, and that's a delight. More of a delight when the cake cools and it becomes hard to tell where the cake stops and the icing begins.

Because I came to the party late, I had a chance to ramble through a bunch of recipes and stories. My favorite story comes from an interview with Michelle Lopez, founder of the *Hummingbird High* blog and the author of a lovely book, *Weeknight Baking*. Michelle told the *New York Times* that when her family moved from Manila to Houston, five different neighbors welcomed them to the area with homemade cakes. They all brought a Texas Sheet Cake! Having looked at a passel of recipes for the cake, I'm guessing that they were all pretty similar. I don't know that I've ever seen a cake that's so consistent across bakers. There are ways to tweak the recipe (see Playing Around for a few modest ideas), but there's good reason not to: it's great just the way it is.

Makes 15 servings

FOR THE CAKE

2 cups (400 grams) sugar

2 cups minus 2 tablespoons (257 grams) all-purpose flour

1 teaspoon baking soda

¾ teaspoon ground cinnamon (optional but really nice)

½ teaspoon fine sea salt

½ cup (120 ml) buttermilk (well shaken before measuring), at room temperature

2 large eggs, at room temperature

1 teaspoon pure vanilla extract

16 tablespoons (8 ounces; 226 grams) unsalted butter, cut into chunks

Scant ½ cup (40 grams) unsweetened cocoa powder (see page 182)

1 cup (240 ml) very hot water

2 teaspoons instant espresso powder (optional but recommended)

FOR THE TOPPING

12 tablespoons (6 ounces; 170 grams) unsalted butter, cut into chunks

Scant ½ cup (40 grams) unsweetened cocoa powder (see page 182)

⅓ cup (80 ml) heavy cream

3 cups (360 grams) confectioners' sugar, sifted if very lumpy

¾ cup (90 grams) chopped toasted pecans

A word on the cocoa: As I usually do in my recipes, I used Dutch-processed cocoa (Valrhona) and I loved the cake I made with it. However, this is a typically American recipe and so natural cocoa would be the traditional pick. Use what you like or what you've got—your cake will be good with either type.

A word on the measurements: Measures like 2 cups minus 2 tablespoons are not my style, and I apologize for that. But it was really the best that I could do to get the volume equivalents of the weights the recipe needed.

To make the cake: Center a rack in the oven and preheat it to 350 degrees F. Butter a half sheet pan (13 x 18 x 1-inch high) or coat it with baker's spray.

Whisk the sugar, flour, baking soda, cinnamon, if you're using it, and salt together in a large bowl.

In a 2-cup measuring cup or a bowl, whisk the buttermilk, eggs and vanilla together until well blended.

Put the butter in a medium saucepan and melt over medium heat. Add the cocoa, lower the heat and whisk until you've got a smooth mixture. Pour in the water, stir in the espresso powder, if you're using it, and bring the mixture to a boil. Boil, stirring nonstop, for 30 seconds.

Pour the hot cocoa mixture into the bowl with the sugar and flour and whisk to stir everything together. Don't worry about being thorough—it's okay if there are a couple of spots of flour here and there. Give the buttermilk mixture a stir, pour it into the bowl and gently mix and fold it into the batter—at first the batter will seem thickish, and then it will be thinnish, which is just how it's meant to be. Pour the batter into the sheet pan and shimmy the pan around to get the batter into the corners.

Bake the cake for 19 to 21 minutes, or until it's evenly puffed and pulls away from the sides of the pan when gently tugged; a toothpick inserted into the center should come out clean. Transfer the pan to a rack.

Meanwhile, make the topping: About 5 minutes before the cake is due to come out of the oven, melt the butter in a medium saucepan over medium heat. Turn the heat to low, add the cocoa, grab a small whisk and stir until it's blended in. Add the cream and whisk until you've got a smooth, glossy mixture—it will look like a gorgeous ganache. Turn off the heat, leaving the pan on the warm burner, and whisk in the confectioners' sugar until the topping is smooth. Stir in the pecans.

As soon as the cake has come out of the oven, pour the hot topping over it and smooth it with an offset icing spatula or a table knife. Let the cake cool in the pan on the rack until it comes to room temperature—or until the look of the cake and the smell of the chocolate beats your patience and self-restraint. The cake is scrumptious warm.

Cut the cake into squares or rectangles large or small. Serve plain or on a plate with whipped cream or ice cream.

Playing Around

You can swap the buttermilk for sour cream or yogurt thinned with whole milk—add enough milk to ⅓ cup yogurt or sour cream to make ½ cup. You can omit the instant coffee and go for an even stronger coffee flavor by using 1 cup hot strong coffee instead of the hot water. And if you'd like to get a little more icing per slice, carefully cut the hot cake into portions—leave them in the pan—and then pour the hot topping over the top. The topping will meld with the cake, but a little will also seep into the cuts, giving you a bit more icing when you get to the "sides." Finally, if you'd like, instead of mixing the toasted pecans into the topping, spread the icing over the cake and then sprinkle the chopped nuts over the top. Or put nuts in *and* over the topping.

Storing: Left in the pan and covered, the cake will keep for 3 to 4 days at room temperature. You can store it in the fridge for a little longer, but my own druthers is to have it at room temperature or to freeze it. Well wrapped, it can be frozen for up to 1 month. Thaw overnight, in the wrapper, in the fridge (or for less time at room temperature) and serve at room temperature.

♥ A TREASURED FAVORITE

Bill's Carrot Cake, The Sheet Cake Edition

As much as I love to play around with recipes, that's how faithful I've been to the original Bill's Big Carrot Cake. Could my friend Bill Bartholomew really have given me the recipe four decades ago? It's possible, even if it seems inconceivable. Mostly it's exciting that a recipe can be so good for so long. The original cake (see Playing Around) was a triple-decker, strong on cinnamon and delightfully chockablock with nuts, raisins and coconut. Of course it had a cream cheese frosting. And, of course, it was perfect for parties—I've lost count of how many rounds of "Happy Birthday" were sung with this cake in the center of the table. I had no reason to tweak the recipe in any way, so I didn't until the question of pineapple began to pop up. Repeatedly. This cake never had pineapple in it, but so many carrot cakes that mean something to my friends did, and so, at last, I took the recipe back into the kitchen.

While I added pineapple—I used the canned pineapple rings that I loved as a child—I subtracted some sugar, and I omitted all of the nuts and raisins, and the cinnamon, too. I replaced the cinnamon with coriander and ginger, spices that seemed more suited to the tropical flavor of pineapple, and changed the shape of the cake: instead of three towering layers, I made a slab cake you can carry to a party or a picnic. You can also split it in half and stack it (see Playing Around)—two layers of cake and two layers of frosting, and still a lot of room for candles.

A word on the carrots: You need about 3 cups grated carrots, and it's best to have more carrots, by weight, on hand than you might need. Start with about 12 ounces of carrots—large carrots are easier to work with here. If what you have is 3 large carrots, you can coarsely grate them by hand on a box grater. If the carrots are small, though, you may prefer using a food processor. Or just make it really simple and buy shredded carrots.

A word on the pineapple: I used canned pineapple rings packed without added sugar. I drained them well, lightly patted them dry and chopped them into small pieces. The pieces should be discernible in the cake, but not chunky. If you'd like, you can use an equal amount of crushed pineapple. Again, drain the pineapple well.

Makes 12 to 16 servings

FOR THE CAKE

2 cups (272 grams) all-purpose flour

2 teaspoons baking powder

1½ teaspoons baking soda

1 teaspoon fine sea salt

1 teaspoon ground coriander

1 teaspoon ground ginger

1½ cups (300 grams) sugar

1 cup (240 ml) neutral oil

4 large eggs, at room temperature

About 3 cups (300 grams) lightly packed coarsely grated or shredded carrots (from about 3 peeled large carrots; see below left)

⅔ cup (80 grams) packed sweetened coconut, such as Angel Flake

4 canned pineapple rings, drained (about 5 ounces; 150 grams), patted dry and chopped, or ½ cup (about 5 ounces; 150 grams) crushed pineapple (see below center)

FOR THE FROSTING

6 ounces (170 grams) full-fat cream cheese, at room temperature

6 tablespoons (3 ounces; 85 grams) unsalted butter, at room temperature

¼ teaspoon fine sea salt

1½ teaspoons pure vanilla extract

2¾ cups (330 grams) confectioners' sugar, sifted if lumpy

Large coconut flakes or sweetened coconut, such as Angel Flake, toasted or not, for finishing (optional)

To make the cake: Center a rack in the oven and preheat it to 350 degrees F. Coat a 9-x-13-inch baking pan with baker's spray, or butter the interior, dust with flour and tap out the excess, and line the bottom with parchment paper.

Whisk together the flour, baking powder, baking soda, salt, coriander and ginger.

You can use a stand mixer fitted with the paddle attachment or a hand mixer, if you like, but you can easily make the batter by hand. Working in a large bowl with a whisk, beat the sugar and oil together until thoroughly blended (beat on medium speed if you're using a mixer). One by one, add the eggs, whisking (or beating) well after each goes in—you want a very smooth mixture. Switch to a flexible spatula if you're working by hand (or turn the mixer to low) and gradually incorporate the dry ingredients in four or five additions. You're always aiming for smooth. When the batter is homogeneous, add the carrots, coconut and pineapple and stir to evenly distribute these add-ins. Scrape the batter into the pan and gently swivel the pan to even it.

Bake for 35 to 39 minutes, or until the cake (it will be soft) is golden and pulls away from the sides of the pan when gently tugged; a tester inserted into the center of the cake will come out clean. Transfer the pan to a rack and let sit for 10 minutes, then run a knife around the edges of the pan and unmold the cake onto the rack; peel away the paper. Leave the cake upside down to cool to room temperature. Alternatively, you can leave the cake in the pan to cool—a good idea if you plan to take it somewhere.

To make the frosting: Working in the bowl of a stand mixer fitted with the paddle attachment, or in a large bowl with a hand mixer, beat the cream cheese, butter and salt on medium speed until smooth and satiny. Reduce the mixer speed to low and beat in the vanilla, then gradually add the sugar, beating well after each addition. You want a voluptuous frosting, so beat away.

To finish the cake: Swirl the frosting over the cake and, if you'd like, sprinkle over a little coconut.

You can serve the cake immediately, but I think it's better if you pop it into the refrigerator for about an hour. And, contrary to what's true for most cakes, this one is really good cold. Some would say better—decide for yourself.

Storing: The unfrosted cake can be covered and kept at room temperature for up to 2 days or frozen for up to 1 month; thaw in the wrapper. Once the cake is frosted, it's best stored in the fridge, where it will keep for at least 3 days. The frosting can be made up to 3 days ahead and refrigerated—beat it well before using.

Playing Around

Bill's Big Carrot Cake, The Classic Three-Layer Extravaganza

Replace the coriander and ginger with 2 teaspoons cinnamon. Omit the pineapple. When you stir in the carrots and coconut, add 1 cup coarsely chopped walnuts or pecans (toasted or not) and ½ cup moist, plump raisins or dried cranberries. Divide the batter among three 9-inch round cake pans (coated with baker's spray or buttered and floured and lined with parchment paper). Bake in a 325-degree-F oven for 40 to 50 minutes. For the frosting, use 8 ounces (226 grams) cream cheese, 4 ounces (113 grams) butter, 3¾ cups (454 grams) confectioners' sugar and 1½ teaspoons vanilla or ½ teaspoon lemon extract. Fill the layers with frosting, frost the top and frost the sides as well or leave them bare. Chill to set.

Playing Around

Bill's Double-Up Carrot Cake

For the most dramatic reading of this slab cake, cut it in half to make 2 layers. Cutting it horizontally would be the most logical thing to do, but you could cut it the long way for a very different look. Fill the layers and top with frosting (use the large batch from The Classic Three-Layer Extravaganza, opposite), then leave the sides bare or cover them with frosting, too. This cake is particularly attractive if, instead of smoothing the frosting over the cake layers, you pipe puffs of frosting. Leave the sides bare to show off the puffs. Sprinkle coconut on top—or don't. Chill before serving.

baby
CAKES

Makes 12 cupcakes

- 1 cup (136 grams) all-purpose flour
- ½ cup (42 grams) unsweetened cocoa powder (see headnote)
- 1 teaspoon baking powder
- ½ teaspoon fine sea salt
- ¼ teaspoon baking soda
- 8 tablespoons (4 ounces; 113 grams) unsalted butter, at room temperature
- 1 cup (200 grams) sugar
- 2 large eggs, at room temperature
- 2 tablespoons neutral oil
- 1 teaspoon pure vanilla extract
- ½ cup (120 ml) whole milk, at room temperature

FOR FINISHING

- Cream Cheese Frosting (page 264), Everyday Buttercream Frosting (page 262) or Glossy Chocolate Glaze (page 265)
- Sprinkles, chocolate shavings or chocolate pearls for decoration (optional)

Devil Dark/Angel Light Cupcakes

These cupcakes raise two existential questions: Must a cake with deep chocolate flavor be dense? Can there be a devilishly chocolaty cake that is angel light? The answers are "No" and "Yes," and the proof is in the cupcakes. What I love about them is that they're cake at its best. They do all the things that any cupcake does—look cute; hold up frosting, and birthday candles, too; and travel easily to your kid's school or your neighbor's potluck. The extra is that the cake is so good that it plays high as well as it does everyday.

Although this is my own recipe, I'm truly not sure what makes it so good. It might be the mix of butter and oil. For sure, the balance between flour and cocoa powder makes a difference. (I like Dutch-processed cocoa here, but natural will work as well.) And waiting a little bit longer than usual to turn the cupcakes out of the pan helps to lock in the texture. Even if I could lay out all the elements of success, I'd still want to believe that a little of it is magic.

Center a rack in the oven and preheat it to 350 degrees F. Line the 12 molds of a regular muffin tin with cupcake papers. Alternatively, you can butter and flour them (tap out the excess flour) or use baker's spray, but the paper liners are nice here—more partyish, too.

Put the flour in a bowl and sift or strain the cocoa powder over it. Add the baking powder, salt and baking soda and whisk to blend.

Working in the bowl of a stand mixer fitted with the paddle attachment, or in a large bowl with a hand mixer, beat the butter on medium speed until smooth and light, about 2 minutes. Add the sugar and beat for another 2 to 3 minutes, scraping the bowl and beater(s) as needed. One by one, add the eggs, beating for a minute after each one goes in. The batter might look a little curdly—keep mixing and scraping until it's fluffy and reminds you of frosting. Lower the speed and beat in the oil, followed by the vanilla. Whirl it around for a couple of seconds on medium speed, then scrape and admire your smooth, shiny batter. Working on low speed, add one-third of the dry ingredients and mix until they almost disappear, then add →

half of the milk; scrape as you go. Once the milk has been added (it may curdle the batter or make it look a bit grainy, but it'll be fine in the end), mix in half of the remaining flour until it's almost incorporated, then blend in the rest of the milk, followed by the last of the dry ingredients. Give everything a final stir with a flexible spatula, making sure to catch whatever might be at the bottom of the bowl.

Divide the batter evenly among the muffin molds. I like to use a scoop for this job, but a spoon is just as easy.

Slide the muffin tin into the oven and bake for about 20 minutes, or until the tops of the cupcakes are dry and feel springy when you prod them gently and, most important, a tester inserted into the center of a couple of cupcakes comes out clean. Transfer the tin to a cooling rack and let stand for 20 minutes (longer if it's more convenient), then remove the cakes from the molds and let cool to room temperature on the rack.

For finishing: Pipe or spread the tops of the cupcakes with frosting or dip them into glaze. Top with decorations, if you'd like.

Storing: Wrapped well, the bare cupcakes will keep for about 4 days at room temperature; wrapped airtight, you can freeze them for up to 1 month—thaw in the wrappers. If you've topped the cupcakes with a freezeable frosting—most buttercreams and ganache are in that category—then you can freeze them topping and all. The topping might look a little dull when thawed, but a few puffs of heat from a hair dryer will restore its shine.

Buttermilk Cupcakes for Everything

I love this recipe because it takes the cake part of cupcakes seriously—at heart it's a light, lovely and inherently elegant buttermilk cake. It's soft and tender and perfect in its simplicity. Like their chocolate sister, Devil Dark/ Angel Light Cupcakes (page 190), these little cakes can be eaten straight up, but that goes against their raison d'être. They're made to be topped. Dip them in Glossy Chocolate Glaze (page 265); pipe on a crown of Cream Cheese Frosting (page 264); swoosh them with buttercream (page 262) or Whipped Cream (page 284); or swipe them with Mixed Citrus Curd (page 275).

Makes about 18 cupcakes

1¾ cups (238 grams) all-purpose flour

2 teaspoons baking powder

¼ teaspoon baking soda

¼ teaspoon fine sea salt

10 tablespoons (5 ounces; 140 grams) unsalted butter, at room temperature

1 cup (200 grams) sugar

3 large eggs, at room temperature

1 large egg yolk, at room temperature

2 teaspoons pure vanilla extract

¾ cup (180 ml) buttermilk (well shaken before measuring), at room temperature

FOR FINISHING

Cream Cheese Frosting (page 264) or any other frosting or glaze you like (see headnote)

Sprinkles, candied peel and/ or chocolate shavings—all optional, all fun

If your oven's center rack isn't large enough to hold two muffin tins, position the racks to divide the oven into thirds. Preheat the oven to 350 degrees F. Line 18 muffin cups with cupcake papers (don't worry about the empties). Alternatively, butter and flour the cups (tap out the excess flour) or use baker's spray.

Whisk the flour, baking powder, baking soda and salt together.

Working in the bowl of a stand mixer fitted with the paddle attachment, or in a large bowl with a hand mixer, beat the butter and sugar together on medium speed for 3 to 4 minutes, until light; give the bowl and beater(s) a good scraping now and then. One by one, add the eggs and yolk, beating well after each one goes in, then beat in the vanilla—the batter may be on the verge of curdling or may even curdle; just carry on. Turn the mixer off, add one-third of the flour mixture and, beating on low speed, mix until it almost disappears into the batter. With the mixer still on low, beat in half of the buttermilk. Turn the mixer off, scrape, add half of the remaining dry ingredients and, again, mix until just about incorporated. Repeat the process with the remaining buttermilk and flour mixture.

Using a spoon or scoop, divide the batter evenly among the muffin cups—each one should be about three-quarters full.

Bake the cupcakes for 19 to 21 minutes (if the pans are on two separate racks and you think they need it, rotate the pans top to bottom and front to back at the 10-minute mark), or until the tops feel springy when poked and a tester inserted into the center of a few cakes comes out clean. These bake up pale—it's fine.

Transfer the pans to racks and let the cakes rest for 10 minutes, then unmold them and let cool to room temperature on the racks.

To finish the cakes: Pipe or spread the tops of the cupcakes with frosting or dip them into glaze. Top with decorations, if you'd like.

Storing: Bare cupcakes can be kept covered at room temperature for about 2 days. Or, depending on what you use to frost or glaze the cupcakes, they might be better kept covered in the fridge. If you've chilled them, pull them out of the refrigerator about 30 minutes before serving. Plain cupcakes can be wrapped and frozen for up to 1 month; thaw in the wrapper. If you've topped the cupcakes with a freezeable frosting—most buttercreams and ganache are in that category—then you can freeze them topping and all. The topping might look a little dull when thawed, but a few puffs of heat from a hairdryer will restore its shine.

Makes 30 little cakes

FOR THE SYRUP

¾ cup (180 ml) water

⅔ cup (160 ml) honey

½ cup (100 grams) sugar

6 tablespoons (3 ounces; 85 grams) unsalted butter, cut into 6 pieces

Peel (white cottony pith removed) from 1 clementine or 1 small orange

3 whole star anise

FOR THE DRY INGREDIENTS

2 cups (278 grams) all-purpose flour

1½ teaspoons baking powder

1½ teaspoons ground cinnamon

½ teaspoon ground ginger

¼ teaspoon ground cardamom

¼ teaspoon freshly ground black pepper

¼ teaspoon baking soda

¼ teaspoon fine sea salt

About ¼ cup (80 grams) apricot jam or orange marmalade

FOR THE ICING

½ cup (60 grams) confectioners' sugar

3 to 4 teaspoons water

Nonnettes

Nonnettes are small cakes that turn up in French pastry shops at about the same time as bûches de Noël, Christmas trees, wreaths and Advent calendars filled with chocolates. They're a beloved classic, as plain and sturdy as the Yule log cakes are fancy and frilly. The smallest member of the pain d'épices family, a branch of the gingerbread clan, nonnettes are a surprise as much for what they aren't as for what they are. They are neither soft nor cakey. They are not delicate. And they're not shy. What they are is boldly spiced, more honey-flavored than sweet and more adorable than their cousins, pain d'épices loaves and slabs, because they're mini muffin sized. Also because they can be—as in this recipe—topped with jam before they're slid into the oven.

The cakes are made like quickbreads—the wet ingredients are mixed into the dry with a few strokes—but here the wet ingredients are a honey-and-butter syrup flavored with orange peel and star anise. No eggs, no oil, no milk or cream and really not much butter. The dry ingredients, basically flour and leavening, have the spices—cinnamon, ginger, cardamom and freshly ground black pepper. It's a heady mix that makes a surprising cake.

As easy as these cakes are to make, they require one often problematic element: patience! The syrup has to steep for 1 hour; the batter has to chill for 1 hour (it can go longer); and the cakes should sit for 1 day. Of course you can eat the cakes as soon as they're cool enough to handle—and maybe you should taste one then, just for contrast—but they don't really become what they're meant to be until they've had a good rest. After a day, the spice is more prominent and the texture sidles closer to the original cakes—it becomes a little bready, a little gingerbready and a lot like the Grandmothers' Honey Cake (page 95).

To make the syrup: Stir the water, honey, sugar, butter, citrus peel and star anise together in a small saucepan and set over medium-low heat. Once the sugar dissolves and the butter melts, turn up the heat and bring the mixture to a boil. Turn off the heat, cover and allow the syrup to infuse for 1 hour. →

To make the cakes: Whisk together the flour, baking powder, cinnamon, ginger, cardamom, pepper, baking soda and salt in a large bowl, then make a well in the center. Hold a strainer over the bowl and pour in the syrup; discard the zest and spices. Gently mix the wet and dry ingredients—think muffins, meaning you want to get everything blended but you don't want to be overly diligent: a few dry spots are better than a beaten batter. Press a piece of plastic wrap against the surface of the batter and refrigerate it for at least 1 hour (or for up to 8 hours).

When you're ready to bake: Preheat the oven to 400 degrees F. These are baked in mini muffin tins. Since the recipe yields 30 nonnettes and most mini tins make either 12 or 24 little cakes, you'll probably have to bake these in batches—not a problem, because the batter can sit in the refrigerator while you're baking the first batch and the bake time for each batch is short. If you're baking one tin at a time, center a rack in the oven; if you're baking more than one tin and they won't fit on one rack, position the racks to divide the oven into thirds. Coat the insides of the molds with baker's spray and then give the tops of the pans a light spray, too. The dollops of jam tend to bubble up and out of the cakes, so if you spray the surface of the pans, you'll have an easier cleanup.

Divide the batter evenly among the molds; each mold should be about two-thirds full. Then each cake needs some jam. Working with a small spoon—if you've got a demitasse spoon, it'll be just right for this job—put a tiny bit of jam in the center of each mound of batter, pressing the tip and the back of the spoon into the batter to make a little nest for the jam. (If you'll be baking another batch after this one, you can get it ready while the first batch is baking.)

Bake for 14 to 16 minutes, or until the nonnettes are golden and puffed, the jam is bubbly and a tester inserted close to the center of a couple of cakes comes out clean. Transfer the muffin tin(s) to a rack and immediately make the icing.

To finish the cakes: Put the confectioners' sugar in a small bowl and stir in the water a little at a time, using as much as you need to get a thin glaze. Brush the glaze over the hot nonnettes and allow the cakes to cool in the tins before unmolding. If the jam has bubbled over and burned and stuck to the pan, or if some of the jam has hardened around the edges of the cakes, use scissors to snip it away.

It's impossible to resist eating at least one cake as soon as it's cool enough, but a freshly baked nonnette is not a peak nonnette—to get the full flavor, you should wait at least 1 day. Wait, and you'll really taste the spices; the texture will also change—the cakes will become a little drier, almost bready, and that's the way they're supposed to be.

Storing: Packed in a closed container, the nonnettes will keep for up to 10 days. They'll get drier—and deliciously dunkable—and more like the cakes that are sold throughout France for Christmas.

Walnut Mini Loaves

These little cakes, slender and low, pull off the trick of being comforting and munchable but still grown-up. It's the combination of pleasantly bitter walnuts and (instant) espresso that earns them their adult rating. Their insides are tender; their thin crust is light; and their flavor is layered and a touch mysterious—the spice blends in so nicely that while you know there's something there, you might have a hard time pinning it down: a good excuse to have another bite. The cakes are easy to love in their plainness and difficult to resist when topped with streusel.

For extra crunch and the best countertexture to the soft crumb, I like to bake the streusel before scattering it over the cakes. That you can make and bake the streusel ahead puts these squarely in the realm of doable-in-the-morning. (See Playing Around for the streusel version.)

Makes 8 little cakes

- ⅓ cup (30 grams) walnuts
- ½ cup (100 grams) plus 1 tablespoon sugar
- ¾ cup (102 grams) all-purpose flour
- 1½ teaspoons instant espresso powder
- ¾ teaspoon baking powder
- ¼ teaspoon baking soda
- ¼ teaspoon fine sea salt
- ¼ teaspoon ground cardamom or freshly grated nutmeg (both so nice with walnuts)
- ½ cup (120 grams) full-fat sour cream, at room temperature
- 2 large eggs, at room temperature
- ½ teaspoon pure vanilla extract
- 6 tablespoons (3 ounces; 85 grams) unsalted butter, melted

Center a rack in the oven and preheat it to 350 degrees F. This recipe makes enough batter to fill eight 2¼-x-4-inch mini loaf pans (or molds) or 8 regular-size muffin molds (see Walnut Mini Cakes, page 201). For these, I use a large pan that contains 8 mini loaf molds, like a muffin tin; if you have individual pans, place them on a baking sheet. Coat the pans (or molds) with baker's spray or butter the interiors, dust with flour and tap out the excess.

Put the walnuts and 1 tablespoon of the sugar in a mini food processor (or a full-size processor, if that's what you've got) and pulse until the nuts are finely ground but not pasty—think fluffy walnut flour; set aside.

Whisk together the all-purpose flour, espresso powder, baking powder, baking soda, salt and cardamom or nutmeg.

Working in a large bowl, whisk the remaining ½ cup sugar and the sour cream together until smooth. Add the eggs one by one, whisking after each one goes in, until smoothly incorporated. Beat in the vanilla. Whisk in the melted butter, working with a little energy to be certain to blend it in thoroughly. Switch to a flexible spatula and stir in the flour mixture. When the flour has almost disappeared, add the ground walnuts and stir until the batter is creamy and homogeneous. Divide it among the eight pans (or molds). →

Bake for 18 to 21 minutes, or until the cakes (they'll only be a scant 1 inch high) are golden and pull away from the sides of the pan when gently tugged and are puffed; a tester inserted into the centers of one or two cakes should come out clean. Transfer the pan(s) to a rack and let the cakes rest for 5 minutes, and then, if necessary, loosen them by running a table knife around the edges of the loaves. Turn the cakes out, flip them right side up onto the rack and let them cool to just-warm or room temperature.

Storing: Wrapped, the cakes will keep for about 4 days at room temperature or for up to 1 month in the freezer; thaw in the wrappers.

Playing Around

Crumb-Topped Walnut Mini Loaves

Just before sliding the pan(s) into the oven, top each loaf with a scattering of either Quick Brown Sugar Streusel (page 277) or All-Purpose Streusel (page 278). If you use All-Purpose Streusel, think about baking it before topping the cakes with it—the crumbs will be extra crunchy, and that's nice here.

Walnut Mini Cakes

Bake the cakes in 8 regular-size muffin tins for 20 to 22 minutes. Because of the molds, these little cakes will bake higher, and you'll get more cake per bite. Given the moreness, I think these are particularly nice topped with crumbs for a little textural back-and-forth.

Makes 14 or 15 madeleines

10 tablespoons (5 ounces; 140 grams) unsalted butter

¾ cup (102 grams) all-purpose flour

1¼ teaspoons baking powder

¼ teaspoon fine sea salt

½ cup (100 grams) sugar

2 large eggs, at room temperature

2½ tablespoons whole milk, at room temperature

2 teaspoons pure vanilla extract

A word on pans: While the shell shape is traditional, you can easily bake the cakes in a mini muffin tin. You can also use the batter to make baby mads in a mini madeleine pan. No matter what shape pans you use, and even if they're nonstick, they need to be buttered and floured or coated with baker's spray; see Playing Around.

A word on quantity: Because the batter, which has to be chilled, can stay in the refrigerator for a couple of days, you can bake as many madeleines as you want whenever you want.

Extra-Buttery Vanilla Madeleines

It's odd for me to think that I got my first madeleine pan fifty years ago. I bought it at Bridge Kitchenware in New York City, which was an adventure, since Fred Bridge, the proprietor, frightened me—he was as famous for his imperiousness as he was for his inventory, and he had a way of making you feel that you had to prove you were worthy of purchasing anything in his store of wonders. Plus, the pan was a splurge, since we were living on a tight budget. And it was a folly: I was not much of a baker, I'd never made madeleines and I'd only tasted one in my life. But many years later, I still have that pan and I've accumulated a stack of others. I've eaten madeleines in villages and big cities around the world, made them hundreds of times and never stopped tinkering with the recipe, not because any one recipe wasn't good, but because the very simple cakes invite variation.

By tradition, madeleines are baked in special pans so that they emerge with ridged and rippled undersides, recalling scallop shells (the centuries-old emblem worn by pilgrims making their way to holy shrines). And also by tradition, the top side of the cakes shows off a majestic bump. The bump is a baker's pride—that it's easily achieved doesn't diminish its beauty or its covetedness. The cakes are honey-brown on the bottom, darker and a bit firmer around the edges and paler on top. Inside, the crumb is light and tender, like a rich, buttery sponge cake, simple but memorable. In this, my newest riff on the recipe, there's an abundance of butter that's hot when it goes into the batter. I've also given the cakes a decidedly vanilla flavor.

The cakes are good served almost hot or warm, and even though received wisdom suggests that they be eaten on the day that they're baked, I find them a pleasure the next day and the day after that. Yes, you can follow the author Proust's now-legendary example and dip your slightly less-than-fresh madeleine into a cup of tea, but you might also follow my husband's example and split and toast the cakes, then butter them while they're hot. Don't underestimate the delights of butter on butter. →

Put the butter in a small saucepan and melt over low heat; remove from the heat. Because the butter should be hot when it goes into the batter, you'll need to keep it warm or quickly reheat it when it's time for it. If you want to use a microwave for this, melt the butter just before you need it.

Whisk the flour, baking powder and salt together.

Put the sugar in a medium bowl, drop in the eggs and whisk vigorously for a minute or two, until blended and slightly paler. Whisk in the milk, followed by the vanilla. For the rest of the mixing, you can stay with the whisk or switch to a flexible spatula. Add half of the flour mixture and stir it in, mixing until smooth. Mix in the remainder of the dry ingredients, and when they're all in, give the batter a couple of brisk strokes to complete the blending. You'll have a thick, smooth, velvety batter—lift the whisk or spatula, and the batter will fall back into the bowl in a quickly dissolving ribbon.

If necessary, reheat the butter now. Blend in the hot butter a little at a time—I usually incorporate it in four or five additions. Toward the end, you might have to whisk or stir energetically for just a beat or two to get all of the butter in—you'll be rewarded with a lustrous batter.

Press a piece of plastic wrap against the surface of the batter and chill for at least 2 hours, preferably at least 5 hours, or for up to 2 days. Alternatively, you can spoon the batter into the prepared madeleine molds, cover and keep chilled for up to 6 hours. You want the pans and batter to be cold when they go into the hot oven.

When you're ready to bake: Center a rack in the oven and preheat it to 425 degrees F. My preference is to bake one pan at a time, but if you want to bake two, you should position the racks to divide the oven into thirds.

If you haven't already portioned the batter into pans and tucked them into the refrigerator, generously butter one or two madeleine pans, dust with flour and tap out the excess. (If you've got just one pan, bake in batches; keep the remaining batter refrigerated until ready to use and prep the cooled pan before baking.) Alternatively, you can coat the pan with baker's spray. For mads, my preference is a nonstick metal pan and butter and flour rather than spray. And yes, I'm kind of overly cautious with madeleines: I butter and flour even nonstick pans. If you're using a silicone pan, prep it and, if necessary, put it on a baking sheet to steady it.

Divide the batter evenly among the molds. The batter won't fill the molds completely and it may not look level, but it will quickly even out in the oven.

Bake for 10 to 12 minutes, or until the cakes have dramatic bumps on top—poke a couple gently, and they'll spring back—and are deeply golden around the edges. Remove the pan from the oven, turn it over and rap it against the counter to set the cakes free. If any are reluctant to pop out, help them along with the tip of a table knife. Serve the madeleines hot or warm, or allow them to cool to room temperature on a rack.

Storing: There's no question that mads are at their peakiest peak shortly after they're baked, but they're still very good—if different—a day later (even two). Fresh madeleines can be wrapped airtight once cooled to room temperature and frozen for up to 1 month. Thaw the cakes in their wrapper and then, if you'd like, give them a quick warm-up in a hot oven.

Playing Around

Mini Muffin-Tin Mads

Oddly, whereas I think prepping madeleine pans with butter and flour is better than spray, I'm fine with baker's spray for mini muffin tins—you'll get about 24 little cakes. Portion the batter out evenly and bake at 400 degrees F for about 14 minutes—in addition to checking the color and poking the tops, you can test for doneness with a toothpick—it should come out clean.

Baby Mads

Use a mini madeleine pan, and you'll get 28 to 30 little cakes from this batter. Start checking them for doneness after they've been in the oven for 8 minutes.

Brown-Butter Madeleines

Use an additional 1 to 1½ teaspoons butter and cook the butter until it's a deep golden brown. When I pour the butter into the batter, I usually include whatever dark bits have fallen to the bottom of the pan, but personal preference rules here.

Citrus Madeleines

Adding freshly grated lemon zest to madeleine batter is almost traditional. Grate the zest over the sugar and use your fingers to rub everything together. Orange zest is nice, too, as is adding a bit of orange-blossom water or the teensiest drop of lemon or orange oil.

Tea-and-Honey Madeleines

Rub a tablespoon of loose tea (an aromatic tea is a good choice) into the sugar, add 1 tablespoon honey to the batter and reduce the milk to 1½ tablespoons. The madeleines will be a tad less light, but still lovely.

Jam-Glazed Madeleines

If you'd like to glaze the mads, bring some jam or marmalade to a boil in a saucepan with a splash of water, stirring to melt the jam, and have it ready to go when they come out of the oven. Delicately brush a coat of glaze over the shell sides of the cakes. Glazed madeleines aren't great for dipping, but they make good treats.

Chocolate-Glazed Madeleines

The easiest way to glaze the mads is to melt chocolate chips, because they set the best. (Alternatively, and more professionally, you can use tempered chocolate.) Let the cakes cool a bit, then dip each one shell side down into the chocolate; set on a rack to dry. You can speed up the drying process by putting the glazed mads in the refrigerator for a few minutes, but don't keep them in for too long or you'll spoil their texture.

Ginger Zucchini Cakes

Don't let the fact that these look like giant dome-topped muffins—or the fact that they're made in a giant muffin tin—push you into a muffin mindset. These are cakes! Big-enough-to-share cakes. Good-enough-to-hoard cakes. Light-and-bright-and-liltingly-gingered cakes. Cakes that will keep you nibbling. I was delighted when the first batch came out of the oven: they were better-than-I-had-dreamed-they-would-be cakes. In fact, for me, the cakes were ground-shifting—they weren't at all like the heavy zucchini loaves of my childhood, the kind that were supposed to be good for you. I love that their flavor is spunky, that their crumb is soft and that they have a pucker because they've got yogurt, tart dried cranberries and that ginger. I love that they're adorable—pudgy and round and grabbable. And I especially love that they take to a drizzle of icing or a brush-over of melted jam. So many batches later, these little cakes haven't lost a whit of their power to delight.

A word on the zucchini: Because you don't need all that much and because I think that grating zucchini is annoying no matter how little you need, I try to make quick work of it. I find that the easiest and neatest way to get the job done is to use a Microplane-type grater. My favorite for this job is an extra-coarse grater meant for soft cheese, carrots and, yes, zucchini, but graters with small holes work well, too. I grate the zucchini onto a plate or a piece of parchment and then have very little to clean up. That said, it's best to grate the zucchini just before you start to mix the batter—freshly grated zucchini keeps its color and doesn't ooze liquid. If you do end up with a little zuke juice, drain it off and pat the zucchini dry.

A word on the cranberries: Dried cranberries are nice in these cakes because of their color and chew, but you've got other choices. They can be replaced by raisins, dark or golden; dried currants; tiny snippets of dried apricot; or even chopped nuts—toast them first to bring out their flavor. But if you're not a fan of any of these add-ins, just leave them out.

A word on finishing: Of course these are delicious plain, but I really like them with a simple topping, either a sugar icing or a gloss of melted marmalade—take your pick.

Makes 6 cakes

2 cups (272 grams) all-purpose flour

1¼ teaspoons ground ginger

1 teaspoon baking powder

¾ teaspoon fine sea salt

½ teaspoon baking soda

2 large eggs, at room temperature

½ cup (100 grams) sugar

½ cup (100 grams) brown sugar

½ cup (120 ml) neutral oil

⅓ cup (about 75 grams) plain whole-milk Greek yogurt, at room temperature

1½ teaspoons pure vanilla extract

1 cup (not packed; about 130 grams) freshly grated zucchini (see below left)

⅔ cup (80 grams) moist, plump dried cranberries (see below center)

FOR THE ICING (optional)

1 cup (120 grams) confectioners' sugar

About 2 tablespoons milk or water

OR

FOR THE GLAZE (optional)

About ⅓ cup (about 100 grams) lemon or ginger marmalade

Center a rack in the oven and preheat it to 350 degrees F. Butter six molds of a jumbo muffin tin, coat them with baker's spray or line them with extra-large cupcake papers (which you can make yourself; see page xx).

Whisk the flour, ginger, baking powder, salt and baking soda together.

Working in a large bowl, whisk the eggs and two sugars together until well blended. Whisk in the oil, making sure it's incorporated, and then whisk in the yogurt and vanilla. When you've got a lovely thick batter with a pretty sheen, switch to a flexible spatula and mix in the flour in two additions, gently stirring and folding it in. Just before the last of the flour has disappeared, add the zucchini and cranberries and stir to get them thoroughly mixed in.

Divide the batter evenly among the molds. I find a 4-ounce scoop is a handy tool for this.

Bake the cakes for 32 to 35 minutes, or until they're golden and domed and easily pull away from the sides of the molds with a gentle tug; a tester inserted into the centers of a few of the cakes will come out clean. Transfer the tin to a rack and let the cakes rest for 5 minutes, then unmold them, turn the cakes right side up and let them cool to room temperature on the rack. While the ginger flavor will be more present if you wait for them to cool, the draw of warm cake might be overwhelming—go ahead and succumb.

To ice the cakes (optional): If you're making the icing, put the confectioners' sugar in a medium bowl, sprinkle over most of the milk or water and stir until smooth. Gradually stir in more liquid, as needed, until you have an icing that falls thickly off the tip of a spoon. Spread the icing over the cakes' domes, drizzle it in squiggles or go rogue (it's what I do) and essentially spatter-paint the tops with icing.

To glaze the cakes (optional): If you haven't iced the cakes and would like to glaze them, put the marmalade in a small saucepan, add a splash of water, stir and bring to a boil. Let the marmalade bubble for a minute or so, until it looks slightly thickened and easily spreadable, then pull the pan from the heat and use a silicone brush or regular pastry brush to glaze the tops of the cakes. Or, if you prefer, heat the marmalade in a microwave—put it and a splash of water in a microwave-safe bowl, cover and cook in short spurts, stirring between spurts. Be careful: Sputtering hot jam is a hazard.

Storing: The cakes will keep covered at room temperature for about 2 days. If you haven't iced or glazed them, you can wrap them airtight and freeze them for up to 1 month; thaw in the wrapper.

Pancakelettes

Makes 12 muffins

1½ cups (204 grams) all-purpose flour

¼ cup (50 grams) sugar

1½ teaspoons baking powder

½ teaspoon fine sea salt

¼ teaspoon baking soda

1 cup (240 ml) buttermilk (well shaken before measuring), preferably at room temperature

3 tablespoons neutral oil

2 large eggs, at room temperature

⅔ cup (about 100 grams) blueberries (or other small or chopped fruit; see headnote)

FOR FINISHING (optional)

Demerara, raw or sanding sugar for sprinkling

Maple syrup for glazing

Confectioners' Sugar Icing (page 270) for glazing

The first time I used this recipe was to make pancakes with my then-two-year-old granddaughter Gemma, and they turned out wonky! She mixed and ladled out the batter and I griddled, and we ended up with mini pucks that were a bit too thick for pancakes, but it seemed like they'd be just right for muffins. And they were! Every time I make them, Gemma says, "This is my recipe!" and, really, it is.

The recipe makes muffins that are on the smallish side, just right for lunch boxes, snacks, and kid-size appetites and hands. They're also wholesomely plain—if you want to jazz them up a bit, I've got some suggestions; see Playing Around. For reasons of sentimentality and also in the service of deliciousness, I kept the blueberries that Gemma and I put into the pancakes, but you could certainly speckle the muffins with a different berry, small bits of plump dried fruits or even mini chocolate chips. The batter itself isn't sweet, so the add-ins and toppings can be. And while I swipe the tops with maple syrup—an homage to their having been pancakes—they could take a dusting of demerara or sanding sugar prebake or a drizzle of icing once they cool.

Center a rack in the oven and preheat it to 425 degrees F. Coat 12 standard muffin wells with baker's spray (first choice for easy release) or use paper liners.

Working in a large bowl, whisk the flour, sugar, baking powder, salt and baking soda together.

In another bowl, whisk together the buttermilk, oil and eggs.

Pour the wet ingredients over the dry and, using a flexible spatula, gently mix until the batter is blended—if there are a few dry spots here or there, leave them: muffin batters like a casual mix. Stir in the berries, mixing just enough to run them through the thick batter.

Divide the batter evenly among the muffin molds—I like a scoop for this job, but a spoon will do. If you want to sugar-coat the muffins, sprinkle the tops with demerara (or raw or sanding) sugar. →

Bake for 14 to 16 minutes, or until the muffins rise (they won't be very big, but they'll definitely puff), the tops spring back when poked and the sides pull away from the pan when gently prodded; a tester inserted into the center of a muffin or two will come out clean. Transfer the pan to a rack and leave the muffins in the tin for 5 minutes, then turn them out and set them right side up on the rack. If you're going to glaze them with a little maple syrup, do it now, while they're hot; if you're going to ice them, wait until they're cool. The muffins are good warm or at room temperature.

Storing: Kept in a covered container, the muffins will be good for about a day—they get heavier with time. If they're not peak when you want to serve them, slice them in half and toast or grill them, or give them a quick warm-up in an oven or microwave. If you haven't topped them, you can wrap them well and freeze them for up to 1 month; thaw in the wrapper.

Playing Around

Citrus-Scented Pancakelettes

Put the sugar in a large bowl and grate over the zest of a lemon or lime or a small orange (a tangerine or clementine would work). Use your fingers to smush the zest into the sugar until it's fragrant. Add the rest of the dry ingredients to the bowl and carry on with the recipe.

Spiced, Herbed or Drop-of-Extract Pancakelettes

A little bit of spice perks up the pancakelettes, and that would be good paired with citrus, too. Try ¼ teaspoon ground cinnamon, ginger or cardamom; ⅛ teaspoon freshly grated nutmeg; or even a pinch of ground star anise—whisk the spice into the flour mixture. You can also rub 1 teaspoon minced fresh thyme, rosemary or mint into the sugar, just as you would with the zest for the Citrus-Scented Pancakelettes above. Or, if you'd like, add ½ teaspoon pure vanilla extract, ¼ teaspoon pure almond extract or just a drop of pure lemon extract, which can be strong, with the liquid ingredients.

Bran-Berry Muffins

There's an old-timeyness to these muffins, a flavor of childhood, a look reminiscent of snacks for hikes and road trips. They're just sweet enough to seem like a treat and just hearty enough to tide you over from breakfast to a coffee break, when you might want another. The flavor of wheat is strong—it's the bran and the whole wheat flour (think Wheaties). The texture is satisfying, not dense or heavy (potential bran muffin hazards). And there's a touch of tang in the background—that's the bit of honey and the yogurt. I think these muffins are best with berries—blueberries or raspberries—but they're also excellent with their most classic companion, raisins. I even like them with astringent fresh cranberries. (See Playing Around for swaps.) Have them plain or with butter or jam or both. Have them with a thick slice of cheddar. And when they're just a little stale, have them toasted.

Makes 12 muffins

- 1¼ cups (170 grams) whole wheat flour
- ¾ cup (102 grams) all-purpose flour
- ½ cup (30 grams) wheat bran or wheat germ (see below)
- 2 teaspoons baking powder
- ¾ teaspoon fine sea salt
- ¼ teaspoon baking soda
- ⅔ cup (133 grams) sugar
- 2 large eggs, at room temperature
- 3 tablespoons honey
- ⅔ cup (160 ml) whole milk, at room temperature
- ½ cup (115 grams) plain yogurt, at room temperature
- ½ cup (120 ml) neutral oil
- 1½ cups (about 225 grams) blueberries or raspberries (chopped if giant size)
- Wheat bran or wheat germ for sprinkling (optional)
- Turbinado, raw or sanding sugar for sprinkling (optional)

Center a rack in the oven and preheat it to 400 degrees F. Drop a dozen cupcake liners into the wells of a regular muffin tin or coat them with baker's spray.

Put both flours, the wheat bran (or germ), baking powder, salt and baking soda in a medium bowl and whisk to blend—you want to make sure that the leavenings are evenly incorporated. Whisk in the sugar.

In another medium bowl, whisk the eggs, honey, milk and yogurt together. When they're fully combined, whisk in the oil. It may take a few determined strokes to blend in the oil—don't be timid.

Pour the wet ingredients over the dry, switch to a flexible spatula and stir everything together until mostly, but not completely, blended. Mix in the berries—again, no need to fret about being thorough. (With muffins, undermixing is better than overmixing.)

Divide the batter evenly among the muffin molds—the batter will fill them to the brim. If you'd like, sprinkle the tops with bran (or germ) and turbinado (or raw or sanding) sugar. →

A word on wheat bran and wheat germ: The bran is the outer part of the wheat kernel, the part that's mostly removed during milling. The germ is the innermost part. Both the bran and germ taste sweet and nutty. They're also both feathery light, highly nutritious and easily available. And, as I discovered when I reached for bran and grabbed germ, they're interchangeable in this recipe.

Bake for 20 to 22 minutes, or until the muffins have risen—they'll develop adorable little peaks—and are firm to the touch. A tester poked into the centers of a few muffins should come out clean. Transfer the tin to a rack and let the muffins rest for 5 to 10 minutes, then turn them out and let them cool on the rack until just warm or at room temperature.

Storing: When the muffins are cool, you can wrap them and keep them at room temperature for about 2 days or freeze them for up to 1 month. Thaw them in their wrappers and then, if you'd like, warm them in the oven or split and toast them.

Playing Around

Jumbo Bran-Berry Muffins

You can use this batter to make 6 jumbo muffins. Line the muffin wells with cupcake papers or make your own (see page xx). Bake these extra-large muffins at 400 degrees F and start checking them at 30 minutes—they'll probably need at least 5 minutes more, especially if they've got juicy fruit in them.

Raisin-Bran Muffins (and a few other ideas)

Raisins, the traditional add-in for bran muffins, are still a good one, as long as you start with moist, plump raisins: use about 1¼ cups (200 grams). If the raisins are a bit hard, dunk them in a bowl of hot water or, if you want to add a little extra flavor, hot tea. Soak for about a minute, drain and pat dry before stirring them into the batter. If you want to use (yes, moist, plump) dried cranberries, snipped dried apricots, prunes or cherries, do it.

Bran-Cran Muffins

These tip between warm and cozy and bright and tart. For the best results, start with 1½ cups (about 150 grams) cranberries. You can use them whole, or you can give them a quick coarse chop—it's easiest (and a little less messy) to chop cranberries when they're frozen. If you're using frozen berries, there's no need to defrost them.

Less-Wheaty Bran-Berry Muffins

For a muffin that's not quite as hearty, use 1 cup (136 grams) whole wheat flour and 1 cup (136 grams) all-purpose flour.

Gemma Cakes

When my first granddaughter's first birthday came around, I knew that whatever I baked for her had to have strawberries—they were Gemma's favorite, the treat she reached for every time. I considered a strawberry shortcake and even a strawberry cheesecake, but I wanted her to have a cake that would be hers alone. One the right size for her to hold in her little hands. And one the right size for a small candle. Cupcakes would have been right, but mini cupcakes were right-er. Perfect, in fact. Vanilla is the primary flavor—there's pure vanilla extract and white chocolate, which adds a different vanilla-like note—but you can tilt the recipe floral by adding a bit of berry to each cake (that was imperative for me, but it's optional for you) and a touch of rose water (also optional). I dipped the cakes in melted white chocolate and showered them with pastel sprinkles, but you needn't be so summery. The cakes, which are tasty on their own, will take to fluffy frosting and are very good with a milk-chocolate topping. They're also very good even when you're not celebrating a birthday. And even when you're not a baby.

Makes 24 baby cakes

FOR THE CAKES

- 3 to 6 strawberries, hulled, or other berries, depending on size (optional; see below)
- ⅓ cup (67 grams) sugar
- ¼ teaspoon fine sea salt
- 2 large eggs, at room temperature
- 1½ teaspoons pure vanilla extract
- ¼ teaspoon rose water (optional but highly recommended)
- 1 tablespoon light corn syrup
- ⅔ cup (90 grams) all-purpose flour
- 6 tablespoons (3 ounces; 85 grams) unsalted butter, melted
- 3 ounces (85 grams) white chocolate, melted and still fluid
- 1 tablespoon whole milk

FOR THE TOPPING

- 3 ounces (85 grams) white chocolate, finely chopped
- 1 teaspoon neutral oil
- Food coloring (optional)
- Sprinkles or decorative sugar (optional)

A word on the berries: I think it's delightful to have a snippet of fruit inside the cakes—a surprise and a nice way to change up the texture and flavor. I chose strawberries for the cake because they were Gemma's favorite fruit at the time, but any soft berry will work. However, unless you've got teensy blueberries, you'll have to cut the fruit down to Lilliputian size. Of course, the berries are not necessary—the cakes are lovely on their ownsome.

To make the cakes: Center a rack in the oven and preheat it to 400 degrees F. Line a mini muffin tin that has 24 molds—or two 12-mold tins—with cupcake papers (my choice here—so cute for a birthday) or use baker's spray to lightly coat the insides.

If you're using strawberries, you'll want a small chunk for each cake, so slice the berries into pieces that are about ¼ inch wide and short enough to be hidden by a little batter when dropped into the molds. Set aside.

Working in a large bowl, whisk the sugar and salt together, then drop in the eggs. You want to beat the mixture until it's foamy and slightly thickened—which will take about 2 minutes—so if you're not feeling energetic, pull out your hand mixer (or do this job in a stand mixer fitted with the paddle or whisk attachment). Stir in the vanilla, rose water (if using) and corn syrup.

Switch to a flexible spatula and gently blend in the flour in two or three additions; you'll have a thick batter. Pour in the melted butter—do this in three or four additions—and stir until it's blended in. The batter will be stretchy and a bit slippery—unusual, but fine. Gorgeous, too. Pour the melted chocolate over →

the batter, stir it in gently until fully incorporated and stir in the milk.

Spoon about 1 teaspoon of batter into each muffin cup and then drop in a berry, if you're including fruit. Divide the remaining batter evenly among the cups, covering the bits of berry. Some of the berries may pop up during baking and that'll be fine, but it's good to spend a second here to poke them down and cover them as best as you can.

Bake for 11 to 13 minutes, or until a tester inserted into the center of a few of the cakes comes out clean—try not to hit a berry. Transfer the pan to a rack and let rest for a minute or two, then gingerly remove the cakes and let them cool to room temperature on the rack.

To make the topping: This is a good job for a microwave, but you can certainly make the topping in a small saucepan set over the very lowest heat (or in a double boiler, if your heat source is exuberant). Melt the chocolate with the oil in a small microwave-safe bowl in a microwave set to half power. White chocolate is fragile—it burns quickly—so work in short spurts and stir often to make certain the topping is smooth. Or, if you do this in a saucepan, remove the pan from the heat as soon as the chocolate is melted (if the topping's in a double boiler, leave it over the hot water with the burner turned off). If you'd like to tint the glaze, stir in a bit of food coloring. Start with a mini drop and blend it in, then decide if and how much more you might want.

Dip the top of each cake into the chocolate, twirling the cake to even the topping and allowing the excess to drip back into the bowl or pan. If the chocolate thickens and won't coat the cakes evenly (it usually keeps its consistency, but if necessary), give it a touch of heat, stir and carry on. Return the cakes to the rack and, if you'd like, scatter over some sprinkles or decorative sugar—it's best to do this when the chocolate is wet.

You can refrigerate the cakes for about 10 minutes to set the chocolate, or leave them at room temperature. Chilled or not, the chocolate will never really set fully—I think that's nice.

Storing: Kept in a covered container at room temperature or in the fridge, the cakes will hold for about 2 days. They can be frozen—with or without the chocolate topping—for up to 1 month. Freeze them until solid and then wrap them well. If they're chocolate-coated, unwrap the frozen cakes, place them on a baking sheet and let thaw at room temperature. If they're not glazed, thaw them in their wrappers.

VV's First Birthday Cake

A Banana-and-Malt Baby Cake

Makes 4 grown-up servings or 8 baby servings

FOR THE CAKE

½ cup (68 grams) all-purpose flour
3 tablespoons malted milk powder
½ teaspoon baking powder
¼ teaspoon fine sea salt
¼ teaspoon ground cinnamon
⅓ cup (80 ml) whole milk
1 tablespoon unsalted butter
1 large egg, at room temperature
½ cup (100 grams) brown sugar
1 teaspoon pure vanilla extract

FOR THE FROSTING

4 ounces (113 grams) cream cheese, at room temperature
8 tablespoons (4 ounces; 113 grams) unsalted butter, at room temperature
1½ teaspoons pure vanilla extract
¼ teaspoon ground cinnamon
¼ teaspoon fine sea salt
2 cups (240 grams) confectioners' sugar, sifted if lumpy

1 medium banana for the filling
Half a lemon
Chocolate shavings or curls for the top (optional)

Although Gemma was just a little over two years old when her sister, VV, was about to celebrate her first birthday, she wanted to make her a cake—and I wanted to make it with her. I had no idea if VV would like cinnamon or brown sugar (like her sister, she hadn't had sugar until she had the first taste of her birthday cake) and certainly no idea if she'd like malted milk. But I knew that she loved bananas and so I built the warm, caramel, almost toasty flavors of the cake around the fruit. And I made the cake in the most adorable pan: a six-inch round. I love that size for small treats, and I love that with the right recipe, you can bake one layer, split it and create a cake that looks as celebratory as the occasion you're marking.

The cake itself is a hot-milk brown-sugar sponge, which means that you make a thick cake batter and then pour in a mixture of hot milk and butter, which thins the batter and guarantees a light, tender, springy crumb with a pleasantly surprising chew. If you've never made a cake this way, I think you'll be delighted. I also think you'll love the almost-grilled vanilla flavor that you get from malt powder—perfect with brown sugar and excellent with bananas. I like to swoop frosting across the middle and top of the cake and leave the sides bare—the better to see the scallops of fresh banana peeking out around the cake's belly. For even more banana flavor, cook up a quick banana jam (see Playing Around) and add it to the banana and frosting in the middle of the cake. The jam won't win any beauty contests, but it gets a blue ribbon for flavor.

To make the cake: Center a rack in the oven and preheat it to 325 degrees F. Butter and flour a 6-inch round cake pan with sides that are at least 2 inches high—this cake rises proudly—or coat it with baker's spray.

Whisk the flour, malt powder, baking powder, salt and cinnamon together.

Using a small saucepan or working in a microwave with a microwave-safe container, combine the milk and butter and heat until the milk just bubbles and the butter is melted. Turn off the heat but keep the pan on the burner or the bowl in the microwave—you want the mixture to stay hot.

Working in the bowl of a stand mixer fitted with the paddle attachment, or in a large bowl with a hand mixer, beat the egg and sugar together on medium speed until thoroughly blended, about 3 minutes. Blend in the vanilla. Spoon in the flour mixture—do this in two additions—and mix on low until it disappears into the thick batter. With the mixer running on low, pour in a little of the hot milk-butter mixture (you want to warm the batter slowly and gently), then steadily pour in the rest and blend until smooth—the batter will thin dramatically. Pour the batter into the pan and swivel the pan to level.

Bake for 23 to 26 minutes, or until the cake is beautifully brown, springs back when gently poked and pulls away from the sides of the pan with a light tug; a tester inserted into the center of the cake will come out clean. Transfer the pan to a rack and let the cake sit for 5 minutes, then run a table knife around the edges of the pan if necessary and unmold the cake onto the rack. Invert onto another rack (or don't—it can remain upside down) and let the cake cool to room temperature.

To make the frosting: Working in the bowl of a stand mixer fitted with the paddle attachment, or in a large bowl with a hand mixer, beat everything *except* the sugar together on medium speed. Add the sugar and pulse the mixer on and off to start blending it. (Consider covering the mixer with a kitchen towel before you do this to contain the inevitable sugar storm.) Then beat the frosting on medium speed until it's smooth and velvety.

To frost the cake: Cut the cake in half through its middle and swirl some frosting over the bottom layer. (If you're using the banana jam—see Playing Around—you might want to put some on top of this layer of frosting before you cover it with banana slices.) Cut the banana into thinnish slices and toss them with a little bit of lemon juice. Arrange the banana slices over the frosting (or the frosting and jam)—I think it's pretty if you let a bit of the slices peek out beyond the edges of the cake, like frilly scallops. (This only works if you won't be frosting the sides—if you're frosting the whole cake, keep the bananas within the bounds of the cake.) You can cover the banana slices with a little frosting, if you'd like. Pop on the top of the cake, settling it gently into the frosting. Swoop and swirl the top with frosting and cover the sides—or don't. Then, if the spirit moves you, scatter chocolate shavings or curls over the top.

When it's just assembled, the cake is very tender, and the frosting is soft. I think that's when it tastes best, but it's not when it's easiest to cut. If you'd like, put the cake in the fridge to firm slightly before slicing it.

Storing: The cake should be filled and frosted on serving day, but you can bake the cake ahead, wrap it and keep it at room temperature for up to a day or freeze it for up to 1 month; thaw in the wrapper. The frosting can be made up to 4 days ahead and kept refrigerated—give it a good beating before spreading it on the cake.

Playing Around

Banana Jam

Slice a medium banana into a small saucepan and add 2 tablespoons brown sugar, a squirt of lemon or lime juice and 1 tablespoon water. Set over medium heat and bring just to a bubble, stirring and mashing the fruit. Lower the heat and simmer the mixture, still stirring, until you have a thick jam (it won't be smooth). Scrape the jam into a bowl, stir in ¼ teaspoon pure vanilla extract and taste—add more lemon or lime juice if you think it needs it. Press a piece of plastic against the surface of the jam and refrigerate until cold. This makes about ⅓ cup—perfect for a baby-size cake.

Making a birthday cake for someone you love is a joy. Making a first birthday cake is also an honor. Sadly, I didn't realize that when I was planning our son's cake years ago. When his first birthday came around, I was too young, too busy, too tired, too worried about all the wrong things to think of anything but the details of the party. I was anxious about chairs and tables, about the guest list and party favors. I didn't breathe deeply until I started baking the cake—it's the effect that baking still has on me. And I didn't really think about the son I was baking for until I was deep into mixing and folding, whipping and smoothing. Then the work became a mediation on the year we'd been through—the journal I'd meant to keep but didn't. In the end, as much pleasure as I derived from the process, I'd made the wrong decision about the cake. Or maybe I made the decision I was meant to make in 1980: while the cake sported a "1" made of chocolate—Michael did that!—it wasn't a cake for Joshua or any of the other babies who gamboled about in the dining room. I'd made a boozy coconut cake that I served to the grown-ups and cookies for the kids. The kids seemed happy. The grown-ups seemed happy. It was a great party. Joshua grew up fine—actually, he grew up to love cookies more than cake, probably having nothing to do with his first birthday. Certainly I don't take credit for being prescient. But when I was asked to make a first birthday cake for Gemma, our first granddaughter, I thought about the undertaking in a very different way. I wanted it to be completely and idiosyncratically hers. I knew she wouldn't remember it, and I knew she wouldn't care what it was, but I knew that I would.

It's nice to have a second chance—we don't always. That I got a third chance with VV would have been the cherry on the cake, except when VV turned one, her favorite fruit was banana.

Makes 9 shortcakes

FOR THE CAKES

1 cup (136 grams) all-purpose flour

1 teaspoon baking powder

½ teaspoon fine sea salt

1 cup (200 grams) sugar

1 medium orange

½ cup (120 ml) whole milk

2 tablespoons (1 ounce; 28 grams) unsalted butter

2 tablespoons olive oil

1 teaspoon pure vanilla extract

½ teaspoon Fiori di Sicilia (or an additional ½ teaspoon vanilla extract)

2 large eggs, at room temperature

FOR THE BERRIES

About 3 cups (about 500 grams) strawberries, hulled and cut into bite-size pieces

3 to 4 tablespoons sugar

A squirt of lemon juice, if you'd like

FOR THE CREAM

2 cups (480 ml) very cold heavy cream

1½ tablespoons confectioners' sugar

3 tablespoons very cold sour cream

Juice of 1 orange for moistening the cakes

♥ A TREASURED FAVORITE

Charlotte Russe Shortcakes

When I was a kid growing up in Brooklyn, just off the avenue where everyone shopped—and where there were three bakeries within easy walking distance of one another—there was a snack stand, long and narrow and open to the street. I think it may have sold hot dogs and burgers, but what I remember most was the glass case with cakes called Charlotte Russe—I only later discovered that this variation on the French classic was a specialty of New York City. Michael and I lived in the same neighborhood and we both remember the cakes and loved that they came in white cardboard cups (I remember the top being zigzagged like a jester's cap) with bottoms that you pushed up to reveal the next layer of cake. We both remember the sponge cake and the whipped cream. So much whipped cream. And the maraschino cherry on top. I think I remember berries in the cake, but there probably weren't any. Still, while I didn't set out to re-create a childhood memory, when I made these shortcakes, both Michael and I said "Charlotte Russe" after the first bite. It's that slightly springy sponge cake and all that whipped cream. Don't you dare stint!

The base cake is a hot-milk sponge with a little olive oil. It's a riff on a very old-fashioned cake, an easy cake to make and so cute baked in jumbo muffin tins. The cakes' tops dome a bit and bake to a lovely gold color. I flavored the cake with orange zest, vanilla and a little Fiori de Sicilia, a fragrant citrus-vanilla extract (if you don't have it, you can add more vanilla), cut it into three layers (although two layers are pretty as well), gave each cut side a squirt of fresh orange juice and then went to town filling the layers with whipped cream and sugared berries. For Gothamites, these shortcakes might be a wink to their childhoods. To everyone else, they'll be a fanciful delight.

A word on working ahead: You can make the sponge cake ahead of time (see Storing) and prepare the berries and cream in advance, but once you've assembled the shortcakes, you'll want to serve them within an hour or two—keep them refrigerated until then. You can sugar the berries and keep them covered at room temperature for a couple of hours or in the fridge overnight. The cream can be made a few hours or even up to a day ahead, covered tightly and refrigerated. If you make it more than 2 hours ahead, you might want to spoon it into a strainer set over a bowl and cover the whole setup with plastic wrap before refrigerating it. In either case, give the cream a quick whip with a whisk before using.

To make the cakes: Center a rack in the oven and preheat it to 350 degrees F. Coat the interior of 9 jumbo-size muffin wells with baker's spray or butter them, dust with flour and tap out the excess. You may need two pans or to bake in batches.

Whisk together the flour, baking powder and salt.

Put the sugar in the bowl of a stand mixer or in a large bowl that you can use with a hand mixer. Grate the zest of the orange over the sugar (save the orange—you'll need the juice when you put the shortcakes together), reach into the bowl and use your fingers to mash and press and smush the ingredients together until the sugar is fragrant and tinged orange. If you're using a stand mixer, attach the bowl to the stand and fit it with the whisk attachment.

In a small saucepan, bring the milk and butter just to a boil; remove from the heat and set aside in the pan. (You can do this in a microwave, if you want.)

Add the olive oil and extracts to the sugar and mix just to blend—there's not much liquid, so it'll be pasty, but that's fine. Drop both eggs into the bowl and mix on medium-high speed for about 4 minutes, until the mixture is pale and light. Turn off the mixer, spoon in one-third of the flour mixture and mix on low speed only until it disappears into the batter. Add the remainder of the dry ingredients in two additions, mixing on low and scraping the bowl and beater(s). Check that the milk and butter mixture is still hot—give it a quick warm-up if necessary—and, with the mixer on low, slowly and steadily pour the liquid into the batter, mixing just until it's blended in. Scrape the bowl and divide the batter among the 9 cupcake molds. The batter will come only about halfway up the sides of the wells.

Bake for 18 to 21 minutes, or until the cakes have risen and are golden and a tester inserted into the centers of a few cakes comes out clean. Transfer the tin(s) to a rack and wait for 2 to 3 minutes, then run a table knife around the edges of the cakes and unmold them onto the rack. Turn right side up and let cool to room temperature. You can assemble the cakes just before serving time or no more than 2 hours ahead (see above and Storing).

To make the berries: Mix the berries and sugar together in a bowl and let sit for at least 15 minutes—you want the sugar and berry juice to form a little syrup. Stir the berries a couple of times and, if you'd like, give them a squeeze or two of lemon juice for zip.

To make the cream: Working in the bowl of a stand mixer fitted with the whisk attachment, or in a large bowl with a hand mixer, beat the heavy cream until it just starts to thicken. Beat in the confectioners' sugar and then beat in the sour cream. If you want to spoon the cream between the cake layers and have it be soft and cushiony, stop beating when it holds gentle waves. If you want to pipe it Charlotte-Russe style, beat until it's thick and holds its shape.

To assemble the cakes: I like making tall shortcakes for the drama—I cut each cake into three layers—but double-deckers are lovely, too, and also a bit easier to both assemble and eat. Whatever you choose, slice the cakes using a gently serrated knife. Then, for each layer, squeeze a little orange juice on the cut side of the cake, top with whipped cream—spooned or piped—and some berries. Top the shortcake with a crown of cream and a few berries, or just one in the center, and, if you'd like, a drizzle of the syrup that accumulated in the bottom of the bowl of berries.

Serve immediately! With a big spoon and a bigger smile.

Storing: Without the whipped cream and berries, the little cakes can be wrapped and held at room temperature for up to 2 days or can be frozen for up to 1 month; thaw in the wrappers.

Playing Around

Old-Fashioned Charlotte Russe

The Charlottes of my childhood probably didn't have strawberries. To make one that comes closer to the old-timey original, cut each cake into two or three layers, pipe whipped cream over the cut side of each layer, pipe a pretty rosette of cream on top and finish with a maraschino cherry.

SALTY CAKES

Fauxcaccia Squares

Makes 9 servings

- 2 large tomatoes or a mix of large tomatoes and grape or cherry tomatoes
- 1⅓ cups (181 grams) all-purpose flour
- 1¼ teaspoons baking powder
- ½ teaspoon dried thyme or oregano or 1 teaspoon minced fresh thyme or oregano
- ½ teaspoon fine sea salt
- ¼ teaspoon freshly ground black pepper
- Pinch of red pepper flakes
- 3 large eggs, at room temperature
- ⅓ cup (80 ml) olive oil, plus more for brushing
- 3 tablespoons honey
- 4 ounces (113 grams) feta or mozzarella, patted dry and cut into small pieces
- A few thin onion slices (red or white)
- A few sprigs of thyme (optional)
- Fleur de sel or flaky sea salt for sprinkling
- Grated Parmesan for dusting

The first time I made this savory cake (don't be fooled by the name; this isn't a bread and there's no yeast in the mix), I was on a mission to salvage the last of the too-many tomatoes I'd bought at the farm stand. But the second time—and every time thereafter—it was because it is so good. The cake itself is a little peppery, a tad sweet, dotted with cheese—sometimes I choose feta, sometimes melty mozzarella—and meant to play a supporting role. Literally. It's a thin layer, but it's got substantial flavor, sufficient heft and the good manners to hold up the tomatoes and allow them to shine.

Choose whatever tomatoes look good to you. I think the cake is prettiest when you've got a mix of color, sizes and shapes, but that's not a requisite. I also like to finish the cake with a few rings of onion, some fresh herbs and a dusting of Parmesan. Think focaccia or even pizza when you're topping the cake. If you like these squares as much as I do, you'll find other vegetables to use on top. Play around with what you have and what you like (see page 230 for some ideas), but just remember to slice the vegetables thin so that they'll cook in the short bake time.

I like to serve squares of this cake just as I would focaccia: as a snack, a nibble with aperitifs or alongside soup or a salad. If you can, serve it shortly after it's baked, while it's still warm; if not, it'll still be good at room temperature or rewarmed for just a few minutes in a hot oven.

Center a rack in the oven and preheat it to 350 degrees F. Butter or spray the interior of a 9-x-9-inch baking pan. Run a piece of parchment paper over the bottom and up two opposite sides of the pan, leaving enough overhang so that you can use the paper as handles to lift the baked cake out of the pan.

Cut the larger tomatoes into slices—if the tomatoes are really large, consider cutting the slices in half—and halve the smaller ones. Place them between paper towels and let them drain for the few minutes it takes you to prepare the batter.

Whisk the flour, baking powder, herbs, fine sea salt and two peppers together in a large bowl. →

In another bowl, whisk together the eggs, oil and honey. Pour the wet ingredients over the dry, grab a flexible spatula and stir everything together until mostly, but not completely, combined. Drop in the pieces of cheese and stir to incorporate and finish blending the batter.

Scrape the batter into the pan and use the spatula to spread it evenly. Because the batter is thick and the layer will be thin, you'll need to poke and prod and cajole it into the corners.

Arrange the tomatoes on top in whatever pattern you like—there's no right way here, but you do want to be sure that there'll be a little tomato in every bite. Scatter over the onion slices and brush the top lightly with olive oil. If you're using the fresh thyme sprigs, arrange them on the cake. Season the top sparingly with fleur de sel and dust with Parmesan.

Bake the cake for 20 to 22 minutes, or until it starts to pull away from the sides of the pan and a tester inserted into the center comes out clean. The cake will be pale. If you'd like it to have a bit more color—I always do—crank up the broiler, slide the cake back into the oven and broil just until you get the color you want. Depending on where the cake is in relation to the broiler element (I have a top broiler and keep the cake on the center rack), it may color in a minute, or you may need about 3 minutes—just stay close! Transfer the cake to a rack and wait for 5 minutes, then run a table knife around the edges of the cake and lift it out of the pan, using the parchment handles, and slide it off the paper and onto the rack. Let it settle and cool a bit before cutting and serving.

Storing: The fauxcaccia is at its peak shortly after it's baked and best the day it's made. If you can't swing baking and then serving it that quickly, let it cool, wrap it and set aside at room temperature. You can keep it this way for a day. When you're ready for it, pop it into a hot oven (a toaster oven is ideal for this) just to warm it.

Playing Around

Zuccaccia

Replace the tomatoes with thin slices of yellow squash and green zucchini—a mandoline's handy here. Keep the onions, use the thyme and, if you'd like, add slivers of garlic.

Ratatouille Cake

Use small tomatoes and add thin slices of zucchini and eggplant (salt the eggplant slices, leave for 15 minutes and then pat dry before using); small pitted olives, or chunks of olives; and slivers of garlic. A little minced fresh rosemary is nice along with the thyme.

Apple-Cheddar Corn Cake, Maple Syrup, Too

It all started because I had a forlorn apple on the counter and didn't know what to do with it. I'm still not sure what quirk of mind led me from save-the-apple to a corn cake with cheese, chile powder and some maple syrup, but happiness ensued. I'm calling it a cake rather than cornbread because when it's warm, the crumb is soft, like a tea cake. That's also when the cheese is at its showiest, stretching as you pull a slice from the square. And warm is when the bit of maple syrup that you brush across the top of the cake is at its most enticing, when it shines and sticks to your lips for a second, giving you a reason to lick them. Once the cake cools, its appeals are different, but not diminished: at room temperature, the texture is more like traditional cornbread and, in fact, the taste of corn is more pronounced. So is the quiet heat of the pepper. And while the cheese won't pull, it will, like all the other ingredients, have more flavor.

I love that this cake, a child of playing around, can be played around with even more; see page 232 for some ideas to get you started on variations.

Makes 9 servings

- 1 medium-large apple (about 8 ounces; 226 grams), peeled
- 1½ cups (192 grams) cornmeal, preferably yellow
- ¾ cup (102 grams) all-purpose flour
- 2¼ teaspoons baking powder
- 1½ teaspoons fine sea salt
- ½ teaspoon baking soda
- About ½ teaspoon freshly ground black pepper
- ¼ teaspoon piment d'Espelette or cayenne, or to taste
- 1¼ cups (300 ml) full-fat buttermilk (well shaken before measuring), at room temperature
- ¼ cup (60 ml) maple syrup
- 2 large eggs, at room temperature
- 8 tablespoons (4 ounces; 113 grams) unsalted butter, melted
- ¾ cup (3 ounces; 85 grams) shredded sharp cheddar, preferably orange (for color contrast), thick-cut if possible, plus more for sprinkling
- About ¼ cup (2 ounces; 56 grams) cheddar cut into small cubes (about ¼- to ½-inch)
- About ¼ cup (60 ml) pure maple syrup for topping

Center a rack in the oven and preheat it to 400 degrees F. Coat a 9-x-9-inch baking pan with baker's spray; line the bottom with parchment, or butter and flour it, tap out the excess flour and line it.

Using the large holes of a box grater or Microplane grater with large holes, shred the apple into a bowl. You should have about ¾ cup.

Working in a large bowl, whisk together the cornmeal, flour, baking powder, salt, baking soda, black pepper and chile pepper.

In another bowl or a large measuring cup, whisk together the buttermilk, maple syrup and eggs. Pour the wet ingredients over the dry and whisk together just until blended—there's no need to be energetic. Switch to a flexible spatula and stir in the melted butter, taking care to get to the bottom of the bowl as you mix. Lift the grated apple out of the bowl and press out as much juice as you can, then stir the apple into the batter, followed by the shredded and cubed cheese. →

Scrape the batter into the pan, nudge it into the corners and smooth the top. Scatter over some more shredded cheese.

Bake for 22 to 25 minutes, or until the cake is golden brown and pulls away from the sides of the pan when gently tugged; a tester inserted into the center of the cake will come out clean. Transfer the pan to a rack and let the cake rest for 5 minutes.

While the cake is resting, bring the maple syrup to a boil and then remove from the heat. Boiling thickens the syrup a bit, but it's not a necessary step—you can use room-temperature syrup.

Run a table knife around the edges of the cake, turn it out onto the rack, peel away the paper and turn the cake right side up onto another rack. Brush the cake with the maple syrup, using enough to just coat the cake—think of it more as a glaze than a soak.

The cake has to wait for at least 15 minutes before you can serve it. I love the cake when it's hot, but be warned: it will be completely delicious but a little ragged around the edges, because it's hard to make neat cuts in a hot cake. The cake is also nice warm or at room temperature, or toasted, griddled or reheated.

Storing: Wrapped, the cake will keep at room temperature for up to 2 days and for up to 1 month in the freezer; thaw in the wrapper. For extra deliciousness, reheat before serving.

Playing Around

Follow the basic recipe but think about add-ins such as cubelettes of cooked ham (I use a ham steak for this), crisp bacon bits, very finely diced chile or bell peppers or sliced scallions or spring onions (include some of the greens). Chopped herbs are always a good idea—think cilantro, basil or dill. Or use oregano, rosemary and/or thyme, and if you do, switch the cheese to something more Italian, like mozzarella, Fontina or Taleggio, with some grated Parm on top. Do that, and you might want to swap honey or hot honey for the maple syrup.

Maybe-This, Maybe-That Ham and Cheese Loaf

There are so many ways to play around with this cake that I gave up trying to find a name that would describe all of its possibilities. At its core, it's a savory loaf with cheese—three different kinds. And while I like to swing Italian and use mozzarella, Fontina and Parmesan, it's just as good with Comté or Gruyère, cheddar and something very meltable, like Brie. It's got bits of roasted red peppers, the kind you might find on an old-school antipasto platter, but you could go spicy—I love this with Calabrian chiles or pepperoncini (you'll want fewer of them)—or head for Provence and use olives. And I like the loaf with different kinds of ham. Sometimes I buy a ham steak and cut it into cubes; sometimes I give small chunks of pancetta a quick brown, drain them and toss them into the batter; and sometimes, especially if I've already got it on hand, I'll add bits of bacon. When I'm making the loaf for vegetarians, as I often do, I nix the meat and add some chunky toasted nuts (coarsely chopped walnuts or hazelnuts) for texture. The recipe gives you lots of room to stretch.

Lots of ways to serve it, too—it can turn up at the kind of breakfast that runs into lunch; it can be an afternooner, good when you want something that's a treat but not a sugary one; it's a happy match for a bowl of soup or a salad, or both; and it shines in the early evening when you pair it with an aperitif. White wine is what I usually serve, but if you've gone Italian, consider doubling down on the theme with a sparkling Lambrusco.

The loaf is nice offered in slices—whole or halved—or in fingers. And if it seems a smidge stale, toast it lightly.

Makes 8 to 10 servings

- 2 cups (272 grams) all-purpose flour
- 1 tablespoon baking powder
- ¾ teaspoon fine sea salt
- ½ teaspoon crushed red pepper flakes, or to taste
- 2 large eggs, at room temperature
- 1 large egg white, at room temperature
- ½ cup (120 ml) whole milk, at room temperature
- ¼ cup (60 ml) olive oil
- 2 tablespoons honey
- ⅔ cup (3 ounces; 85 grams) Italian Fontina cut into small (¼- to ½-inch) cubes
- 1 cup (4 ounces; 113 grams) shredded low-moisture mozzarella (see below)
- 3 tablespoons shredded Parmesan, plus more for sprinkling
- ½ cup (3 ounces; 85 grams) cooked ham or browned pancetta cut into ¼-inch cubes
- ¼ cup (about 2½ ounces; 70 grams) finely chopped roasted peppers, patted dry
- 3 tablespoons snipped fresh chives (or thinly sliced scallions)
- 1 teaspoon finely chopped fresh thyme

A word on the mozzarella: If you love fresh mozzarella, as I do, you might be tempted to use it in the batter. I did, and it was a mistake—the fresh cheese is too wet for this cake. Choose a low-moisture mozzarella, the kind that's typically used for pizza.

Center a rack in the oven and preheat it to 350 degrees F. Coat an 8½-inch loaf pan with baker's spray or butter, then run a piece of parchment paper over the bottom and up the long sides, leaving enough overhang to use as handles for lifting the cake out of the pan. →

In a large bowl, whisk together the flour, baking powder, salt and pepper flakes.

In another bowl, whisk together the eggs and egg white, milk, olive oil and honey. Pour the liquid ingredients over the flour mixture and, using a flexible spatula, stir a few times, just to get things started. Add the three cheeses, ham, roasted peppers, chives and thyme and, using as few strokes as possible, mix them in. Be gentle, and don't be too diligent—it's better to have a few dryish spots than to overmix the batter. Scrape the batter into the pan and plunge your spatula up and down in it a few times to get it to fill the corners. Even the top with the spatula and sprinkle with shredded Parmesan.

Bake for about 50 minutes, or until the top is golden brown and a tester inserted into the center comes out clean. Because of all the cheese, you can easily mistake a bit of it for a wet spot, so test in a few places. Transfer the pan to a rack and let sit for about 5 minutes, then run a table knife around the edges of the cake and use the paper to lift the loaf out of the pan. Gently peel away the paper, return the cake to the rack, right side up, and let the cake cool until it's just warm or at room temperature.

Storing: Wrapped well, the cake will keep for about 3 days at room temperature. It can be frozen for up to 1 month; thaw in the wrapper.

Harissa-Lemon Loaf

Makes 8 to 10 servings

- 1 small lemon (about 4 ounces; 113 grams), preferably organic, scrubbed (see below left)
- ¼ cup (about 40 grams) black or green olives (see below center), pitted
- 2 cups (272 grams) all-purpose flour
- 1 tablespoon baking powder
- ½ teaspoon fine sea salt
- 2 large eggs, at room temperature
- 3 tablespoons sugar
- 1 tablespoon honey
- 2 teaspoons harissa sauce or about half as much paste (see below center)
- ⅓ cup (80 ml) neutral oil
- ½ cup (120 ml) whole milk, at room temperature

Harissa is a blend of spices found often in the cuisines of North Africa and the Middle East. In harissa country, every spice vendor has a proprietary blend; every cook has her or his own preference. Whether you buy harissa as a ground-spice blend, a paste in a tube or a sauce in a jar (my preference for this recipe), the base ingredient will be chiles and the mix will be spicy. After that, it can be a potpourri—there'll usually be garlic and cumin and there may even be rose petals, a lovely addition. Taste it once, and you'll recognize it the next time. Love it, and you'll want to keep a steady supply in your kitchen.

It was while I was trying to get the right amount of harissa in a tagine that I wondered if I could make a savory cocktail loaf with harissa and a couple of the other ingredients I add to the dish, specifically lemons and olives. The answer to the question is yes! When the harissa is mixed into a batter and baked, some of its heat is mellowed—you get more of the chiles' sweetness than their fire. Because you use the whole lemon—everything but the seeds—there's plenty of sharpness. And because the olives hold their own in the oven, their distinctive salty edge remains. With dreams of tagines in my head, I thought about adding chickpeas to the mix, but then I had a better idea—cut the cake into chunky strips and make them scoopers for hummus. For tzatziki and baba ganoush, too. Happily, the cake is just as perfect for what I'd originally intended it to be—a straight-up nibble with drinks.

A word on the lemons: You're going to use every bit of the lemon except the seeds, so it's best to choose organic fruit. I've made this using preserved lemon, *citron confit*, and loved it—the preserved lemons are salty and have a different type of acidity than the fresh fruit. If you want to try this, drain 1 or 2 small preserved lemons, discard the seeds and give the rind and pulp a medium-fine chop. If you'd like, add a teaspoon of the brine to the batter.

A word on the olives: Any olive will be good here, but I like this cake with oily black Greek olives.

A word on the harissa: Harissa paste comes in small tubes and is easy to keep on hand—refrigerated, it'll last almost forever. If you use the paste instead of a sauce, use a smaller amount, maybe 1 teaspoon—it's stronger and less nuanced than most sauces. Taste it and see what you think. If you've got a favorite spoonable harissa sauce, use it (I love New York Shuk's Signature Harissa).

Center a rack in the oven and preheat it to 350 degrees F. Coat the interior of an 8½-inch loaf pan with baker's spray and then run a piece of parchment paper over the bottom and up the two long sides, leaving enough of an overhang to serve as lifters when the cake is baked. Or, if you prefer, butter the pan and line it.

Cut the lemon in half or into quarters, pick out the seeds and chop or dice it, peel and all, medium-fine. It's hard to give a size for the pieces here, so just consider what might be a pleasant bit to come upon when you're eating the loaf. I usually end up with 3 to 4 tablespoons of lemon. Chop the olives the same way (maybe going more medium than fine)—you'll probably have about ¼ cup. Precision doesn't count here.

Whisk the flour, baking powder and salt together in a large bowl.

In a smaller bowl, whisk the eggs, sugar, honey and harissa together. When they're well mixed, blend in the oil, followed by the milk—the mix will be sloshy, and that's fine. Pour the wet ingredients over the flour mixture, switch to a flexible spatula and stir until the dry ingredients are mostly moistened. Fold in the lemon and olives. If you've got a few dry spots, leave them—with this loaf, a couple of dry patches are better than an overmixed batter. Scrape it into the pan and plunge your spatula up and down in a few places, especially in the corners, to even everything. The batter will only come about halfway up the sides of the pan.

Bake for 48 to 53 minutes, or until the cake is golden, rises, has cracked and can be nudged away from the sides of the pan; a tester inserted into the center of the cake will come out clean. Transfer the pan to a rack and wait for 5 minutes, then run a table knife around the edges of the cake and lift it up and out of the pan with the parchment handles. Gently peel away the paper, return the cake to the rack, right side up, and leave it to cool to room temperature.

Storing: Wrapped well, the cake will keep for about 3 days at room temperature. If you think the cake is a little stale, toast the slices—it will bring the flavors to life again. You can freeze the cake for up to 1 month; thaw in the wrapper.

Corn Toasties

Makes 12 jumbo toasties

- 1 cup (144 grams) yellow cornmeal
- 1 cup (136 grams) all-purpose flour
- 2 teaspoons baking powder
- 1 teaspoon fine sea salt
- ½ teaspoon baking soda
- 2 large eggs, at room temperature
- 1⅔ cups (400 ml) buttermilk (well shaken before measuring), preferably at room temperature
- 3 tablespoons (1½ ounces; 42 grams) unsalted butter, melted and cooled for a few minutes
- 3 tablespoons olive oil
- 3 tablespoons honey

When I first made the batter for this recipe, I turned it into muffins—good corn muffins. Then I made it into a sturdy-crusted cornbread baked in a cast-iron skillet—also really good. Finally, I poured it into a jumbo muffin tin, and it became what I think it was meant to be all along: toasties, a more polished, less sweet version of the supermarket corn cakes of my childhood. They're barely 1 inch high, so you can eat them out of hand, toast them whole or split them, slather them with butter or use them as the base of a shortcake or a sandwich—think BLT or an open-faced peak-of-summer tomato treat. They've got a natural sweetness (the corn), a pleasingly rough texture (which you'll get even from finely milled cornmeal) and a sunshine-gold color (yellow cornmeal is best here). I've played to the toasties' savory side by adding olive oil, a little honey and a fair amount of buttermilk: a simple but complex flavor combination. And there's a light crispness—and a beautiful honeycomb pattern—that turns up in all the parts of the adorable little cakes that have pressed against the pan.

This is the plainest version of the recipe, but you can jazz it up with add-ins, toppings and spreads. Take a look at Playing Around for a few ideas.

Center a rack in the oven and preheat it to 400 degrees F. Butter the interior of 12 jumbo-size muffin wells or lightly coat them with cooking spray. You may need two pans or to bake in batches.

Working in a medium bowl, whisk together the cornmeal, flour, baking powder, salt and baking soda.

In another bowl, whisk together the eggs, buttermilk, butter, olive oil and honey. Pour the wet ingredients over the dry, switch to a flexible spatula and stir everything together. Work quickly, but not furiously; you don't want pockets of dry ingredients, but you needn't fuss over a few lumps here and there. Divide the batter evenly among the muffin wells—they'll be only about half-full.

Slide the muffin tin(s) into the oven, close the door and immediately turn the temperature down to 375 degrees F. Bake the cakes for 15 to 18 minutes, or until they are springy to the touch, pull away from the sides of the tin(s) when →

prodded and are golden brown around the edges; a tester poked into the center of a few of the cakes should come out clean. Transfer the tin(s) to a rack and allow the cakes to settle for 2 minutes before unmolding. I'd tell you to wait until they cool a bit before serving, but the temptation to dig in may be too great.

Storing: These are really best the day they're made, but they are still very good a day or two later if you store them in a tightly sealed container at room temperature. Of course, if they go a little dry, you can toast them. For longer storage, wrap them well and freeze for up to 1 month; thaw in the wrapper.

Playing Around

Toasted Toasties

You can toast these whole or split them in half. Cut in half, they're great for shortcakes (make them open-faced or use the tops to cap them) or open-faced sandwiches. Cut in half, toasted and then sliced in half again, so that each cake makes four pieces, they're a good base for something savory to serve with wine—think cream cheese and smoked salmon, crab salad, butter and anchovies, or cheese, soft and creamy or hard. Also think about something as simple as a swipe of mayo and a thick slice of the juiciest summer tomato you can wrangle. i like that with a dusting of spicy furikake, the Japanese seaweed-and-sesame-seed sprinkle often served over rice.

Skillet Cornbread

You can make a beautiful thick cornbread with this batter using a 9½- or 10-inch cast-iron skillet. If you'd like, melt 4 tablespoons of butter in the skillet, then pour off 3 tablespoons for the batter and swirl the remaining tablespoon around the skillet to coat the bottom and sides. Alternatively, you can simply butter, oil or spray the pan. Bake the cornbread for about 25 minutes, or until it tests done.

Corn Toastie Muffins

Make the batter as described and divide among a dozen regular muffin cups. Bake for 17 to 20 minutes.

Add-ins

Toasties, muffins and cornbread welcome all kinds of additions, from bits of bacon (cooked crispy) to chiles, fresh (finely chopped) or dried (add chile flakes by the pinch). Corn kernels are an easy add-in, as are chopped scallions (add some of the greens), fresh herbs (think chives, thyme, dill or tarragon, or cilantro—perfect with chiles, especially jalapeños) or dried spices. When it comes to spices, I like a bit of harissa powder, smoked paprika or sumac. Of course you could add grated or chopped cheese to the batter, or top the toasties, muffins or cornbread with grated cheese before baking (or just after).

Miso-Cheddar Scone Cake

Makes 16 scones

2 cups (272 grams) all-purpose flour

1 tablespoon baking powder

1 tablespoon sugar

½ teaspoon fine sea salt

¼ teaspoon baking soda

1½ tablespoons miso paste, dark or light (see headnote)

1 tablespoon pure maple syrup, plus 1 to 2 tablespoons for brushing

1 cold large egg

¾ cup (180 ml) cold whole milk

8 tablespoons (4 ounces; 113 grams) cold unsalted butter, cut into small bits

4 ounces (113 grams; about 1 cup) shredded sharp cheddar, plus (optional) more for sprinkling

Umami, the fifth flavor—sweet, sour, salty and bitter are its four sisters—is harder to recognize than its sibs and just as difficult to describe. It's often defined as "savory," and I like that word for it, but I like "moreish" more. When something has umami, it has the power to captivate, to make you want bite after bite, to invite you to have more. Miso is quintessentially moreish, a poster child for umami and the ingredient that, along with cheddar and maple syrup, makes this pull-apart scone cake stand out. I love the combination, love how unexpected it is, love that it's right for breakfast or an afternoon snack and love how, when the batter is scooped into a springform pan in concentric rings, it bakes into a daisy cake.

I use dark miso for the cake—its flavor is stronger—but if you prefer lighter white miso, or if that's what you've got, carry on! And I use sharp cheddar. Aged cheddar has more umami than a younger cheese, but supermarket shredded cheddar will give you good flavor and has the additional virtue of easy availability. Finally, if you can, serve these when they're just minutes out of the oven or still warm, or at least the day they are made. If you do need to hold them, give them a quick reheat in a hot oven.

Center a rack in the oven and preheat it to 375 degrees F. Coat the interior of a 9½- or 10-inch springform pan with baker's spray, then remove the springform ring from the base and set it aside until you're ready to put the pan in the oven.

Whisk the flour, baking powder, sugar, salt and baking soda together in a large bowl.

Put the miso and 1 tablespoon of maple syrup in a medium bowl and stir until blended and smooth. Beat in the egg and milk.

Drop the bits of cold butter into the bowl with the dry ingredients; reach in and use your fingers to press and mash the butter into the flour. You're aiming for a bumpy, lumpy, uneven mixture—it's good to have pieces of flour-coated butter visible here and there. Add the cheese and, using your fingers, run it through the ingredients. Pour the liquid ingredients on top and use a fork to stir them in, going down to the bottom of the bowl and turning and tossing the mixture. You don't want to →

beat it, and you don't want to be too thorough. You're looking to moisten most of the dough, but if you've got a few dry spots here and there, that's fine. The dough will be heavy and sticky.

I like to use a large cookie scoop, one with a capacity of about 3 tablespoons, to portion out the dough. If you prefer, use a spoon. Scoop the dough onto the base of the springform pan: start at the outer edge and scoop out 9 scones, trying to leave a little space between them (extra points if you can leave a little space between the dough and the edge of the pan bottom). Then scoop out an inner ring of 6 scones and finish with a scoop in the center, to make a total of 16 scones. Attach the sides of the pan to the base and lock the springform. If you'd like, sparingly sprinkle the tops of the scones with a little cheese.

Bake for 22 to 24 minutes, or until the scones have puffed—they'll have baked together into a pretty flower—and are golden. The tops will feel firm and a tester inserted into the centers will come out clean. Transfer the pan to a rack, unlock and remove the ring and brush the tops of the scones with maple syrup. Let the cake rest for 5 minutes or so, then lift it off the pan's base and onto the rack. The cake is ready to enjoy now, when it's only just warm or when it's reached room temperature.

Storing: Like all quickbreads, this cake is best the day it is made. If you have any scones left over, wrap them and then rewarm them the next day in a 350-degree-F oven before serving.

Makes 8 servings

About 1 pound (450 to 500 grams) small to medium zucchini

1 cup (136 grams) all-purpose flour

1¼ teaspoons fine sea salt

1 teaspoon baking powder

½ teaspoon freshly ground black pepper

2 large eggs, at room temperature

⅓ cup (80 ml) whole milk, at room temperature

¼ cup (60 ml) olive oil

3 to 4 tablespoons minced fresh tarragon and/or chives

About 2 ounces (60 grams) goat cheese, cut into small bits or crumbles (see below)

Finely grated Parmesan for dusting (optional)

A word on the cheese: Since I often have a log of softish goat cheese in the fridge, it's what I'll grab for this, but you can use a firmer, more crumbly cheese. You want a cheese with some tang and acidity, but how strong it should be is your choice. You can also skip the chèvre and go for feta (make sure you press it to get out the moisture), robiola or even low-moisture mozzarella.

Zucchini and Chèvre Invisible Cake

This is the Apple Custard Cake's (page 71) salty, tangy, cheesy, made-for-summer flip side. It's a classic of the invisible-cake clan, earning its membership because the cake's scant amount of batter and small dabs of goat cheese seemingly disappear into the recipe's abundant zucchini. And, like the best invisibles, it shows off another bit of culinary wizardry: under heat, the hodgepodge of sliced squash manages to arrange itself into beautiful layers. The cake is reminiscent of a crustless quiche, but wobblier and more puzzling: it looks rough and rustic, but somehow elegant, too. Make sure to slice the zucchini into very thin rounds—a mandoline is perfect for the job.

Center a rack in the oven and preheat it to 375 degrees F. Coat an 8½-inch loaf pan with baker's spray or butter, flour it and tap out the excess. Run a piece of parchment paper over the bottom of the pan and up the two long sides, leaving enough overhang so that you can use the paper to lift the cake out of the pan. Put the pan on a baking sheet to catch any possible drips as it bakes.

If you're slicing the zucchini by hand, do it now: using a sharp knife, slice the zucchini into rounds that are thin enough to bend but not so thin that they break. You should have about 2 cups of slices. If you're using a mandoline or other slicer, wait until the batter is mixed to slice the zucchini.

Working in a bowl that's large enough to hold all the ingredients, whisk together the flour, salt, baking powder and pepper.

In another bowl, whisk together the eggs, milk and olive oil. Pour the wet ingredients over the dry and, using a flexible spatula, stir to blend—you'll have a thick, pancake-like batter. Stir in the herbs. If you haven't cut the zucchini yet, set the mandoline or slicer over the bowl and slice the squash into it, stopping a few times to mix everything together. If you've already sliced the zucchini, stir it in. Either way, you'll have so much zucchini that you might think it will be impossible to coat the slices with batter—but you can do it! Keep stirring, and when you've succeeded, blend in the goat cheese. Scrape the unruly mix into the pan, plunging your spatula into the batter in several places to settle it and ensure that it fills the corners, then rap the pan against the counter. Dust the top with some Parmesan, if you'd like.

Bake for 75 minutes, or until the cake is browned and evenly puffed; a tester plunged into the center should go through the zucchini easily. You might see some bubbling around the edges of the pan, and that's fine. Transfer the cake to a rack and wait for 15 minutes—don't be concerned when your cake settles and sinks a bit; that's its nature—then carefully run a table knife around the edges of the cake to loosen it; the cake is fragile, so go gingerly.

Leave the pan on the rack for 2 hours (the cake might still be warm at that point) before using the paper to lift the cake out. Peel away the paper and set the cake on a cutting board; if the paper gives way, just turn the cake out onto the cutting board, peel away the paper and then invert it onto the board. Let the cake cool to room temperature before serving it or wrapping it and tucking it into the refrigerator.

The cake is good at room temperature or chilled. Either way, it's fragile and most easily cut and most fully enjoyed in thick slices.

Storing: Wrapped well, the cake will keep in the fridge for up to 2 days.

Pop-the-Cork Nibblets

I loved these from the instant I first made them. They were born in Paris and made to surprise friends who expect that when they come to my place for dinner, they'll be greeted at the door with chilled wine and hot gougères, the cheese puffs that have become my signature. I thought that I'd change things up a bit and make them something just as small and delightful as gougères, as cheesy, as subtly salty and as irresistibly munchable. And so I made these nibblets with blue cheese, a few spoonfuls of grated Parmesan and some tiny cubes of soft, sweet prunes, a dried fruit that goes really well with salty blue cheese (see Playing Around for other choices). As I'd hoped, they were as good with white wine as my old standbys and perfect with sparkling wine. And while I made them to serve before dinner, I've also found myself snacking on them in the afternoon and liking them with salad at dinner. I never expected they'd be an anytime treat, but how nice that they are! Also nice: They come together quickly, bake quickly and are good hot from the oven, at room temperature or even gently reheated.

Makes 24 small cakes

- About 2 ounces (about 60 grams) blue cheese (or other cheese; see below), cut into small bits
- ⅔ cup (90 grams) all-purpose flour
- 8 moist, plump pitted prunes (about 70 grams)
- ¾ teaspoon baking powder
- ¼ teaspoon fine sea salt
- 1 large egg, at room temperature
- 1 large egg white, at room temperature
- 2 tablespoons honey
- ¼ cup (60 ml) whole milk, at room temperature
- ⅓ cup (80 ml) neutral oil
- 3 tablespoons finely grated Parmesan, plus about 2 tablespoons for sprinkling
- 3 tablespoons finely chopped walnuts, preferably toasted (optional)

A word on the cheese: If you love blue cheese, go all out with something bold, like Roquefort, Gorgonzola or Saint Augur. But if you don't love blue cheese, don't use it. The nibblets are great with aged Gouda or Mimolette, an older Comté or a strong cheddar—all cheeses with personality. For something milder, try a medium-soft goat cheese, a young Brie or robiola. The most important consideration when you're making a choice is simply what you like.

Center a rack in the oven and preheat it to 350 degrees F. Lightly coat 24 mini-muffin molds with baker's spray—spray works better than butter (or even paper liners) for these.

If you're using a cheese that's soft and sticky, put it in a small bowl or on a plate and toss it with 1 teaspoon of the flour; set aside. Using scissors, snip each prune into 6 pieces—set aside, or mix with the cheese.

Whisk the remaining flour with the baking powder and salt.

Working in a large bowl, whisk the egg, white and honey together until blended and foamy. Pour in the milk and whisk to combine. Add half of the dry ingredients and whisk gently to incorporate. When the batter is homogeneous, whisk in the remaining flour mixture—you'll have a creamy batter that will fall off the whisk in ribbons. So pretty. Still working with the whisk, stir in the oil in three additions. The batter will be creamy and shiny. Switch to a flexible spatula and stir in the Parmesan cheese, followed by the other cheese you're using, floured or not, and the prunes. If you're using the nuts, stir them in. →

Divide the batter evenly among the muffin molds, making sure to get a few chunky bits in each mold. I use a small cookie scoop for this job, but a spoon will work. Sprinkle the tops with grated Parm, using just enough to lightly dust each nibblet.

Bake for 12 to 14 minutes, or until the little cakes are puffed and golden; a tester inserted into the center of a few cakes should come out clean. Transfer the muffin tin(s) to a rack and let sit for 2 to 3 minutes, then run a table knife around the edges of each cake and gently remove them from the tin. The cakes can be served now, or when they're only just warm or have cooled to room temperature.

Storing: Lightly covered, the nibblets will hold overnight at room temperature—you can give them a quick reheat in a 350-degree-F oven or a microwave. Packed airtight, they'll keep for up to 1 month in the freezer; thaw in the wrapper and warm before serving.

Playing Around

I like adding something sweet to the mix here, but there's no law that says that the fruit has to be prunes. Snipped dried apricots, dried pears or dried apples are nice stand-ins—just make sure that the fruit is soft (soak it in hot water for a minute to soften if necessary, then drain and pat dry). And if you want the nibblets to be even more savory and even a bit saltier, consider pancetta: cook a few spoonfuls of cubed pancetta (make the cubes tiny) just long enough to render the fat, then drain, pat dry and let cool before mixing it into the batter.

New York Dutch Baby

I was a new cook when I learned how to make a Dutch baby. I'm not sure who gave me the idea—for sure I didn't think of it on my own—but since then, I've been convinced that every new cook should be taught how to make one. Make a Dutch baby early in your culinary life, and I'm sure that you'll remember it as something that made you feel like a kitchen star. You can't go wrong with this recipe, mostly because there is no right: Every Dutch baby has its own personality. Every Dutch baby comes out of the oven looking only like itself. And they all look great.

The batter is similar to one you'd use to make pancakes or crepes—just flour, eggs and milk. It's the add-ins and toppings that change its personality. And it's the way you cook it that makes it a Dutch baby: you melt butter in a heavy skillet—cast iron is my first choice—pour the batter into the hot pan and watch as the batter quickly starts to set, then slide the pan into the hot oven and wait, preferably sitting cross-legged in front of the oven window, so that you can watch the magic. At first it's kind of slow, and then, as though set to time-lapse, the batter bubbles and lifts, rising dramatically, puffing in high swoops, dipping in valleys, browning here, glistening with butter there. It's a thrill.

For this baby, I've gone all New York, channeling the classic bagels with lox, making the batter with herbs, scallions and everything-bagel mix or poppy seeds. And then, as soon as it comes out of the oven, topping it with smoked salmon, crème fraîche, onions and all the fixings. You can play fast, loose and fun with this recipe—I've given you a few ideas for different kinds of pancakes (see Playing Around)—but there is one Dutch baby rule that's unbreakable: you must put your people on high alert—you want them gathered in the kitchen so that they don't miss the moment when the extravagantly puffed pancake emerges from the oven.

Makes 2 servings for supper, 4 for a snack or starter

FOR THE PANCAKE

4 large eggs, at room temperature

¾ cup (180 ml) whole milk, at room temperature

¾ cup (102 grams) all-purpose flour

¾ teaspoon fine sea salt

¼ teaspoon freshly ground black pepper

About ¼ cup (about 40 grams) minced mixed fresh herbs, such as dill, chives and cilantro

1 to 2 tablespoons everything-bagel mix or 1 tablespoon poppy seeds

2 scallions, trimmed and very thinly sliced

5 tablespoons (2½ ounces; 70 grams) unsalted butter

FOR THE FINISHING TOPPINGS—MIX AND MATCH

Small soft lettuce leaves

4 thin slices (about 4 ounces; 113 grams) smoked salmon

Thinly sliced red onion

Thinly sliced radish

Sliced or chunked tomato

Capers, rinsed and patted dry

Olive oil for drizzling

Crème fraîche for drizzling

Sprigs of fresh dill and a few chives

Lemon wedges

To make the pancake: Center a rack in the oven and preheat it to 425 degrees F. Have a 10- to 12-inch cast-iron or other heavy ovenproof skillet at hand.

Working with a blender (stand or immersion), whir the eggs, milk, flour, salt and pepper together until smooth, stopping to scrape as needed. Drop in the herbs, seed mix and scallions and pulse just to incorporate—the bits of scallions are nice. If you prefer, you can mix the batter in a food processor, or in a bowl with a whisk, taking care to beat out any lumps of flour.

Cut the butter into a few chunks, toss them into the skillet and set the skillet over medium-high heat (you want to melt and bubble the butter and heat up the skillet, too). When the butter is melted—it's fine if it browns a bit—carefully tilt the pan to coat the sides. Pour the batter into the pan—it will sizzle, and some of the butter may slip over onto the batter, and that's okay.

Immediately slide the pan into the oven. Once you've closed the oven door, don't open it for 20 minutes—the development of the Dutch baby's characteristic mountains and valleys depends on undisturbed heat. Take a look at the 20-minute mark—it will probably be perfect. You want the pancake to puff above the rim of the skillet, feel firmish to the touch and be golden and gorgeous. Go by gorgeous—it's the best test of doneness. (You may have a little butter skimming the pancake's dips—it's normal.)

While the pancake bakes, assemble your topping ingredients.

To finish: As soon as the pancake comes out of the oven (and the oohs and aahs have quieted down), decide if you'd like to top the pancake in the kitchen or take the toppings to the table and make it a do-it-yourself adventure. If you're taking charge, working quickly, arrange the lettuce and salmon over the pancake's contours, then scatter over (depending on what you've chosen) the onion, radish, tomato and capers. Drizzle with a bit of olive oil and crème fraîche and finish with the herbs and lemon wedges.

Serve the instant the pancake is ready. You can bring it to the table in the skillet or gingerly tug it onto a serving plate.

Playing Around

Niçoise Baby

Omit the everything-bagel mix in the batter and channel a salade Niçoise for the topping—include canned tuna, tomatoes, black olives, cooked green beans, capers, onions, a little lettuce and a few anchovies. Drizzle with crème fraîche just before serving.

Italian-ish Baby

Omit the everything-bagel mix and use basil and/or rosemary in the batter. Top the baked baby with torn pieces of mozzarella or burrata and slices of mortadella. Finish with dollops of pesto, a small handful of arugula and drizzles of olive oil.

Makes about 10 servings

3 tablespoons white sesame seeds, plus (optional) 3 tablespoons for coating the pan

1½ cups (204 grams) all-purpose flour

2 teaspoons baking powder

¼ teaspoon baking soda

3 tablespoons sugar

1 lemon

4 teaspoons sumac

1 tablespoon za'atar

1¼ teaspoons fine sea salt

3 pinches red pepper flakes, such as Marash, Urfa Biber or Aleppo (or 1 to 2 small pinches chile flakes)

½ cup (about 115 grams) thick plain whole-milk Greek yogurt

3 tablespoons honey

3 large eggs, at room temperature

½ cup (120 ml) olive oil

4 ounces (113 grams) feta, patted dry if necessary and cut into very small cubes

Feta, Sumac and Za'atar Loaf

I had the idea for this cake when we were on the Greek island of Sifnos—which was also the source for a wonderfully unusual cheesecake (see page 175), as well as the first place where I tasted a cake made with crumbled phyllo instead of flour (see page 162). There, thick, creamy, tart yogurt was an everyday delight and wild herbs were the fragrance in the air. Greece is the land of yogurt, olive oil and feta cheese, lemons and honey, sumac and za'atar, all the ingredients that pack this savory loaf with flavor and make it as aromatic as a breeze off the Aegean.

The loaf's texture is light, like a springy sponge cake, with the intermittent crunch of tiny sesame seeds. Its flavor is determinedly herbal, but sparked by citrus, rounded by honey and salty because it's dotted with cubes of feta. And I love its look—it's burnished nut-brown outside, tweedy on the inside and, because I coat the pan with sesame seeds before pouring in the batter (optional, but lovely and a quiet echo of the seeds that are baked into the cake), appealingly bumpy all around.

Serve chunky slices or fingers of the loaf with salads, with mezze, with hummus, with roasted peppers, with olives, with tea, with wine. Especially with wine.

Center a rack in the oven and preheat it to 350 degrees F. If using the sesame seeds for the pan, butter or spray an 8½-inch loaf pan and then coat the inside with the 3 tablespoons seeds; the coating doesn't have to be even, just do your best. If you don't want to sesame-coat the cake, butter or spray the pan and run a piece of parchment paper over the bottom of it and up the long sides.

Whisk the flour, baking powder and baking soda together.

Put the sugar in a large bowl and grate the lemon zest over it. Halve the lemon and squeeze 1 tablespoon of juice into a separate bowl. Add the sumac, za'atar, salt and pepper flakes to the sugar and then reach in and smush everything together with your fingers until the sugar is moist and fragrant. Whisk in the yogurt and honey until blended, then whisk in the eggs one at a time, mixing well after each one goes in. Working with the whisk or switching to a flexible spatula, stir in the dry →

ingredients one-half at a time, mixing until the batter is homogenous. Pour in the olive oil and, with a spatula, stir and fold it into the batter, mixing until you have a lovely smooth mixture. Gently fold in the sesame seeds and feta. Scrape the batter into the pan and run the spatula over the top to even it out.

Bake for 50 to 55 minutes, or until the cake has risen—the top will crack, and that's nice—is deeply golden brown and is pulling away from the sides of the pan. A tester inserted into the center of the cake will come out clean. Transfer the pan to a rack and wait for 5 minutes, then carefully turn it over and remove the pan. You'll lose some of the seeds if you used them—it's unavoidable—but the lion's share will stay put and give you the little moments of crunch that make this cake such fun. Turn the cake right side up and leave it on the rack to cool to room temperature before slicing or wrapping it.

Storing: Like most cakes with herbs and spices, this one is best the day after you bake it. Wrapped well, it keeps for about 4 days at room temperature. If it seems a little stale, you can toast the slices. You can also keep it in the freezer for up to 1 month; thaw in the wrapper.

Seaweed and Furikake Muffins

I know that muffins made with toasted seaweed snacks and furikake, a Japanese seasoning traditionally sprinkled over rice, sound kooky, but they're serially munchable if you like the savoriness of these ingredients, which are salty, a touch sweet (furikake usually has some added sugar) and packed with umami. I like the muffins alongside soup or softly scrambled eggs or with green tea. I like them warmed with butter, and I like them even more warmed and dabbed with seaweed or miso butter (see Playing Around). If you decide to butter them and then drizzle them sparingly with a little honey, you'll tip the balance and want to have them as an afternoon pick-me-up.

A word on seaweed snacks: While you could use sheets of toasted nori, seaweed snacks, sometimes sold as *gim*, are toasted and seasoned with oil and salt, which is nice for these muffins. Some snacks come seasoned with sesame seeds or spices—if that appeals to you, opt for them. They need to be cut before you mix them into the batter, something I find easiest to do with scissors. Cut them in half the long way and then snip into thin strips.

A word on furikake: Furikake is a mixture of crushed nori, sesame seeds, sugar and salt, meant to be sprinkled over rice. It can include many other ingredients, such as bonito flakes, poppy seeds, wasabi, mushroom powder and/or dried chiles. What kind of furikake you use in these muffins is up to you.

Makes 12 muffins

- 2 cups (272 grams) all-purpose flour
- 2 tablespoons very finely grated Parmesan
- 1 tablespoon baking powder
- ½ teaspoon fine sea salt
- 10 rectangles (about 2¼ x 3¼ inches) roasted seaweed snacks, snipped into small pieces (see below left)
- 3 tablespoons furikake (see below center), plus more for sprinkling
- 2 large eggs, at room temperature
- ¾ cup (180 ml) whole milk, at room temperature
- ½ cup (120 ml) neutral oil
- 1 tablespoon Asian roasted sesame oil

Center a rack in the oven and preheat it to 400 degrees F. Coat the interiors of 12 standard muffin wells with baker's spray or butter them. (You could bake the muffins in paper liners, but they won't release as well.)

Whisk the flour, Parm, baking powder and salt together in a large bowl, then whisk in the seaweed and furikake.

In a medium bowl, whisk together the eggs, milk and both oils. Pour the wet ingredients into the bowl with the dry, switch to a flexible spatula and briskly stir the two mixtures together. Thoroughness is neither needed nor rewarded with muffins, so if you see specks of flour here or there, ignore them. Divide the batter among the wells. Sprinkle a pinch of furikake over each muffin.

Bake for 17 to 19 minutes, or until the muffins have crowned and, most important, test done—a tester inserted into the center of a few of the muffins should come out clean. Transfer the tin to a rack and wait for 3 minutes, then turn the muffins out onto the rack. Give them a little time to gather themselves before digging in—they're very good warm or at room temperature.

Storing: Like most muffins, these are best the day they are made, but you can keep them covered at room temperature overnight or wrap them well and freeze them for up to 1 month; thaw in the wrapper. If you'd like, warm them in an oven or microwave before serving—heat boosts their flavor.

Playing Around

Miso Butter

Soften 4 tablespoons unsalted butter and mash it with 1 to 2 tablespoons white miso—taste as you go. Finish with freshly ground pepper and a little salt, if you think it needs it, and spread sparingly (miso is a big flavor) on warm muffins.

Seaweed Butter

You can finely chop seaweed snacks to make this butter or use nori flakes. Soften 4 tablespoons unsalted butter and mash it with the finely chopped seaweed or the flakes. Start with about 1½ tablespoons of seaweed and taste as you go. I think the butter tastes best when the muffins are warm.

FROSTINGS, FILLINGS, CREAMS, CRUNCHES and EXTRAS THAT ARE FUN

Everyday Buttercream Frosting

Makes about 2 cups

16 tablespoons (8 ounces; 226 grams) unsalted butter, at room temperature

2 cups (240 grams) confectioners' sugar, sifted if lumpy

¼ teaspoon fine sea salt

1 tablespoon pure vanilla extract

1 to 2 tablespoons whole milk, as needed

Squirt of lemon juice (optional)

A word on mixing: You'll get a lighter, fluffier frosting if you use an electric mixer (stand or hand).

A word on piping: You can pipe the frosting as soon as it's made, but you'll get better results if you chill it for about 30 minutes, either in the bowl or, better yet, in the piping bag you'll be using.

This is the all-American buttercream of small cupcakes and big layer cakes—and everything in between, too. And it can be just about anything. It's a basic delicious vanilla buttercream that you can flavor many ways, a soft, luxurious buttercream that spreads in swirls and stays satiny smooth. Happily, as soft as it is, it's pipeable. (See Playing Around for a few flavor ideas, as well as a firmer buttercream that you can pipe more precisely.) Also, it's tintable—use your favorite food coloring to get the shade you want.

Working in the bowl of a stand mixer fitted with the paddle attachment, or in a large bowl with a hand mixer, beat the butter and sugar together on low speed until smooth, scraping the bowl and beater(s) early and often. You might want to drape a towel over the bowl and beater(s) at the beginning of the process—confectioners' sugar flies! Mix in the salt and vanilla and then up the speed to medium and beat until the frosting is light and swoopy, about 3 minutes. If you'd like the frosting to be a bit thinner, beat in some milk a little at a time, as needed. Taste, and if you think you want a touch of acidity, beat in a few drops of lemon juice.

The buttercream is ready to use now, or it can be covered tightly—press plastic wrap against the surface of the frosting—and refrigerated.

Storing: The frosting will keep in the refrigerator for about 4 days. It gets hard and won't be luxurious and spreadable again until it comes back to room temperature, so leave it covered on the counter and be patient.

Playing Around

A Firmer Everyday Buttercream

Adding more confectioners' sugar to the buttercream will stiffen it for piping. Add another ½ cup (60 grams).

Dark Chocolate Buttercream

Beat about 1 cup (170 grams) chopped chocolate, melted and cooled (the cooled part is important), into the finished buttercream. Since the buttercream is very sweet, I think bittersweet chocolate is a good choice. No matter which chocolate you use, the color of the buttercream will be light, but the flavor will be true. With this frosting, you can omit the vanilla or use just ½ teaspoon; don't add lemon juice.

White Chocolate Buttercream

Beat about ⅔ cup (116 grams) chopped best-quality white chocolate, melted and cooled, into the finished buttercream. White chocolate carries hints of vanilla, so you can either omit the vanilla extract or just add ¼ to ½ teaspoon; don't add lemon juice.

Lemon Buttercream

Grate the zest of 1 lemon into the butter, add the sugar and beat. Omit the vanilla, add 1½ tablespoons lemon juice, then taste and decide if you want more.

Coffee Buttercream

Dissolve 4 teaspoons instant espresso in 1 tablespoon very hot or boiling water. When it's cool, beat it into the buttercream. Omit the vanilla extract and lemon juice.

Freeze-Dried-Fruit Buttercream

Once your buttercream is mixed and beautiful, you can use either freeze-dried fruit powder or pulverized freeze-dried fruit to color and flavor it. It's hard to give an exact amount here, so go by color and taste, especially if you're using the powder. If you're using freeze-dried fruit, start with ¼ cup and pulverize it with ¼ cup of the confectioners' sugar.

Cream Cheese Frosting

Makes about 2⅔ cups

- 8 ounces (226 grams) full-fat cream cheese, at cool room temperature
- 8 tablespoons (4 ounces; 113 grams) unsalted butter, at room temperature
- ¼ teaspoon fine sea salt
- 1½ teaspoons pure vanilla extract
- 3¾ cups (450 grams) confectioners' sugar, sifted if lumpy

A word on piping: If you want to pipe the frosting, cover and refrigerate it for about 30 minutes; better yet, refrigerate it in the piping bag you'll be using.

I think of cream cheese frosting as the chameleon of the frosting world—it's a good match for just about every cake. In fact, my friend Ellen Einstein (she of the Grandmothers' Honey Cake, page 95), who owned the beloved Sweet Sixteenth Bakery in Nashville, told me that cream cheese frosting was their all-purpose topper—they frosted everything from mini cupcakes to towering birthday cakes with it, and it was always right.

Working in the bowl of a stand mixer fitted with the paddle attachment, or in a large bowl with a hand mixer, beat the cream cheese, butter and salt on medium speed until smooth and satiny. Reduce the mixer speed to low and beat in the vanilla, then gradually add the sugar, beating well; you want a voluptuous frosting, so beat away. The frosting is ready to use.

Storing: You can cover the frosting tightly and keep it in the refrigerator for a couple of days. Bring it to room temperature and give it a few brisk beats to soften it if you won't be piping it.

Glossy Chocolate Glaze

Makes about ½ cup

4 tablespoons (2 ounces; 56 grams) unsalted butter, cut into 8 pieces

4 ounces (113 grams) bittersweet or semisweet chocolate, chopped

1½ tablespoons light corn syrup

This is the recipe you'll reach for whenever you want a thick glaze with a full chocolate flavor and a shine that looks pro even if all you had to do to get it was to heat three ingredients together.

Set a heatproof bowl over a pan of gently simmering water, making sure the bottom of the bowl does not touch the water. With the pan over low heat, drop in the pieces of butter, followed by the chocolate and corn syrup. Heat, stirring frequently, until the butter and chocolate are melted and the glaze is smooth and shiny. Be careful not to overheat it—you don't want to break the emulsion. Remove from the heat.

The glaze is ready to use, but if you want a thicker glaze, let it stand for 5 to 10 minutes before using. Pour out a little to test its viscosity.

Storing: It's best to use the glaze soon after it's made, but it can be kept in the refrigerator for about 5 days. Heat it very gently—use the same bowl-over-hot-water method—stirring to bring it back. You can also freeze the glaze. Pack it airtight, then defrost it overnight in the refrigerator and reheat over gently simmering water.

Makes about 2 cups

8 ounces (227 grams) semisweet or bittersweet chocolate, finely chopped

1 cup (240 grams) full-fat sour cream, not very cold (see below)

A word on the sour cream: Make sure that you use full-fat sour cream and that it's not straight-from-the-fridge cold—slightly warmer cream will make your frosting smoother and easier to blend.

Sour Cream–Chocolate Frosting

A thick, pipeable, full-on chocolate frosting with a subtle sour cream tang that sneaks in with each bite.

The chocolate needs to be melted, and the best way is to put it in a large microwave-safe bowl and warm it for 30-second intervals with the oven at half power—scrape and stir often. It should take 1½ to 2½ minutes—hard to say precisely. The next best way is to put the chocolate in a heatproof bowl set over a pan of gently simmering water—making sure the bottom of the bowl isn't touching the water. Stir over low heat until it's melted. Since chocolate is so delicate, you want to keep a close eye on it and catch it when it's almost melted—then remove it from the heat and stir to finish melting it on the counter.

Add the sour cream in two additions, stirring it into the chocolate thoroughly. The mixture will thicken as you stir. By the time all the sour cream is incorporated, the frosting should be thick and shiny and ready to be spread, swirled or piped.

Storing: The frosting can be covered and kept at room temperature for up to 8 hours or refrigerated for up to 4 days. If you've chilled the frosting, you'll have to bring it back to room temperature before using it. Unfortunately, the best way to do this takes the longest—let it sit out until it comes to temp, which can take an hour or more. You can go directly from the fridge to a mixer—give the frosting a few beats to bring it around to spreadability— but just know that the frosting might lighten in color (a small price to pay for convenience).

Any-Kind-of-Chocolate Dip-or-Not Glaze

Makes about ½ cup

6 ounces (170 grams) chocolate (milk, semisweet, bittersweet or good-quality white), finely chopped

2 teaspoons neutral oil

Food coloring (optional)

This is the ideal glaze to use for cupcakes and baby cakes—it's what I use to finish the Gemma Cakes (page 215)—because, while you can certainly pour it over a cake, it creates a smooth, flavorful finish when you put it in a bowl and dip the tops of the little cakes into it.

Glaze is perfect when you don't want the muchness of frosting. You can use whatever kind of chocolate you like, but if you make it with white chocolate, you can tint it.

Melt the chocolate and oil together in a microwave oven using low or half power (heat in spurts and stir often) or in a heatproof bowl set over a pan of gently simmering water—make sure the bottom of the bowl doesn't touch the water. The glaze is ready to use as soon as it's blended.

If you're using white chocolate and want to color it, now's the time.

Refrigerate whatever you've glazed for 15 to 30 minutes to set the chocolate.

Storing: Tightly covered, the glaze will keep in the refrigerator for about 4 days; reheat gently before using.

Makes about 2 cups

- 1 cup (240 ml) plus 2 tablespoons heavy cream
- 8 ounces (227 grams) bittersweet or semisweet chocolate, finely chopped
- 4 tablespoons (2 ounces; 57 grams) unsalted butter, cut into 4 pieces, at room temperature

Chocolate Ganache

Ganache is a magical emulsion of chocolate and heavy cream. Used just after it's made, when it's warm and fluid, it can be poured over a cake to become a glaze. Chill it, and it can be a frosting.

Rinse a medium saucepan with cold water, but don't dry it (this will help keep the cream from scorching). Pour in the cream and bring it just to a boil.

Remove the pan from the heat and add the chocolate. Wait for 30 seconds and then, using a small flexible spatula and beginning in the center of the pan, start stirring the chocolate and cream together. Continue to stir in increasingly wider concentric circles until you have a thick, shiny, smooth mixture. Piece by piece, stir in the butter until it's melted and the ganache is smooth. (If you're having a problem emulsifying the ingredients, put the pan over very low heat for just a minute or so.)

If you want the ganache for a glaze, now's the moment to use it. If you want it for frosting a cake, you'll need to wait until it thickens. You can leave the ganache on the counter, stirring occasionally—this takes a while. Or you can refrigerate it, checking on it and stirring frequently. If you miss the perfect moment, you can always gently reheat the ganache.

Storing: Tightly covered, ganache will keep in the fridge for about 5 days or in the freezer for up to 1 month. Let it come to room temperature before using. You can also warm the ganache in a microwave (work on low power, in short spurts, and stir often) or in a bowl over simmering water. No matter what you do, be gentle—too much heat, and the ganache may separate.

Yogurt Topping

Makes about 1 cup

- ¼ cup (60 ml) very cold heavy cream
- ½ cup (115 grams) cold very thick plain yogurt (see headnote)
- 1 tablespoon confectioners' sugar, or a tiny bit more, to taste (optional)

Keep this topping in mind when you want something fast, easy to make and luscious to finish a plain cake. It's nothing more than yogurt and cream, but it sets beautifully and it takes to a touch of whimsy. Look for thick whole-milk Greek yogurt or, better yet, an ultrathick Icelandic yogurt, like Skyr. I like to use berry yogurts for both their flavor and their color. I sometimes add a splash of liqueur or rose water or a drop of extract to flavor the topping—go easy on the extra liquid—and a bit of sugar. Make a simple version once and then play around ever after.

You can easily double this recipe.

Working in a medium bowl, whip the cream until it holds soft peaks. You can use a hand mixer or a stand mixer fitted with the whisk attachment to do this, but if your cream is very cold, it shouldn't be hard or take you more than a couple of minutes to do the whipping by hand with a whisk. Give the yogurt a stir to loosen it, then fold it into the cream. Taste a dab, and if you want a bit of sugar, add it now. Ditto for any flavoring (see headnote).

The topping is ready to use as soon as it's mixed. If you have to keep it for a couple of hours, cover it and put it in the refrigerator; drain off any liquid that has accumulated before using it, and give it a few beats with a whisk if necessary. You can also line a small strainer with a piece of dampened cheesecloth (or a paper towel), set it over a bowl, spoon in the topping, cover the setup and refrigerate it for up to a day.

Storing: The topping is best used soon after it's made, but it has surprising stayability—it can be refrigerated in a covered bowl (in the strainer or not) for about 1 day.

Makes about ½ cup

1 cup (120 grams) confectioners' sugar, sifted

About 1 tablespoon liquid, such as milk, water or juice, more as needed

Confectioners' Sugar Icing

The simplest way to dress up a plain cake. This recipe multiplies easily.

Put the sugar in a medium bowl and, little by little, gradually stir in the liquid. In the beginning, it will look hopeless. It seems impossible that such a small amount of liquid will moisten the sugar, but just keep going. If you want a thinner icing, add more liquid by the drop. I usually want an icing that falls slowly and steadily from the tip of a spoon, but you may want it thicker or thinner—it's easy to adjust the liquid and get what you like.

Storing: This is not meant to be kept—use the icing as soon as it's made.

Playing Around

Chocolate Icing

Whisk 3 tablespoons unsweetened cocoa powder into the sugar. To get a fall-off-the-spoon consistency, you will probably need more water or milk—start with 1½ tablespoons and add more liquid as you work, if necessary.

Vintage Boiled Caramel Icing or Sauce

Makes about 1 cup

- 8 tablespoons (4 ounces; 113 grams) unsalted butter, cut into chunks
- 1 cup (200 grams) brown sugar
- ¼ cup (60 ml) evaporated milk (or half-and-half or heavy cream)
- 1 teaspoon pure vanilla extract
- ¼ teaspoon fine sea salt

This recipe was a footnote on an old (1950s? 1940s?) handwritten apple cake recipe that my friend Ellen Einstein sent me. I made it to pour over and serve alongside the First-of-Fall Apple Bundt (page 129) and then continued to make it to pour over lots of things, including vanilla ice cream. It's sweet, of course, but its caramel flavor—more butterscotch, really—brings back the joys of simpler times. Childhood, too.

The original recipe called for evaporated milk, a common pantry staple in many households back then, but since you use just a small amount, it's nice to know that you can make the sauce with an equal measure of half-and-half or heavy cream.

Put all of the ingredients in a medium saucepan and bring to a boil over medium-high heat. Boil, stirring frequently, for 2 minutes. The icing/sauce will be smooth and have thickened a bit.

The caramel pours most easily if you use it as soon as it's made; wait, and it will thicken. If it seems too thick, just warm it gently in a saucepan over low heat or in a microwave in short spurts on reduced power.

Storing: Tightly covered, the sauce will keep for about 5 days in the fridge. Warm in a microwave or in a saucepan over low heat before using.

Makes about 2 cups

2 cups (480 ml) whole milk

6 large egg yolks

½ cup (100 grams) sugar

⅓ cup (43 grams) cornstarch, sifted

1 tablespoon pure vanilla extract

3½ tablespoons (1¾ ounces; 50 grams) unsalted butter, at room temperature

Vanilla Pastry Cream

A thick, rich pastry cream, one meant to hold up as a cake filling. It's smooth, creamy and velvety but sturdy enough to slice through. See opposite for the chocolate version.

Rinse a medium saucepan with cold water, but don't dry it (this will help keep the milk from scorching). Pour in the milk and heat over medium heat until you see bubbles around the edges of the pan.

Meanwhile, working in a medium bowl, whisk the yolks, sugar and cornstarch together. Whisking nonstop, drizzle in about a quarter of the scalded milk. When the yolks are warm (and the risk of scrambling them has passed), whisk in the rest of the milk in a steady stream. Pour the mixture back into the saucepan and set the pan over medium heat. Whisking energetically and constantly, bring the mixture to a boil, taking care that you're getting into the corners of the pan, then lower the heat a bit and cook for another minute or two, still whisking—you'll see a few bubbles breaking on the surface and that's what you want. Pull the pan from the heat and if the pastry cream isn't smooth, push it through a strainer into a clean bowl. Stir in the vanilla.

Let sit for about 5 minutes, then whisk in the butter bit by bit.

Press a piece of plastic wrap against the surface of the cream and refrigerate until it's cold, about 3 hours. Keep refrigerated until needed.

Storing: Well covered, the pastry cream will keep for about 3 days in the fridge. Whisk it vigorously to loosen it before using it as a filling.

Chocolate Pastry Cream

A cake filling that's thick, spreadable, sliceable and lick-the-whisk good (and also good as a pie filling).

Makes about 2½ cups

- 2 cups (480 ml) whole milk
- 4 large egg yolks
- 6 tablespoons (72 grams) sugar
- 3 tablespoons cornstarch
- ¼ teaspoon fine sea salt
- 7 ounces (200 grams) bittersweet chocolate, melted and still warm
- 2½ tablespoons (1¼ ounces; 35 grams) unsalted butter, at room temperature

Rinse a medium saucepan with cold water, but don't dry it (this will help keep the milk from scorching). Pour in the milk and heat over medium heat until you see bubbles around the edges of the pan.

Meanwhile, working in a medium bowl, whisk the yolks, sugar, cornstarch and salt together. Whisking nonstop, drizzle in about a quarter of the scalded milk. When the yolks are warm (and the risk of scrambling them has passed), whisk in the rest of the milk in a steady stream. Pour the mixture back into the saucepan and set the pan over medium heat. Whisking energetically and constantly, bring the mixture to a boil, taking care that you're getting into the corners of the pan, then lower the heat a bit and cook for another minute or two, still whisking—you'll see a few bubbles breaking on the surface and that's what you want. Pull the pan from the heat, and if the pastry cream isn't smooth, push it through a strainer into a clean bowl.

Whisk in the melted chocolate and let the mixture sit for 5 minutes, then whisk in the butter bit by bit. Press a piece of plastic wrap against the surface of the cream and refrigerate until it's cold, about 3 hours. Keep refrigerated until needed.

Storing: Well covered, the pastry cream will keep for about 3 days in the fridge. Whisk it vigorously to loosen it before using it as a filling.

Makes about 3 cups

7 ounces (200 grams) bittersweet chocolate, finely chopped
2¼ cups (540 ml) whole milk
⅓ cup (67 grams) sugar
4 large egg yolks
3 tablespoons cornstarch
½ teaspoon fine sea salt
2 tablespoons (1 ounce; 28 grams) unsalted butter
1½ teaspoons pure vanilla extract

Dark Chocolate Pudding Filling

This is the filling that I turn to when I'm making the Puff Cake (page 21), but it's ideal for the Paradise Cake (page 11)—and it would have been lovely in VV's First Birthday Cake (page 219), if only she'd liked chocolate then. It's a perfect soft filling and, if you've got leftovers, remember: before it was a filling, it was a spoon dessert—indulge!

You can melt the chocolate in a heatproof bowl set over a pan of gently simmering water (don't let the bottom of the bowl touch the water), in a microwave oven or in a saucepan over direct heat if your burner goes superlow. No matter how you do it, be gentle and remove the chocolate from the heat as soon as it's melted. Set aside.

Rinse a medium saucepan with cold water, but don't dry it (this helps keep the milk from scorching), pour in the milk and stir in half of the sugar. Bring just to a boil.

While the milk is heating, whisk the remaining sugar, the yolks, cornstarch and salt together in a large bowl. Whisking without stopping, slowly drizzle in about ½ cup of the hot milk—keep it slow, so that the eggs don't scramble. Still whisking, add the remainder of the milk in a slow, steady stream.

Rinse out the saucepan with cold water again, pour in the milk mixture and place the pan over medium heat. Whisking nonstop, and making sure to get into the corners of the pan, cook until the pudding thickens and a bubble or two pops on the surface. Lower the heat and, still whisking like mad, simmer the pudding for another 2 minutes. Remove from the heat and whisk in the melted chocolate, followed by the butter and vanilla.

Give the pudding one last whisk, then pour it into a bowl, press a piece of plastic wrap against the surface and refrigerate for about 3 hours, or until cold.

Storing: Covered airtight, the pudding can be kept in the refrigerator for about 3 days. When you're ready to use it as a filling, give it a few vigorous beats with a whisk or spatula to bring it back to a spreadable consistency.

Mixed Citrus Curd

Makes a generous 2 cups

1¼ cups (250 grams) sugar

Enough lemons and other citrus to make ¾ cup (180 ml) juice (see below)

3 large eggs

1 large egg yolk

1 tablespoon light corn syrup

8 tablespoons (4 ounces; 113 grams) unsalted butter, cut into chunks

A word on the zest and juice: It usually takes 4 to 6 lemons to get ¾ cup (180 ml) of juice. Before cutting and juicing the fruit, remove the zest with a Microplane or other rasp-type grater. The zest should be extremely fine so that it blends into the curd easily.

This basic recipe will make an all-lemon or an all-any-kind-of-citrus curd you like, but my favorite is a combo curd. I use equal parts lemon, lime and orange (actually, what I've got in the house most often is clementines rather than oranges) and add the zest as well. If you decide on an orange curd, I'd suggest that you squeeze in the juice from at least one lemon and maybe from a lime, too. These tangier juices will not only give your curd a bit of pop, but their acidity will also help it set nicely.

The curd's texture is velvety and luxurious, ideal for glossing the tops of plain cakes and so good swiped on cakes and muffins—think of curd as a more vibrant stand-in for butter or jam.

Put the sugar in a medium heavy-bottomed saucepan and add the zest. Using your fingertips, smush, rub and press the sugar and zest together until the sugar is moist, fragrant and tinged with color. Add the eggs and yolk and immediately start whisking (since yolks can "burn" when they come in contact with sugar, it's important to get the mixture moving quickly). Whisk in the corn syrup and citrus juice, then drop in the pieces of butter.

Put the saucepan over medium heat and cook, whisking nonstop and making sure to get into the corners (if you're more comfortable with a heatproof spatula or spoon, switch now), for about 8 minutes, until the curd thickens—it won't thicken much (it will get thicker as it cools), but the change is noticeable. When you see a bubble or two come to the surface and pop, you're finished.

Scrape the curd into a heatproof bowl or jar and press a piece of plastic wrap against the surface to seal. Let cool to room temperature, then chill thoroughly before using.

Storing: Kept in an airtight container, the curd will hold in the fridge for about 3 weeks.

Makes a generous 1 cup

- 6 ounces (170 grams) semisweet or bittersweet chocolate (not chips), finely chopped
- ¾ cup (180 ml) heavy cream
- 3 tablespoons light corn syrup
- 2 tablespoons sugar

Hot Fudge Sauce

When you're topping a cake with ice cream, you just might want to top the ice cream with this thick, glossy sauce.

Put all the ingredients in a medium saucepan and cook, stirring constantly, over medium-low heat until the chocolate melts and the mixture comes to a light simmer, about 5 minutes. Still stirring, simmer the sauce for another minute or two, then scrape it into a heatproof container.

The sauce is ready to use now, or it can be covered and refrigerated.

Storing: Tightly covered, the sauce can be refrigerated for about 2 weeks. Reheat gently before using.

Quick Brown Sugar Streusel

Makes about 1¾ cups

- 1 cup (136 grams) all-purpose flour
- ⅔ cup (132 grams) brown sugar
- ½ teaspoon fine sea salt
- ¼ teaspoon ground spice, such as cinnamon (optional)
- 8 tablespoons (4 ounces; 113 grams) unsalted butter, melted
- ½ teaspoon pure vanilla extract (optional)

Turn to this recipe when you want to top something with crumbs but don't have time to give the topping mixture a good chill. Through some trick of nature, this streusel, made with melted butter, is ready to use as soon as it's made. It's faster to pull together than the All-Purpose Streusel (page 278) and a bit crunchier. Streusel is always good; having a couple of streusels to choose from is always better. If you'd like to make a topping that's more like what you'd use for a crisp, take a look at Playing Around.

Stir the flour, sugar, salt and spice, if you're using it, together in a medium bowl. Pour in the butter and the vanilla, if using it, and stir with a fork until the butter has moistened all of the ingredients. If you toss the mixture with the fork, it should break up into clumps.

The crumbs are best used now, but you can cover and refrigerate them for an hour or so (chill them longer, and they'll become hard and difficult to use). When you're ready for them, break up the mixture with your hands and pinch bits of it into uneven nubbins.

Storing: The streusel is best used shortly after it's made.

Playing Around

Oat or Nut Brown Sugar Streusel

For a traditional crisp topping, you can add ½ cup old-fashioned oats—add them to the dry ingredients before you add the melted butter. You can also add chopped nuts—stir about ¼ to ⅓ cup into the flour mixture.

Makes about 1½ cups

¾ cup (102 grams) all-purpose flour

3 tablespoons sugar

1 tablespoon brown sugar

¼ teaspoon ground cinnamon

¼ teaspoon fine sea salt

5½ tablespoons (2¾ ounces; 78 grams) cold unsalted butter, cut into small cubes

½ teaspoon pure vanilla extract

A word on working ahead: After you've pinched the dough into crumbs, it has to be chilled for at least 1 hour (3 is better). Plan ahead.

Storing: Tightly covered, the streusel will keep in the refrigerator for about 2 weeks. It can be kept in the freezer for 1 month; thaw it in the refrigerator.

All-Purpose Streusel

This is the use-it-for-anything, grab-it-whenever-you-want-sweet-crunch streusel. Make sure your butter is cold before you start to work.

For extra crunch, bake the streusel; see Playing Around.

You can make the streusel using an electric mixer, but making it by hand is fast and easy. Regardless of the method, begin by whisking the flour, both sugars, the cinnamon and salt together, either in the bowl of a stand mixer or in a bowl that you can use with a hand mixer—or your hands. Drop in the cubes of cold butter and toss all the ingredients together with your fingers until the butter is coated.

If you're working with a mixer (use the paddle attachment for a stand mixer), beat on medium-low speed until the ingredients form moist, clumpy crumbs. Squeeze the streusel, and it will hold together. Sprinkle over the vanilla and mix until blended.

Or, if you're working by hand, squeeze, mash, mush or otherwise rub everything together until you have a bowl full of moist clumps and curds. Squeeze the streusel, and it will hold together. Sprinkle over the vanilla and toss to blend.

Pack the streusel into a covered container and refrigerate for at least 1 hour, preferably 3 hours, before using.

When you're ready to use the streusel, break up the mixture with your hands and pinch bits of it into uneven clumps.

Playing Around

Baked Streusel

Chill the streusel for at least 3 hours. When you're ready to bake it, center a rack in the oven and preheat it to 350 degrees F. Line a baking sheet with parchment and turn the streusel out onto the sheet. Using your fingers, break the clumps apart or squeeze them together—the size of the streusel is up to you. Spread the clumps over the baking sheet and bake, stirring often, for about 15 minutes, or until the streusel is golden brown. Put the baking sheet on a rack and let the streusel cool to room temperature. Covered, the baked streusel will hold at room temperature for about 1 week or frozen for up to 1 month.

Cocoa Crumbs

If, like me, you love streusely crumbs and you love chocolate, you'll find these crumbs irresistible and you'll want to have them at the ready at all times. You can use the crumbs as you would streusel: make them and refrigerate them for at least 3 hours—you'll get lovely, tender clumplettes. If you'd like more crunch, bake the crumbs after chilling them. Whether they're raw or baked, you can pop them into the freezer—insurance that you'll never be without a terrific topping, even if what you're topping is just a scoop of ice cream.

Makes about 2 cups

- 1 cup (136 grams) all-purpose flour
- ⅓ cup (67 grams) brown sugar
- ¼ cup (21 grams) unsweetened cocoa powder
- 2 tablespoons sugar
- ½ teaspoon fine sea salt
- 7 tablespoons (3½ ounces; 99 grams) cold unsalted butter, cut into small cubes

A word on working ahead: After you've pinched the dough into crumbs, it has to be chilled for at least 3 hours. Plan ahead!

Put the flour, brown sugar, cocoa, granulated sugar and salt in a large bowl. Reach in and toss everything together to mix and to make sure that the brown sugar and cocoa aren't lumpy. Drop in the cubes of butter and squish and squeeze everything together until the mixture is moist enough for you to pinch it into clumps and curds.

Cover the crumbs and refrigerate them for at least 3 hours before sprinkling them over a batter or baking them on their own.

To bake the crumbs: Center a rack in the oven and preheat it to 350 degrees F. Line a baking sheet with parchment paper.

Turn the crumbs out onto the baking sheet and squeeze them into clumps, or loosen them into sandy bits, depending on how you want to use them. Bake for about 15 minutes, tossing the crumbs at the halfway mark, until they've separated into morsels or formed small clusters. Transfer the baking sheet to a rack and let the crumbs cool to room temperature.

Storing: The unbaked crumbs can be covered and refrigerated for up to 1 week or frozen for up to 1 month (if they're loose enough, you might not have to fully defrost them before using). Baked crumbs can be kept in a container at room temperature for at least 1 week or in the freezer for up to 1 month.

Mary Dodd's Homemade Sprinkles

Makes about 1 cup

1½ cups (180 grams) confectioners' sugar

2 teaspoons cornstarch

1 to 2 tablespoons cold water

1 tablespoon light corn syrup

1 teaspoon vanilla extract (see below)

Food coloring—either gel or liquid works well here

A word on the vanilla extract: If you want to make white or pale pastel-colored sprinkles, you might want to use clear imitation vanilla extract. I never recommend it for flavor, but it's useful in this recipe.

A word on working ahead: While it may only take minutes to make the sprinkles, it'll take the sprinkles hours—about 12 of them!—to dry.

Whether you call these sprinkles or jimmies, if you make them yourself, you get to call them the best. You also get an extra helping of the pride and delight that come when you turn out something you thought could only be bought in a store. Everything about making these is fun, especially the chance to choose your own colors and design your own shapes. Thank you, Mary Dodd, for the recipe.

Line three baking sheets with parchment paper.

Working in a medium bowl, whisk 1 cup of the sugar with the cornstarch to get rid of any lumps. Add 1 tablespoon water, the corn syrup and vanilla and whisk until you've got a smooth mixture. Continuing with the whisk or switching to a flexible spatula, mix in the remaining ½ cup sugar and as much additional water as you need to get the mixture smooth again. You're aiming for a consistency that's thick and flowing.

If you're making different-colored sprinkles, divide the mixture among small bowls, one for each color. Drop by drop, stir in the food coloring, adding as much color as needed to get the shade you want. Because the color will fade a little as the mixture dries, you might want to go brighter now.

You need to pipe the mixture and you've got a choice for how to do this—you can fill a zipper-lock bag and snip a tiny hole in one of the bottom corners, or you can use a small pastry bag fitted with a super-narrow tip (such as a Wilton #4).

Pipe long thin lines of the mixture across the parchment sheets; if you'd like, make some dots, too. Stripes and dots are the easiest shapes to make, but experiment and see what else might work for you.

Let stand at (dry, not humid) room temperature for at least 12 hours, or overnight. When what you've piped is absolutely, positively, unequivocally dry, cut the lines into whatever lengths make you happy.

Storing: Sprinkles will keep in a closed container at room temperature for at least 1 month.

Makes a scant 1½ cups

1 cup (240 ml) water

1 cup (200 grams) sugar

1 to 2 tablespoons alcohol (see headnote) or about 1½ teaspoons pure vanilla extract for flavoring (optional)

Simple Syrup/Soaking Syrup

When you want to add moisture and more flavor to a cake, turn to simple syrup. A blend of equal parts (by volume) water and sugar, it's the same syrup that you might already be using to sweeten iced drinks and cocktails. To give it some punch, you can flavor it with herbs or spices or add some booze. A tablespoon or two of a liqueur or other spirit will bring perfume and flavor to the syrup. My favorite add-ins are Kirsch (good with berries and with cherries, its base flavor), Grand Marnier (for orange cakes), limoncello, Campari or Aperol (for citrus cakes) and dark rum (for vanilla cakes and cakes with warm spices). You can also add herbs to the syrup as it cooks; strain them out when the syrup is cool.

Put the water and sugar in a medium saucepan and bring to a boil over medium heat, stirring until the sugar dissolves, then let the mixture burble away for 2 to 3 minutes. Remove from the heat, pour the syrup into a heatproof container and allow it to cool to room temperature. The syrup will not be thick—it's not supposed to be.

If you're adding a flavoring, add it once the syrup is cool. Add a little at first, then taste and add more as you go. Cover the container tightly.

Storing: Kept covered in the refrigerator, it will keep for almost forever.

Mulled Wine Syrup

All the flavors of mulled wine concentrated into a syrup. I first made this to drizzle over the Fall Harvest Cake (page 169) and then kept reaching for it. It's lovely with citrus cakes, with the Classic French Yogurt Cake (page 94) and over ice cream. Also, it makes a nice Kir—put a spoonful or two in a wineglass and pour in sparkling wine or white wine.

Makes about 1 cup

2 cups (480 ml) red wine

1 cup (200 grams) sugar

A 1-inch piece fresh ginger, washed and cut into chunks

1 cinnamon stick

2 whole cloves or 1 whole star anise

A long strip of orange or lemon zest, white cottony pith removed

Stir all of the ingredients together in a medium saucepan and bring to a boil over medium-high heat, stirring until the sugar dissolves. Lower the heat just enough to keep the liquid at a moderate burble and simmer until you've got about 1 cup of syrup. Be patient, this can take between 10 and 20 minutes.

Strain the syrup into a heatproof container—I like a jar for this—and discard the solids. Let cool, uncovered.

You can use the syrup when it's warm—it's nice that way—or at room temperature. Just make sure it is cool before you cover it.

Storing: Tightly covered and refrigerated, the syrup will keep for at least a week. Reheat gently, if you'd like, before using.

Makes about 2 cups

- 1 cup (240 ml) very cold heavy cream
- 2 tablespoons confectioners' sugar, or more to taste, sifted if lumpy
- 1 teaspoon pure vanilla extract (optional but recommended)

Whipped Cream

The key to good whipped cream is cold, cold cream. And restraint—underwhipped trumps overwhipped every time.

Working in the bowl of a stand mixer fitted with the whisk attachment, or in a large bowl with a hand mixer, beat the cream and sugar together on low speed just until the cream starts to thicken. Taste and see if you'd like a little more sugar and, if so, add it now. Continue beating until you're just shy of the consistency you want. I start beating on medium-low speed, then increase the speed to medium/medium-high and beat until the texture of the cream is almost what I want, and then finish the cream by hand with a whisk to avoid overbeating. When you like what you've got, beat in the vanilla (if using).

Storing: Whipped cream is best soon after it's made, but you can keep it refrigerated for a few hours. To hold the cream for up to 24 hours, line a strainer with damp cheesecloth or a couple of damp paper towels, set the strainer over a bowl, scrape in the whipped cream, cover and refrigerate.

Mascarpone Whipped Cream

Adding mascarpone to whipped cream brings a little sharpness to it and also stabilizes it a bit.

Makes about 2 cups

½ cup (113 grams) mascarpone

1 cup (240 ml) very cold heavy cream

2 tablespoons confectioners' sugar, sifted if lumpy

1 teaspoon pure vanilla extract

Put the mascarpone in the bowl of a stand mixer or in a large bowl that you can use with a hand mixer. Using a flexible spatula or a fork, stir just to loosen it. If you're using a stand mixer, fit it with the whisk attachment. Add the cream and confectioners' sugar to the bowl and beat on medium speed until the cream holds medium peaks. With the mixer on low, add the vanilla.

Storing: The cream is best soon after it's made, but you can keep it refrigerated for a few hours. To hold the cream for up to 24 hours, line a strainer with damp cheesecloth or a couple of damp paper towels, set the strainer over a bowl, scrape in the whipped cream, cover and refrigerate.

Acknowledgments

This is my fifteenth book and the fifteenth time that I have the joy of thanking the people who make both my work and me better. Also the fifteenth time that I have to face the truth: I can never thank them enough.

I always tell people that I'm the luckiest author on earth, because I work with the most talented people. What makes me even luckier is that I've worked with many of them for many years.

David Black has been my agent and friend for more than twenty years. He's my smartest counselor. Even my husband, Michael, who's known me since I was sixteen and is no slouch in the smart department, will stop me mid-fret, mid-moment of worry, mid-tizzy, mid-dip and say, "Call David—he'll know what to do!" We both know that if a problem can be untangled, David's the person who'll do it. David came into my life when I was most confused about my work. That I've made eight books since then and loved working on each one is in enormous measure thanks to David's encouragement, intelligence, ferocious determination and unfailing support. He's always on my side! And always funny—never underestimate the power of a laugh. Special thanks to Anna Zinchuk, David's assistant, for her easy competence and her endless patience.

It was David who brought me to the legendary editor Rux Martin two decades ago, and Rux who put me in Sarah Kwak's capable hands. Sarah has a deep passion for cookbooks and a love for the food that can be made from them. She's a writer's editor, taking pleasure in good sentences and the unexpected but right word, and she has a brilliant eye for design. Thank you, David, Rux and Sarah.

As I was finishing the recipes for this book and wrapping up loose ends, Mary Dodd, who tests all of my recipes, said to me, "After almost fifteen years of working together, we hardly have to talk anymore—we just know what the other person is thinking." It's a great privilege to have this kind of relationship, but with this book, we had a lot more to talk about a lot more often, because Mary had new work to do for it. In addition to testing each recipe after I'd finish it, Mary photographed her cakes so that they could be models for Nancy Pappas's stunning illustrations. Neither of us knew what this work would entail, but I knew from the start that Mary would do it splendidly—and she did.

I'm thrilled that I got to work with Nancy Pappas and adore the art that she created for this book. I met Nancy years ago and knew instantly that I wanted to work with her, but I had to wait for the right book—this is it! It's an honor to have her paintings in this book. Nancy understood the beauty to be found in the simplest cakes and painted them with joy. Every time Nancy said that she'd be sending a new batch of illustrations, I felt the kind of excitement a kid feels on Christmas. Even though I now know the work well, it still feels like a gift—the paintings fill me with wonder and delight.

For the fourteenth time—please imagine a slew of exclamation points and then a sad face to mark the one time we missed each other—I get to thank Judith Sutton for copyediting my work. Talk about good fortune! Judith is the behind-the-scenes magician, the good witch of words, the

queen of semicolons and the person who has saved me from myself time and again.

And we're all thankful to Melissa Lotfy for designing this book so beautifully and for finding the right way to balance my recipes with Nancy's exceptional paintings. Melissa and I have worked together before, and with each book, my admiration for her ability to make a book sparkle grows.

Once again, I get to thank Carrie Bachman, whose skill as a publicist is unparalleled. As remarkable as Carrie is at her work, for years I've thought that she could start a business teaching people to be as optimistic, energetic, focused and open to new ideas as she is. I'd be her first client!

Cookbooks have what seem like a million moving parts, each of which needs someone to take care of them, and the team at Harvest are great caretakers. Thank you—Diana Baroni, publisher; Rachel Meyers, associate director, production editorial; Kimberly Kiefer, production manager; Jacqueline Quirk, associate editor; Liz Psaltis, marketing; and Anwesha Basu, publicity.

I am thankful to friends who gave me permission to share their recipes—thank you, Ellen Einstein, Berna Feuerstein, Darra Goldstein, Pierre Hermé, Rosa Jackson, Jaíne Mackievicz and François Perret. And to friends who've shared the ups and downs—and lots of cake—with me. Thank you, Jane Bertch, Nina Brickman, Clo Davis, Leslie Gill, Ellen Madere, Priscilla Martel, Ginny Millhiser, Jennifer McLagan, Hélène Samuel, all the Bake & Tellers and the Tuesdays with Dorie bakers, especially Stephanie Whitten, Mardi Michels and "Brizzy Girl" Gaye. A mountain of hugs to Antonella Iannarino. And thank you to Emily Weinstein and Genevieve Ko, who saw the goodness in my simple cakes and inspired me to write about them for the *New York Times*: you got me thinking and baking and eventually cookbooking.

My mother would touch wood if she said something good about her children—she wasn't a superstitious person, but when it came to us, she wasn't taking any chances. I'm holding on to wood as I write that my family—Michael, Joshua, Linling, Gemma and VV—is my treasure. They are constant. They are caring. They are generous. And they are sweet. My goal is to be just half as kind and loving—and adorable—as they are. I'm still working on it.

Index

Note: Page references in *italics* indicate recipe illustrations.

D

E

R

V

W

Y

Z

About the Author

Inducted into the James Beard Foundation's Who's Who of Food and Beverage in America, **DORIE GREENSPAN** is the *New York Times* bestselling, IACP Award and James Beard Award–winning author of fifteen cookbooks, including *Baking with Dorie, Dorie's Cookies, Around My French Table, Baking Chez Moi,* and *Baking: From My Home to Yours,* and a Substack with a hugely devoted following, xoxoDorie Newsletter. She lives and bakes in New York City, Westbrook, Connecticut, and Paris.

doriegreenspan
doriegreenspan.com

About the Illustrator

NANCY PAPPAS is a Korean American designer and illustrator who works in both digital and traditional mediums. Passionate about enhancing brands and expanding creative ideas, Nancy uses her art to celebrate food, culture, and community, and brings a colorful and versatile style to every project. She lives in Brooklyn, New York.

nkpcreate
nkpcreate.com